SLAPPING LEATHER

ELYSSA FORD AND REBECCA SCOFIELD

SLAPPING LEATHER

Queer Cowfolx at the Gay Rodeo

UNIVERSITY OF WASHINGTON PRESS
SEATTLE

Copyright © 2023 by the University of Washington Press

The chapters in *Slapping Leather* draw on previous work by the authors, including Rebecca Scofield, "Chaps and Scowls: Play, Violence, and the Post-1970s Urban Cowboy," *Journal of American Culture* 40, no. 4 (December 2017): 325–40; Elyssa Ford, "Becoming the West: Cowboys as Icons of Masculine Style for Gay Men," in "Fashion and Style Icons," special issue, *Critical Studies in Men's Fashion* 5, nos. 1–2 (May 2018): 41–53; Rebecca Scofield, *Outriders: Rodeo at the Fringes of the American West* (Seattle: University of Washington Press, 2019); and Elyssa Ford, Rodeo as Refuge, *Rodeo as Rebellion: Gender, Race, and Identity in the American Rodeo* (Lawrence: University Press of Kansas, 2020).

Design by Derek George
Composed in Sentinel, typeface designed by Jonathan Hoefler

All rights reserved. No part of this publication may be reproduced or transmitted in any form or by any means, electronic or mechanical, including photocopy, recording, or any information storage or retrieval system, without permission in writing from the publisher.

UNIVERSITY OF WASHINGTON PRESS
uwapress.uw.edu

LIBRARY OF CONGRESS CATALOGING-IN-PUBLICATION DATA

Names: Ford, Elyssa, author. | Scofield, Rebecca, author.

Title: Slapping leather : queer cowfolx at the gay rodeo / Elyssa Ford and Rebecca Scofield.

Description: Seattle : University of Washington Press, 2023. | Includes bibliographical references and index.

Identifiers: LCCN 2023031443 | ISBN 9780295752129 (hardback) | ISBN 9780295752136 (paperback) | ISBN 9780295752143 (ebook)

Subjects: LCSH: Gay rodeos—United States—History. | Rodeos—Social aspects—United States. | Gays—Social life and customs—United States. | AIDS (Disease)—Research—United States—Finance.

Classification: LCC GV1834.5 .F674 2023 | DDC 791.8/408664—dc23/eng/20230828

LC record available at https://lccn.loc.gov/2023031443

∞ This paper meets the requirements of ANSI/NISO Z39.48-1992 (Permanence of Paper).

FOR EACH OTHER

CONTENTS

ACKNOWLEDGMENTS ix
LIST OF ABBREVIATIONS xi

INTRODUCTION
Framing Gay Rodeo 1

Oral History Vignette
Roger Bergmann, Rodeo Judge and IGRA Past President 12

CHAPTER 1. ORIGINS
The History of the Gay Western Ideal and the Gay Rodeo 14

Oral History Vignette
Bruce Roby, Rodeo Judge 36

CHAPTER 2. "HOOKIN' UP" AT THE GAY RODEO
Normative Masculinity, Queer Sexuality,
and the Authentic Cowboy 38

Oral History Vignette
Brian Helander, IGRA Past President 69

CHAPTER 3. "A EUPHEMISM FOR AN ORGY"
Sex, Sexuality, and the AIDS Crisis 71

Oral History Vignette
Marie Antoinette Du Barry, NMGRA Royalty 103

CHAPTER 4. "DOLLARED TO DEATH"
Gay Rodeo Queens, Camp Events, and the Labor of Inclusion 106

Oral History Vignette
Candy Pratt, IGRA Past President   130

CHAPTER 5. "IT'S MILLER TIME"
Negotiating Gay Political and Consumer Identity at the Rodeo   132

Oral History Vignette
Laura, Champion Cowgirl   166

CHAPTER 6. "FOR ALL GAY PEOPLE"
Outreach, Acceptance, and the Boundaries of Inclusion   168

CONCLUSION
The Future of Gay Rodeo   204

GLOSSARY   211

NOTES   215

INDEX   263

ACKNOWLEDGMENTS

Writing is never done alone. That is especially true for works that are coauthored. As scholars, we initially came to this project individually, and our eventual collaboration produced the book you now read. We are deeply indebted to each other for the time, effort, and trust that we placed in this relationship. In our research and writing, we also have benefited from the support and help of many people. We want to express our gratitude to all the gay rodeo participants who shared their stories with us. Similarly, without the hard work of community archivists like Roger Bergmann and Frank Harrell, this project would not have been possible. Your devoted and meticulous documentation of gay rodeo has been inspirational. We have especially valued our close working relationship with Nicolas and Ryan Villanueva for their gay rodeo expertise and friendship. We would also like to thank all members of the Gay Rodeo Oral History Project, including Court Fund, Dusty Fleener, Rev Detiv, Kenwyn Richards, Devin Becker, and Oliva Wikle. Saraya Flaig, thank you for your initial research into rodeo royalty, which laid the groundwork for our analysis. Renae Campbell, Simon Judkins, and David-James Gonzales, thank you for your work as research assistants at different points throughout the project. Our universities have also provided conference and research support, and we are grateful for that, as well as the countless conference audiences who listened to early versions of this work and provided important feedback. We are immensely appreciative to all of the archivists and staff at the Autry Museum of the American West, the USC ONE Archives, and the University of Nevada, Las Vegas, and our reviewers and editor who helped polish our work. To our friends and colleagues, including Chris Hanson, Rochelle Smith, Adam Sowards, Alyson Roy, Amy Fish, Carla Cevasco, Brett Chloupek, and Sara Lampert, your commitment to our project and our well-being is deeply appreciated. Finally, we must thank our families for sticking with us through archival trips and rodeo visits. This is not just our project; it is thanks to you and your support.

ABBREVIATIONS

AGRA	Arizona Gay Rodeo Association
ARGRA	Alberta Rockies Gay Rodeo Association
ASGRA	Atlantic States Gay Rodeo Association
BSGRA	Big Sky Gay Rodeo Association
CCGRA	Central Canada Gay Rodeo Association
CGRA	Colorado Gay Rodeo Association
CGRA	Comstock Gay Rodeo Association
CSGRA	Cotton State Gay Rodeo Association
CSRA	Cowboy State Rodeo Association
DSRA	Diamond State Rodeo Association
FGRA	Florida Gay Rodeo Association
GGRA	Georgia Gay Rodeo Association
GSGRA	Golden Spike Gay Rodeo Association
GSGRA	Golden State Gay Rodeo Association
HGRA	Heartland Gay Rodeo Association
HSRA	High Sierra Gay Rodeo Association
IAGRA	Iowa Gay Rodeo Association
IGRA	International Gay Rodeo Association
ILGRA	Illinois Gay Rodeo Association
KGRA	Kansas Gay Rodeo Association
LGRA	Liberty Gay Rodeo Association
LSGRA	Louisiana State Gay Rodeo Association
MGRA	Missouri Gay Rodeo Association
MIGRA	Michigan International Gay Rodeo Association
NCGRA	North Carolina Gay Rodeo Association
NGRA	Nevada Gay Rodeo Association
NMGRA	New Mexico Gay Rodeo Association
NSGRA	North Star Gay Rodeo Association
NWGRA	Northwest Gay Rodeo Association
OGRA	Oregon Gay Rodeo Association
PCGRA	Pacific Coast Gay Rodeo Association
PONY	Pennsylvania, Ohio, New York
RRRA	Red River Rodeo Association
SCCGRA	Sacramento Capital Crossroads Gay Rodeo Association

SEGRA	Southeast Gay Rodeo Association
SGRA	Sonoran Gay Rodeo Association
SMRA	Smoky Mountain Rodeo Association
SNGRA	Southern Nevada Gay Rodeo Association
SSGRA	Silver State Gay Rodeo Association
SSRA	Sooner State Rodeo Association
TGRA	Texas Gay Rodeo Association
TSGRA	Tri-State Gay Rodeo Association
UGRA	Utah Gay Rodeo Association
WGRA	Wyoming Gay Rodeo Association

SLAPPING LEATHER

Introduction

FRAMING GAY RODEO

A lone cowboy on horseback stares into a rocky Arizona valley, surrounded by majestic mesas. He represents strength, masculinity, and domination over the untamed lands, peoples, and animals of the frontier. He is America. Yet the sky above fills with a rainbow-colored mist, disrupting this classic image of the US West. Within the rainbow sits a bull rider, and behind the rider is a pink triangle. Originally representing World War II–era Nazi oppression, this symbol was reclaimed in the 1970s by LGBTQ+ people in their fight for civil rights.[1] By embedding the rainbow and triangle within an otherwise traditional rodeo image, gay rodeo made a bold statement that queered not just the rodeo but the West as a whole. This image graced the cover of the 1997 program for the International Gay Rodeo Association's finals rodeo (see figure 1). Just one year after the release of effective HIV/AIDS medications, this program cover can be read as a hopeful imagining of a gay future. In a time when conservative states continued to pass anti-LGBTQ+ legislation and when same-sex sexual contact would remain illegal in parts of the country for another six years, this queer image of the West was truly radical in many ways.

FIGURE 1. *IGRA Finals Rodeo program cover, 1997. The colorful program cover is turquoise with a gold font. The cowboy in a red shirt with white sleeves sits astride a horse, looking out over the Arizona desert. A glowing pink triangle frames a bull rider, with a rainbow of blue, purple, red, orange, yellow, and green filling the entire sky. Courtesy of the Autry Museum of the American West.*

It illustrated how gay rodeo participants leveraged both western and LGBTQ+ iconography to envision new geographies for themselves and future generations.

Slapping Leather: Queer Cowfolx at the Gay Rodeo brings together over a decade of research by two historians of gender and sexuality in the American West. Drawing from multiple archives and over seventy oral history interviews, this work explores the complex history of gay rodeo from the late 1960s through the 2010s as a case study for western cultural performance, LGBTQ+ community building, queer philanthropy, and the creation of a racialized and gendered image of the queer cowboy. Studying gay rodeo provides a look at both the gay male idealization of the cowboy icon and the debates that have developed within this sporting arena as people struggle to embody, rewrite, and redeploy it.

"Slapping leather" is a term that evokes many images. It was often used to refer to the sound of a hand slapping against a pistol holster during a gunfight or the sound of thighs sliding across a leather saddle during a fast ride. One could also dance the "Slappin' Leather" line dance during the 1980s urban cowboy craze, which celebrated the sound of people's hands slapping their leather cowboy boots both in front and behind them. Beyond these common usages, "slapping leather" also suggests the connection between gay rodeo and the emergence of the sexual subculture of leather in the late twentieth century, as some gay men embraced hypermasculinity and advocated for the elimination of effeminate stereotypes of gay men. Gay rodeo offered a space where men could revel in a stylized white masculinity and its material markers. As one gay horseman asserted, "I like the look, smell, and feel of a good man in levis and leather."[2] In our analysis of gay rodeo, *Slapping Leather* examines the broader western and queer cultures that welded together violence, materiality, and sexuality. We map the assumptions, desires, and tensions at the heart of gay rodeo. Sitting at the intersection of queer rural studies and the history of the US West, this competitive arena captures the stories of a group of people dedicated to renarrating these histories by choosing to embody a national symbol, risking the threat of injury and death from homophobic protestors and animal rodeo participants to do so.

Indeed, the fact that people who rodeo risk death is part of what makes this arena such a compelling case study. Western historians have long pointed to the simultaneous development of the real and imagined

Wests and to the violence embedded within both of these visions. At the turn of the twentieth century, "Buffalo Bill" Cody, dime novels, and Fredrick Jackson Turner were waxing poetic about the "frontier" at the same time the US military and extractive industries were systematically plundering the region.[3] Born out of rangeland competitions, rodeos soon circulated across the country, and even globally, alongside Wild West shows and early Hollywood films, contributing to the emergence of the cowboy as an icon of American identity. Yet this new cowboy icon of the popular imagination failed to accurately reproduce the reality of nineteenth-century western ranches and rodeos. White and Black cowboys rode together on cattle drives. Hispanic families owned vast ranches in the Southwest, and Native Americans sometimes adopted ranching and rodeo to conform to American expectations of assimilation, as financial endeavors, and to subversively resist their cultural suppression.[4] As the frontier days drew to a close and as rodeo professionalized over the twentieth century, the sport embraced a narrative of physical hardship and danger that reflected the stories of the "Old West," connecting modern rodeoers to a mythologized and racialized western past in which white settlers pitted themselves against the landscape, animals, and Indigenous peoples.[5] The involvement of women and nonwhite men was ignored and then erased as this new white cow*boy* became the vision of the American cowboy that was remembered, enshrined in both iconography and mythology.

For this new cowboy, being ready to "cowboy up" meant that one was willing to endure the broken bones, punctured organs, and bruised brains that almost all rodeo participants sustain to prove their ability to belong. Studies have shown that rodeoers are far more likely than other athletes to be significantly injured during their careers, and simple safety measures have been difficult to implement, because rodeo was idealized as a sport for rugged, masculine men who embraced danger.[6]

Participating in rodeo also meant being prepared to endanger the safety of the animal performers with whom they worked. As scholar Susan Nance has explained, the willingness to chance death for themselves and other living creatures exposes the persistence of a regional identity centered around the idea of the violent struggle of the frontier.[7] Both encapsulating and eliding a century of racialized, gendered, and species-specific violence, rodeo provides a window into the push and pull of domination and inclusion. This has been especially true for gay rodeoers, who have used the arena to create and embrace a multitude of intersectional identities. Intended to be a site of inclusion that would counter the problematic stereotypes of LGBTQ+ people, particularly those of gay men, gay rodeo also relied on a framework of domination that placed some groups and identities over others, thereby recreating the oppression that all queer cowfolx faced in traditional (i.e., straight) rodeos.

In many ways, as rodeo professionalized, it also narrowed the boundaries of the cowboy. Prior to the 1930s, rodeos often included women in roughstock events and permitted cowboys of color to compete. In 1936, the Cowboys' Turtle Association, later the Professional Rodeo Cowboys Association (PRCA), began the process of unionizing rodeo cowboys and creating sanctioned rodeos. White women and men of color increasingly were systematically excluded from these sanctioned rodeos, both through the elimination of women's events and the enforcement of Jim Crow segregation. In response, Black, Native, and mixed-race men and women formed their own riding associations and rodeo circuits.[8] As mainstream rodeos erased men of color and women of all races from the mythology of the West in the midcentury, a historically inaccurate ideal of white western masculinity solidified in these spaces and informed the imagery gay rodeoers initially drew from in the 1970s and '80s.

At the heart of gay rodeo is the question of racialized masculine performance.[9] While we often use terms like *LGBTQ+* or *queer* to gesture at the idealized inclusiveness of gay rodeo, this has been a competitive arena and community designed predominately by white gay men for their own use. The male founders of the first gay rodeo groups wanted to prove their masculinity, not to remake societal understandings of traditional masculinity but rather to align with white, hegemonic, heteronormative expectations. They wanted to be what ethnomusicologist Kathryn Alexander has described as being "politely different." In Alexander's study, queer country-western dancers strove to emulate the space, dancing, and partnering patterns of mainstream country-western culture, and where they departed, they did so in quiet, respectful ways, attempting to escape notice.[10] Gay rodeoers embraced similar approaches to difference, often attempting emulation rather than revolution. Accordingly, gay rodeos were modeled on the professional circuit and adopted many of the same masculinized notions of the American West.

And yet, despite this desire for societal acceptance, gay rodeo is also meant to be a queer space and has always included elements of campy fun and sexual playfulness. These elements sit uncomfortably alongside the notion of the normative, macho gay man and helped to redefine who had access to these nationalized gendered ideals. Drag queens and special camp events within the rodeo arena, like the wild drag race, which included a mixed-gender team of rodeoers, with at least one in female drag, allowed for gender play and provided the audience with some lighthearted fun.[11] Rodeo programs showcased seminaked male bodies and refused to deny same-sex sexual activity, even in the darkest days of the AIDS epidemic. Indeed, the inclusion of lesbians and gay subcultures promoted alternative sexual cultures and pushed against the traditional boundaries of mainstream, western rodeos.

Even though gay rodeos tried to just be "politely different" and mimicked the professional circuit, their inclusion of difference frequently pushed too far against mainstream rodeo and societal understandings of acceptable gender presentation and sexual desire. Homophobic attacks against gay rodeo claimed that it undermined the legitimacy of rodeo and the cowboy as American ideals. Opposition expanded with the AIDS epidemic, as both fears of contagion and a growing political and religious conservatism swept the country. Gay rodeoers struggled to adjust their image to survive these onslaughts and yet also tried to balance their desire for conformity and acceptance with the proud acknowledgement that they were not just cowboys and cowgirls. They were queer cowfolx, and they adamantly rejected external—and at times even internal—calls to hide that element of their identity.

In creating a space that allowed for intersectional, and sometimes conflicting, identities, gay rodeoers confronted the painstaking realities of building community while their very existence was threatened. Throughout this book, we follow the thread of these dualities and tensions. The desire to emulate professional rodeo and present traditional masculinity conflicted with designing a space meant specifically for queer cowfolx to compete safely and embrace their sexuality openly. Gay rodeo's model of being "politely different" and officially apolitical collided with a disease landscape that pushed participants to act. As the western icon changed in the late twentieth and early twenty-first centuries, the urban cowboy boom coincided with the

LGBTQ+ rights movement, resulting in a space that illuminated clear tensions about identity and visibility politics.

As queer-identifying people claimed their rights to be seen as cowfolx, they also imploded the rural and urban divides that have structured thinking about liberal and conservative politics and queer safety and belonging for the past century. As these binaries between rural and urban have been eroded by both actual queer communities and the scholars who study them, historians and queer theorists have, for the past two decades, resisted the assumption of metronormativity, or the focus on metropolitan spaces, in queer histories. Many early LGBTQ+ studies were anchored in John D'Emilio's foundational assertion that rapid urbanization in the late nineteenth century allowed for the expansion of identities because of the unmooring of the individual from the household economy. As queer rural scholar Colin Johnson has argued, it was not that D'Emilio was saying no same-sex desire existed prior to urbanization, but simply that cities allowed individuals to create communities around their commonalities.

This argument, however, alongside the reality that many of the LGBTQ+ political movements were located in major urban areas, initially led to a dearth of stories about queer people beyond American coastal cities. In the late 1990s and early 2000s, theorists such as J. Halberstam began critiquing the construction of these binaries, and many queer scholars have similarly taken a "rural turn" in their work.[12] More recently in the past decade, a growing number of geographers, sociologists, anthropologists, and historians have also begun examining more liminal spaces, such as the queer suburbs. Noting that most scholars have taken a sweeping approach to nonmetropolitan regions, lumping together small towns, rural communities, and suburban neighborhoods, some geographers have urged scholars to tease out how each of these spaces operate.[13]

Gay rodeoers have always tread these taut divisions, as many themselves fled small towns and rural communities for the perceived safety of the anonymous city.[14] Rather than a comforting sanctuary, however, some found that they did not fit easily there either, because of the culture they carried with them from home. Through country-western bars, square dancing and clogging groups, and gay rodeo, they created spaces that could exist beyond the imagined restraints of both the rural and the urban, occupying zones that were neither strictly urban nor rural. They often hosted rodeos in liminal spaces like the outskirts of big cities—close enough to draw an audience and not too far into the countryside to draw dangerous attention. Their place at the margins shaped their identities of being between: not fully representing country, suburb, or city.

These imagined geographies have been linked intimately with the assumed political orientation of different groups, particularly the association of rural people in the late twentieth century with conservatism, prowar stances, and hypernationalism, versus the progressive, liberal views tied to the (urban) LGBTQ+ community. This dichotomy is based on several sweeping—and erroneous—assumptions: (1) that geography denotes one's political leaning and (2) that queerness means one is urban and liberal. Musicologist and cultural historian Nadine Hubbs has framed this as the urban, elite, gay freedom fighters against the white, working-class "rednecks."[15] But the reality of political life and LGBTQ+ identities is more nuanced and varied. Gay rodeoers from rural backgrounds often eschewed the urban, bar- and club-based gay lifestyle and created their own country-western environment, which provided a sense of comfort and familiarity for these urban transplants. Similarly, not all urban gay rodeoers adopted the liberal views of the gay liberation movement or activist groups like ACT UP. While they believed that queer people had a legitimate claim to the rodeo, organized effectively to oppose homophobic attacks, and engaged in progressive politics through their AIDS fundraising and charitable donations, queer cowfolx also sometimes aligned with their rural, conservative neighbors around issues like gun rights, taxes, and women's rights. Gay rodeo encapsulates both the nostalgia for a bucolic frontier past and the hope for a more inclusive future. Yet studying this space also subverts these assumptions and offers a more complex understanding of queer political realities across geographical locations.

Pulling together threads of gender, politics, and geography, *Slapping Leather* is a book that revels in the uncomfortable tensions that gay rodeo has produced. Its chapters examine how gay rodeo, and more specifically the International Gay Rodeo Association (IGRA), helped construct and contest a particular gender order rooted in the iconography of the cowboy, while also navigating the first decades of the AIDS epidemic, calls for consumer activism, and desires to be inclusive across gender, sexuality, and race. We carefully examine how the rodeo arena became a space that resisted a monolithic narrative of what a rural westerner or a gay community should look like, exposing fracture points among members as the organization attempted to create a unified version of what gay rodeo meant.

Accompanied by oral history vignettes and arranged thematically, each chapter grapples with questions about how the gay rodeo community engaged with the world around them. Chapter 1 introduces readers to the roots of gay rodeo and queer country-western culture in the 1960s and '70s. It follows the history of early gay rodeo and the birth of IGRA as the circuit grew out of a history of queer civic fundraising and a rejection of the effeminacy ascribed to gay men in the midcentury. Chapter 2 delves further into hegemonic masculinity and the desire of gay male rodeoers to align with that vision of gender performance. Yet within these normative gendered notions of gay rodeo, the gay cowboy also embraced explicitly (homo)sexual imagery that disrupted the traditional conservatism of mainstream rodeo and queered notions of cowboy masculinity.

The galvanizing pressure of the AIDS epidemic is explored in chapter 3. Just as gay rodeoers endorsed a public celebration of their sexuality and of queer sexual activity, the AIDS epidemic in the 1980s and '90s brought change to gay rodeo. Forced to confront a growing conservative movement and anti-LGBTQ+ opposition, along with the pressures that AIDS placed on the queer community, gay rodeo brought people together to care for each other, to fundraise for the community, and to push back against the political climate. Chapter 4 provides a closer examination of the fundraising branch of gay rodeo—the royalty titleholders—and of the camp elements of the circuit. The playful humor of the camp events and the royalty contest upended the gender binary and the normative gender roles desired by many gay rodeoers. This led to an uncomfortable relationship in gay rodeo, as some participants criticized these elements of the rodeo as unprofessional and not suitably aligned with the country-western imaginary, while others recognized the centrality of drag queen titleholders to gay rodeo's fundraising mission.

Chapter 5 examines gay rodeo's relationship to formal politics and IGRA's commitment to the neoliberal market as the appropriate place to achieve LGBTQ+ civil rights. Though they carefully avoided political pronouncements in public and many members noted their disdain for more activist—and in their eyes more extremist—queer political activity, gay rodeoers participated in forms of political activism through their AIDS fundraising and their repeated calls for IGRA members to vote with their dollars in pursuing sponsorship opportunities. As they fought for these expanded rights and promoted claims of inclusion regarding their own organization, members of the gay rodeo community faced successes and failures. Chapter 6 illustrates the challenges that gay rodeo experienced around inclusion as IGRA welcomed relationships with specific communities. Notably, gay rodeoers overlapped with groups of men who celebrated masculinity through ideals of the "regular guy," such as bears, with their love of big, hairy male bodies, and leathermen, who used leather to communicate their commitment to toughness and independence. They even intersected with straight rodeoers, who helped shape their desire for a masculine, professional-style rodeo. Those who failed to do so or who contradicted the ideal of an authentically western rodeo, such as lesbians, trans people, and nonwhite participants, were sometimes met with ambivalence or outright hostility.

For each chapter, a corresponding oral history vignette provides personal insight into the lives of queer cowfolx, the struggles gay rodeo has faced, the tensions of intersecting identity claims, and the undeniable importance this arena has held for its participants. Together, these chapters argue that gay rodeo offered people a place to explore many facets of their overlapping identities, even as this space at times invested in historically problematic ideas about the US West, the cowboy icon, and what it meant to be masculine, American, and gay at the turn of the twenty-first century.

In 1997, a rodeo director responded to an IGRA letter asking about the direction gay rodeos should take to keep expanding and professionalizing. In his response, the director asked about the central mission of IGRA: "Do we want IGRA to be a Junior PRCA for Gays? Is our purpose to raise money for the fight against AIDS? Do we want an organization that will simply provide a way for those of us who are interested in Rodeo to pursue our interests in a gay environment?"[16] He did not know the answers to these questions and therefore struggled to imagine what the future of the organization could be. As we have pored over archival material and worked with the community, we have seen similar questions posed. Is the gay rodeo "just a rodeo"? Is it a wholesome place for family fun? Is it a true replication of the American West and a "real" rodeo but for LGBTQ+ competitors? Is it a sexual space for participants to either find sex or establish partnerships and love connections? Is it a site of real or performed masculinity? At various times and in different places, gay rodeo has been all of these. While it has been a site of performed normative masculinity, it also disrupted the hegemonic heterosexuality of the rodeo, a beloved sport and cultural performance for millions of people globally. But beyond just a sport or a country-western performance, gay rodeo remains as it has always been: tenuous and fragile. In encapsulating so many tensions, it represented a truly radical promise that would allow anyone to identify as a cowboy. While it at times failed to achieve all it set out to do, it still provided a much-needed haven for thousands of people.

This, then, is a book about fitting imperfectly. It is about never being gay enough. Never being conservative—or liberal—enough. Never being cowboy enough. Gay rodeo at times is not masculine enough and, other times, is too masculine. As a case study for belonging, *Slapping Leather* illustrates how marginalized groups can come together to resist easy categorization, while sometimes building barbed fences of exclusion themselves.

Oral History Vignette

ROGER BERGMANN, RODEO JUDGE AND IGRA PAST PRESIDENT

I grew up in northwestern Montana, near Glacier National Park. We lived in town, only like a half a block from the downtown area of Kalispell, which, when I was growing up, was a town of about fifteen thousand people. As a youth, I would ride my bicycle to the county fair in August every year, and I'd go in and watch the rodeos.

I graduated from the University of Montana in 1971. The Vietnam War was still going on, but I applied for conscientious objector status with the Selective Service. At the time, I did not realize or accept the fact that I was gay, or I could have used that for a deferment. I ended up going to California for alternate service work with the California Ecology Corps for fifteen years and then transferred to the Forest Service. At this point I still had not accepted my own sexuality. It was about 1981 that I finally went into my first gay bar. I was nervous as could be when I was going in. It was a bar called the I-Beam in San Francisco. As soon as I got into that bar and walked around, I felt totally comfortable and at ease. I felt that, "Yes, it's not just a curiosity. I am gay."

That same year, I saw a flyer on the wall for the National Reno Gay Rodeo, which was the first gay rodeos that were held. They were started in 1976 by a man named Phil Ragsdale in Reno, Nevada. I went to the rodeo in August 1981, and there were about eight thousand people in the stands. A lot of people from San Francisco and Los Angeles would get up there for the rodeo. I went from 1981 every year until their last rodeo around 1985. Those weekends were pretty wild.

In the spring of 1993, I got a phone call from Wayne Jakino, the founding president of IGRA, who said I should run for president. I thought about it for a couple of weeks and called back and said that I would. When the word got out that I was going to run, nobody else did. I was voted in by acclamation. I ran a second year, and then the man that I was dating passed away in 1994. I had planned on not running, so that I could spend time with him. But when he passed away, I decided I would run for a third term, so that I would keep busy. I was president from 1993 through 1995. I became president at a time when country music was still on the rise, and in 1993, interest in rodeo had grown tremendously. Every year I was president we brought in two or three new member associations.

The interest originally was from people in western states that had grown up, if not on a ranch, then near a ranch or knew people that had horses. A lot of the people would watch the rodeo, have a good time watching it, and want to get involved. That's one of the reasons why we have nontraditional rodeo events called the camp events. Goat dressing, steer decorating, and the wild drag race are events where you don't have to ride a horse, you don't have to have really any skill. You just have to have the courage to step into the arena and work with somebody.

Over time there was a change. We saw it fading away. It's been shrinking since 2000. I was president at the peak, with about seven thousand members around the US and Canada. Now I would guess it's around 3,500 or 4,000. When Garth Brooks came back, there was talk, even on the radio—because country-western in the straight community had also faded away—that he was going to start singing again, and he's going to get the interest up again. It didn't really get the numbers to grow within the gay community, and I'm not so sure about the straight community either.

Chapter 1

ORIGINS

The History of the Gay Western Ideal and the Gay Rodeo

"Straights beware," warned a sign outside the 1981 National Reno Gay Rodeo in Nevada. Established in the 1970s and '80s, gay rodeo provided cowboys with a traditional, masculine-styled rodeo but also, as the message to "straights" cautioned, embraced an openly gay identity, from playful camp events to drag queen contests.[1] Heteronormative masculinity existed in uneasy tension with this campy fun. Some participants, like Greg Olson, future seven-year all-around champion, expressed disappointment with the first National Reno Gay Rodeo he attended in 1977. "It wasn't anything like the normal rodeos we always went to and watched back home."[2] Raised on a Nebraska farm, Olson critiqued the emphasis placed on camp events such as greased-pig chasing and wild cow milking. Even more upsetting, these seemed more popular with the crowd than the traditional bull riding and calf roping that he wanted to see.[3]

Whether the participants played with effeminacy in the drag queen contests, engaged in public queerness in the camp events, or desired a strictly masculine environment, like that which Olson sought, there was no hiding the gayness of the gay rodeo. As Roger Bergmann, longtime judge and association president, said about the early years, "Those weekends were pretty wild."⁴ A sense of queered space surrounded participants and visitors, as the rodeo used explicit images of gay male sex in its program and received sponsorships from gay bars, sex clubs, and bathhouses. Despite its internal frictions, the audiences, gay press, and rodeoers clamored for this different type of gay western America. As one newspaper exclaimed in 1982, it was "three days of hot men, hot weather and hot times. Hot Dog!"⁵ While most gay rodeos were urban or urban-adjacent, rodeo in general has been associated with rural spaces for a century and so provided a way for participants to "go country" and escape the metrochauvinism common within urban gay communities in the 1970s and '80s. Yet gay rodeo also adopted and reinforced a more heteronormative, white chauvinism prevalent in the very same rural western communities from which so many of its participants were trying to escape. These events, alongside enthusiast clubs, relied on the norms and strictures of western rodeos and traditional masculinity to gain entry into that conservative world, but as gay men. Through their involvement, whether as riders or viewers, they were able to create a different queer sexual subculture that straddled the urban and rural.

While it is certain that queer cowfolx participated in ranching and rodeoing from the origin of these activities, that history and the identities of those people have proven difficult to uncover. Gay rodeoers sometimes invoke a queer history of the West to demonstrate that they belong, but they have referred to the past less frequently than other circuits. Participants in Black rodeo, Native American rodeo, and Mexican American *charreada* competitions routinely point to a racially diverse western history to illustrate their involvement in that past and validate their claim to a space in the rodeo world.⁶ In contrast, gay rodeo was not established to celebrate a queer ranching history or a historic rodeo involvement specifically rooted in a gay identity. Rather, early promoters in the 1970s framed it as a place to fundraise for your community, be out and proud, and embrace a country-western lifestyle.

Corresponding with the urban cowboy craze and an upsurge in hypermasculine gay male subcultures, gay rodeo expanded and was formalized during the AIDS epidemic in the 1980s. Shifting from some of its earlier, more blatant promotion of sex and redirecting its fundraising toward AIDS research, it became a place dedicated to supporting its members and establishing a safe community in an often-hostile environment. Gay rodeo has welcomed most with open arms, from gay men, lesbians, drag queens, and transgender people to straight riders and even curious onlookers. It is a place that has allowed people to be who they are and who they want to be, largely without judgment. Because of this, it quickly became a refuge for queer people to escape the discrimination they faced in mainstream rodeos and even in broader American society. Yet, despite the credo of acceptance within gay rodeo, not all groups have found the same type of support and community there. Formed *by* gay men *for* gay men, it has had a complicated relationship with straight rodeo as it supported and aligned with traditional gender stereotypes. Particularly, this space often struggled to truly welcome female competitors and to balance its own dichotomous and often contentious relationship between the drag-based royalty pageants and the primarily masculine-presenting male rodeo competitors.

In order to fully understand how gay rodeo has contributed to the development of queer western performance, we must understand its development as a community rooted in the late twentieth century. This chapter examines early groups like the Golden State Cowboys (1969–76) that were formed to be country-western lifestyle and rodeo-enthusiast organizations for members who wanted to forge an identity for themselves as gay men that was separate from other gay communities and interest groups, such as motorcycle clubs and the leather scene. From there, the chapter traces the creation of the Reno gay rodeos in the 1970s, the spread of gay rodeo across western states in the '70s and '80s, the establishment of the International Gay Rodeo Association in 1985, the early explosive success of IGRA over the course of the '80s and '90s, and the subsequent decline of gay rodeo in the 2000s. Embedded throughout this chapter are discussions of gay rodeo's purpose, from fundraising and community development to the promotion of a specific masculine ideal, all of which are connected to the rise and fall of this circuit.

FROM COWBOY ENTHUSIASTS TO RODEO PARTICIPANTS IN THE 1970s

In 1989, a western-themed photospread in *Esquire* magazine claimed, "If you're an American male, buried somewhere deep in your soul is a little bit of cowboy."[7] This claim was at least a century old by the late 1980s. The notion of the West's import to a larger national identity dates well back into the nineteenth century. Cowboys, along with scouts, miners, and trappers, had once been perceived to be the outcasts of Victorian American society. As men who worked in multiracial, homosocial, and untamed nomadic settings, they lacked the cultural and financial capital of the landed, patriarchal "cattlemen." The closing of "the frontier" in the 1890s created an antimodern backlash driven by cultural producers like "Buffalo Bill" Cody, Frederick Remington, Owen Wister, and Theodore Roosevelt. The emergence of western performance walked hand in hand with western identity as Wild West shows, rodeos, and early western films enthralled domestic and international audiences and made heroes of these outcasts. In the aftermath of Reconstruction and at a moment when Jim Crow, anti-Chinese sentiments, and immigration restrictions solidified, the West became intimately associated with a national American identity. Rodeo, together with literature and film, continued to develop the cowboy as the mascot of the imagined West in the twentieth century.[8]

Most importantly, with the rise of television and film, cowboys became imagined as white and heterosexual. Simultaneously, rodeo cowboys increasingly represented "real" cowboys in American culture.[9] As cowboys unionized in the 1930s and '40s with the creation of the Professional Rodeo Cowboys Association (PRCA), Jim Crow segregation and an unwillingness to support women's roughstock events helped push specific groups toward the margins of cowboy culture. The homogenized version of the American cowboy solidified in the postwar period, with John Wayne western films in the 1940s, '50s, and '60s and popular television shows like *Annie Oakley* (1954–57) and *Gunsmoke* (1955–75).

As the West became increasingly mythologized and divorced from actual western experiences, rodeo and Wild West show performers created a highly stylized and overtly gaudy form of attire as each entertainer sought to capture the audience's attention. Western film stars adapted these flashy costumes to the silver screen, wearing custom-made outfits through the 1920s. It was only in 1923 that manufacturer Miller & Co. established the Stockman-Farmer catalogue to sell western clothing to actual working cowboys, and in the 1930s, manufacturing companies, like Rockmount and Levi's, were founded to mass-produce ranchwear. Both performers and early manufacturers gave the look new stylistic flairs and practical nuances. For instance, embellished embroidery on boots was intended for pure show, but snap buttons were meant to tear away if a shirt became dangerously snagged while working on a ranch.[10]

From that point, western wear continued to enjoy periods of mainstream popularity through the twentieth century. Catalogs and newspaper advertisements in the 1950s and '60s appealed to children playing dress-up and adults who worked in the West, along with those who lived in the urban East but craved a form of western authenticity. Just as this earlier interest was spurred by film and television representations of the West, the release of new cinematic westerns in the late 1970s pushed this kind of clothing to even more widespread prominence. The film *Urban Cowboy* in 1980 and the television show *Dallas*, which premiered in 1978 and soon drew audiences of over forty million viewers weekly, are credited with launching this new popular interest in the American West and igniting a western-wear craze.[11]

Designers like Calvin Klein and companies like L. L. Bean sold western-influenced roughwear, and Levi's jeans steadily increased its yearly profits.[12] Country music also moved from a regional genre to national prominence with the Nashville sound of outlaw-country performers like Waylon Jennings and Willie Nelson.[13] Even the elder statesman President Ronald Reagan portrayed himself in the cowboy image, seen most notably in his "Man of the Year" *TIME Magazine* cover in 1981.[14] However, just as the popular enthusiasm for western style and culture peaked in the early '80s, it began a similarly swift decline. The same year as Reagan's cowboy cover, more traditional western-wear companies, like Kauffman's in New York and Rodeo Ben's in Philadelphia, reported a drop in business, and contemporary western-focused lines, like Ralph Lauren, also saw low profits at the start of the new decade.[15]

Yet this expansion of western style from the working ranch to the mainstream fashion scene was not strictly linear. Similar to other trends, such as the fashion, dancing, and music of disco in the 1970s and voguing in the 1980s, which first emerged in gay, urban, Black communities, country-western wear and enthusiasm for aspects of that lifestyle appeared years earlier within similarly marginalized groups. A decade before its rise to popular acclaim in 1978, western wear and culture appeared in the burgeoning gay enclaves of urban, bicoastal America, in places such as Los Angeles, San Francisco, and New York City.[16]

By the 1970s and '80s, gay men and women already used cowboy performance to assert their rights to a place in America's social and political landscape. Gay masculine subcultures, particularly leathermen and bears, became increasing popular in the era, with the cowboy becoming one of the key hero figures of gay masculinity. These subcultures sought to fight the assumed effeminacy of gay men in particular.[17] Gay cowboy culture also allowed men and women who grew up in rural areas, often uncomfortable in urban gay culture, a space to relax. Country-western havens, like Charlie's in Denver, opened up in the early 1980s, and many gay disco bars converted to country and line dancing venues.[18]

The new country-focused bars catered to this growing subculture of gay cowboy devotees, performers, and riders, helping people connect and form rodeo groups as their interests moved beyond just fashion and music. The earliest identifiable gay rodeo organization was founded in 1969, when nine gay men created a western-lifestyle group that would allow them to socialize and attend (straight) rodeos together. After some discussion over the name—Bear State Cowboys, Golden West Riders, and Marlboro Wranglers were proposed—Golden State Cowboys (GSC) was formed in Los Angeles. Though designed to be a social organization, the group was serious about its endeavor and formal in its meetings. The members created a constitution and bylaws, kept regular meeting notes, and held a series of events.[19]

GSC, which existed from 1969 until 1976, intended "to expose and maintain a fitting and proper representation of the American Cowboy image to society, and provide reason for all to respect our individual habit of living." To do this, it planned to "increase public interest and intrigue with our membership" but also "maintain an exposure that will invite recognition and respect." There was some desire to expand interest in the group, but the founders also wanted to be exclusive: membership was limited to twenty-five people. To become a member, applicants had to demonstrate their ability to ride a horse, pay a sixty-dollar annual fee (fairly steep for 1969, as later gay rodeo organizations in the 1980s only had a twenty-dollar fee), agree to wear "complete western apparel" at all events and meetings, and portray the "American Cowboy image."[20]

The organization intended to hold meetings and other western-focused events, but GSC member Brian Smith wrote a formal complaint that it did little in the first couple of years other than "drink beer and attend rodeos in a group." He remarked that GSC was not all that different from other gay groups in the area other than the fact that "(1) we tend to be a little more butch than they, and (2) we can all ride a horse rather than a 'bike.'" The last comment refers to a segment of the growing gay leather scene, which was connected to the gay motorcycle groups that first appeared in the 1950s, '60s, and '70s in California.[21] Unlike the cowboy, who was steady and rugged, the quintessential American hero, the new urban gay biker was dark and dangerous, the antihero. Yet both were masculine, undeniably sexy, and sexual, and quickly became icons within the growing urban communities of gay men. They grew in popularity contemporaneously and shared much in their use of leather and their promotion of sex and hypermasculinity, but tensions between them also existed.

While both of these communities promoted a more traditionally masculine, rather than an effeminate, gay male identity, motorcycle fashion developed a close association with the new leather scene of the 1950s and '60s and its promotion of sexual sadomasochism (S/M), bondage, and kink (see figure 2).[22] This made biker groups one of the most subversive of the new gay sexual subcultures and, even as they and the S/M leather community began to diverge, lingering associations remained. By the 1970s, books like *The Leatherman's Handbook* (1972) and *The Joy of Gay Sex* (1977) helped make leather and S/M more mainstream among gay men, and yet both publications still identified S/M as closely connected to leather and motorcycle culture.[23]

GSC existed in this world of hypermasculine adulation, as the disgruntled member noted. The gay motorcycle culture was centered in California, and GSC in many ways was a reaction to it, as it promoted its own conception of masculinity, one it saw as profoundly different from the gay biker and leather culture of the time. Brian Smith wanted GSC to be something distinct from the dozens of other gay groups in the area. Part of his critique was that he wanted the group to be less self-serving and instead focus on fundraising for charity, but his critiques of drinking and bike culture also suggest that he, and other GSC members, wanted this organization to offer its members an alternate way to be gay men. Rather than adopt the alternative subculture of S/M leather, they wanted to assume the mainstream leather culture of the masculine, heroic cowboy.

FIGURE 2. *Two leathermen at the San Francisco Pride Parade, circa 1988–94. Wearing accoutrements of the leather community—motorcycle caps, vests, and chaps—they are taking in the parade from the mayor's balcony. Some of these elements, like the vests and chaps, also appear in rodeo wear as part of the "brown leather" community, as opposed to the "black leather" men seen here. Courtesy of Shades of LGBTQIA, San Francisco Public Library.*

The organization seemed to take his suggestions, and while it continued to organize excursions to the big western rodeos in California and Arizona, it also began to host its own western hoedown and square dance competition, an annual ranch roundup, and fundraisers such as a Toys for Tots dinner and a Christmas benefit party to buy gifts for senior citizens. Though GSC was meant to be a social group and rodeo enthusiast club, some of its activities were rodeo-like in design. The ranch roundup, which the group sometimes called a rodeo roundup, took place outside of San Diego. Despite Smith's earlier criticism of the group's drinking, plenty of alcohol was still available, including a cocktail hour and "all the beer you can drink." By 1976 a mix of motorcyclists and cowboys attended the roundup, and prizes were offered to participants in both western events and biker events (see figure 3). Even though there had been earlier complaints about the biker groups, there was now a mixing of gay leather masculinities, with bikers and cowboys alike at this "rodeo" roundup. This was not

FIGURE 3. *Golden State Cowboys flyer, 1976. While other GSC flyers hinted at gender play—such as the "Flaming Saddles" hoedown, which included a man wearing a dress, braids, and lipstick but also with unshaven legs and curly chest hair—the 1976 roundup ad is a show of traditional masculinity, with a powerful cowboy looming large on a poster that also promised both "western & bike" events. Courtesy of ONE Archives at the USC Libraries.*

the only time that the gay cowboy and biking cultures bumped into each other. The early gay rodeo programs, which will be discussed in the next chapter, included extensive leather imagery, and the connections to the leather scene are still present at gay rodeos into the twenty-first century.

Despite the intermixing of these gay male subcultures at the 1976 roundup and the group's expanded slate of activities, GSC appears to have folded shortly after this event. Though the specific reasons are unclear, the organization struggled with membership since its founding. One list from 1970 includes only eleven members. With nine of those likely the original charter members, the group had apparently grown little in its first year, and it seems that those membership problems continued.[24] However, just as Golden State Cowboys dissolved, a new gay rodeo organization formed and began to host full-scale gay rodeos that were open to the public. This new group emerged in the bordering state of Nevada, and just a few years later, another gay cowboy group formed in California, though none of the original GSC members appear to have been involved in these organizations. While the members of GSC had worn the clothes and became cowboy icons in style, the new gay rodeo groups were going to help queer people become cowboys in action.

The creation of the first formalized and more widely advertised gay rodeo began in 1975, when Reno businessman Phil Ragsdale decided to plan his own rodeo as a fundraiser for the Imperial Court in Nevada. At the time, Ragsdale was serving as Emperor I of Reno's Comstock Empire Silver Dollar Court, which was part of the larger Imperial Court network. The Reno court had only begun that year, and Ragsdale was the first "Emperor of Reno."[25] The Imperial Court System began a decade earlier, in 1965, as an extension of the drag balls and bars in San Francisco. Initially it focused on its drag roots by electing an empress but in 1972 added the title of emperor for a cisgender gay man who did not appear in drag. In addition to the crowning of the royal court and holding balls, the Imperial Court System was a philanthropic organization, raising tens of thousands of dollars for charity every year. It quickly spread to cities outside of San Francisco and by 1980 included more than fifty chapters across the United States, Canada, and Mexico.[26]

It was with this history in mind and with his own experience in Nevada, a place steeped in western cowboy culture, that in 1975, as emperor, Phil Ragsdale proposed hosting an amateur gay rodeo to raise money for the local senior center and, later, the Muscular Dystrophy Association (MDA). He also wanted it to be a fun event for gay riders and described the same concerns that many in the gay leather community had about the perceived effeminacy of gay men. Ragsdale hoped his rodeo would show the masculine side of gay men to counter these societal stereotypes.[27] With months of planning, he secured the county fairgrounds for October 1976. Local stock contractors were reluctant to rent him animals when they learned it was for a gay rodeo, so he proceeded to purchase his own "wild" stock.[28]

The first Reno Gay Rodeo saw a fairly limited turnout of competitors and fans (40 contestants and 150 spectators) and raised only $1,000, but Ragsdale decided to sponsor another one the following year.[29] In 1977 it became known as the National Reno Gay Rodeo, and he founded and became president of the Comstock Gay Rodeo Association that same year to help produce the event and organize competitors. By 1981, the National Reno Gay Rodeo had become an annual weekend-long festival, accompanied by a parade and a plethora of cowboy-themed parties. Over the first five years, donations for the MDA raised at the rodeo grew to over $40,000 per year. Attendance reached ten thousand spectators, and a public celebrity status was reached when Joan Rivers served as grand marshal of the parade in 1982.[30] Growing out of a longer tradition of LGBTQ+ civic engagement and coinciding with a major surge in country-western trendiness, Reno's early gay rodeos provided participants with a place to line-dance with their same-sex partners, raise money for charity, and cruise for sex and companionship outside of the urban gay bars (see figure 4).

The National Reno Gay Rodeo continued to lead the scene for several years and quickly began to attract riders from other states. Soon, more cowboy groups began to form. The Golden Spikes Gay Rodeo Association was founded in Utah in 1979 and the Pacific Coast Gay Rodeo Association in 1980. The latter was the combined effort of three people who met at the Reno rodeo and wanted to start a group in the Northwest. They joined forces with other enthusiasts trying to form one in the Bay Area and together created the new association. Unlike Golden State Cowboys from a few years earlier, this organization was significantly larger—with upwards of a hundred members—and welcomed women. Four women served on the board of directors, and the

FIGURE 4. *National Reno Gay Rodeo flyer, 1983. A muscled, shirtless cowboy promotes the upcoming gay rodeo. His unbuttoned jeans and skintight chaps—almost nude in appearance—hint at the excitement you would miss out on if you were to fail to make your reservations today. Courtesy of ONE Archives at the USC Libraries.*

association's statement of purpose specifically included "gay men and gay women" whom they wanted "to participate equally and proudly together in organized rodeo events."[31] While the group held a series of events, including a "country and western round-up" and a barn dance, it could not fulfill its goal of staging the first gay rodeo outside of Reno. One was planned for 1981, but the high cost of production, along with opposition from animal rights activists, stalled it that year.[32]

In the meantime, the new organizations continued to travel to Reno, as it was still the only gay rodeo available. However, the growing numbers of riders in other states looked for rodeos closer to home, and everyone involved seemed interested in more opportunities to compete. In 1981 the Colorado Gay Rodeo Association formed, and, within a couple of years, it became the first group to host its own rodeo, held in Denver in 1983.[33]

Even as new rodeos were added, the Reno one expanded and became more elaborate. A newsletter advertised "an Evening of [Women's] Concerts" with guest artists at the 1982 edition. There also was an invitation for anyone with music experience to answer an open call for a marching band, slated to perform five songs at the rodeo. To encourage involvement, anyone who joined the band received free tickets to the entire event. The following year, in 1983, the Reno rodeo grew further to include a talent showcase.[34]

These were heady days of expansion for gay rodeo, with new state organizations and an almost ever-growing event list at the annual Reno weekend. No formal association connected the separate groups, but the Comstock Gay Rodeo Association in Reno, with Phil Ragsdale at the helm, provided centralized direction and leadership. Shortly after organizing, the first Colorado president, Wayne Jakino, contacted Comstock to notify it of the new group and invited representatives from Comstock to attend its meetings. Jakino wrote, "As this is our first contact with your organization, may I wish us both a congenial and prosperous future through the close and continued dialogue. Our group is very anxious to hear from you and receive information from you that we may use to bring our groups together in a working relationship for our common goals."[35]

In these early years, groups worked together and relied on the sharing of knowledge. Just as Colorado had, each new one looked to the Comstock Gay Rodeo Association—and to Ragsdale specifically—for leadership, although they did not always like the direction they received. For instance, in 1982, Comstock and Colorado debated the royalty contest rules. The Colorado association inquired about adding riding abilities as a requirement for the contest, but Comstock refused, responding that it would be too confusing to have various organizations judging the contest differently. Comstock and Ragsdale also controlled the royalty contest in other ways by requiring any city interested in holding one to first register a coordinator with the Comstock association.[36] Ironically, even though the Colorado group asked for leeway on the royalty contest rules and disliked Ragsdale's response that uniformity in requirements and judging was needed, it also implored Comstock in 1982 to standardize the rules for rodeo events.[37]

FORMALIZATION AND EXPANSION IN THE 1980s AND '90s

Amid these early growing pains and power struggles, gay rodeo continued to expand. Cowboys and cowgirls from Texas first participated in the Reno rodeo in 1981. They soon formed their own group, the Texas Gay Rodeo Association, in 1983 and hosted their first rodeo the following year in Houston. In 1984 the Golden State Gay Rodeo Association replaced the Pacific Coast Gay Rodeo Association for the California region, and an Arizona association formed the same year. Like the Colorado and Texas groups, Golden State and Arizona sponsored their own rodeos—Los Angeles in 1985 and Phoenix in 1986—shortly after organizing.

These organizations expanded quickly across the West, often forming after cowboys and cowgirls from those states attended the Reno rodeo. Despite the importance of that original event, the leadership of Phil Ragsdale and Comstock began to crumble, and 1984 was the last year of the National Reno Gay Rodeo. One was planned for 1985, but a combination of financial difficulties and attacks from the Christian Right in Nevada stopped it that year. Ragsdale hoped to revive it the following year, but he was unsuccessful, and the National Reno Gay Rodeo fizzled out and came to an inglorious end.[38]

Even though the dominance of the National Reno Gay Rodeo and the Comstock Gay Rodeo Association was over, gay rodeo was only entering its early stages of growth. By the last Reno event in 1984, gay rodeos already had been held in Denver and Houston, and the first in California was scheduled for 1985. With the growing number of competitions and organizations—and now without Comstock as the central authority—the groups from Colorado, Texas, California, and Arizona formed the International Gay Rodeo Association (IGRA) in 1985 to act as a governing body. Wayne Jakino from the Colorado association played a pivotal role in its founding and became the first president of IGRA. In addition to that position, Jakino provided guidance to several of the new state and regional associations as they were formalized and began to host their own rodeos. The newly birthed IGRA knit together local associations by managing membership requirements, seeking large sponsorships, sanctioning rodeos, training officials, reviewing formal complaints, and standardizing rules. While gay rodeoers were still required to join specific local associations—no one is technically a "member" of IGRA—they found a national, and even international, community through the association.

Once formed, IGRA organized things meticulously. Its rule book included bylaws, standing rules, general regulations for the rodeos, information about prizes, and explanations of each event. In 1986 it underwent a large expansion, with additional sections about fair play and ethics, guidelines for the royalty contest, and information for judges and rodeo directors. Since that time, the rule books have followed much the same format, and many of the rules have remained the same since the very first version in 1984, such as allowing men and women to compete together but judging them separately, offering an all-around title for the top cowboy and cowgirl, dividing events into four categories—roughstock, roping, horse (later called speed), and camp—and requiring contestants to compete in three of the four categories and placing in two of them to qualify for the all-around titles. However, other rules have changed, nonrodeo events have been eliminated or moved to other competitive venues, and the rule book itself has become increasingly complex as gay rodeo attempted to model itself on the professional circuit.[39]

IGRA events largely align with those of professional western rodeo, although gay rodeo has featured several unique events and puts its own spin on others. The first official IGRA rule book from 1984 listed sixteen events: bull riding, wild cow riding, bareback bronc riding, chute dogging, team roping, mounted breakaway roping, calf roping on foot, ribbon roping, barrel racing, pole bending, speed barrels, the Texas flag race, speed racing, wild cow milking, steer decorating, and goat decorating. Some of these early events have changed or been removed. For instance, the speed barrels did not appear again after 1984, and the speed race and ribbon roping were eliminated after 1985. Wild cow milking was replaced with the wild drag race in 1986, wild cow riding was replaced with steer riding in 1989, and goat decorating was renamed goat dressing in 1989.[40]

These events are divided into the four categories of roughstock, roping, speed, or camp. Most appear at other western rodeos, though some, such as bull and bronc riding, have different rules. In IGRA, competitors make a six-second, not eight-second, ride.[41] Other events, such as pole bending, steer decorating, and chute dogging, do not appear at the professional level. IGRA included these options, more frequently seen at youth and high school rodeos, to encourage participation by LGBTQ+ people new to the rodeo world but interested in the country-western lifestyle or looking for a safe space to be themselves. Each of the four categories includes one of these entry-level events so that anyone can participate. In addition, gay rodeo also diverges from western rodeos in its inclusion of camp events: wild cow milking (later the wild drag race), steer decorating, and goat decorating/dressing. Some of these events are unique to gay rodeo while others appear in the western version as events for children or as exhibitions. In gay rodeo, they become a place where the adult contestant can assume the fun, playful events of children—truly queering the traditional masculinity of the rodeo. (These camp events, along with the royalty contest, are discussed in greater detail in chapter 4).

After the creation of IGRA in 1985, gay rodeo grew rapidly, appearing first in western states long associated with this sporting arena and then into other parts of the country. By the end of 1986, there were associations in Arizona, Colorado, Missouri, Oklahoma, California, Kansas, New Mexico, and Texas, and collectively they hosted five regional rodeos. Some states were so large and the rodeo so popular that multiple chapters existed. By 1985, there were five chapters in Texas and at least two in California, though eventually that association would be home to six separate chapters. IGRA used this momentum to expand into other events, with its first official royalty competition in 1986 and its first dance competition in 1987, featuring gay square dancers, cloggers, and two-steppers. The organization also began to plan its first finals rodeo, initially intended for 1986. However, the extensive planning process pushed the rodeo to 1987, when it was held in Northern California, the first in that part of the state.[42]

The 1987 IGRA finals rodeo followed the format of the regional competitions and included a full slate of other events, including dances, a craft and souvenir fair, a grand entry parade, and even an excursion to a local casino. The rodeo program also highlighted the growing concern about AIDS, a cause that gay rodeo had begun to fund years earlier in 1983. By 1987, AIDS groups made up the majority of the circuit's fundraising efforts. Only in the 2000s did IGRA begin to shift its focus away from HIV/AIDS, although it continued to appear as a charity recipient into the 2020s.[43]

The first IGRA finals rodeo attracted a crowd of approximately five thousand.[44] Even though the organization was left with a debt of $4,500 and there were fears that it might have to cancel one of the regional rodeos if there were not enough donations to cover the debt, IGRA moved boldly forward and began to plan the second finals rodeo, which it hoped to bring back to Reno for the first time since the Comstock Gay Rodeo Association had dissolved.[45] Despite these ambitions, the same attacks by the Christian Right—now emboldened by the growing AIDS crisis—that had plagued Phil Ragsdale in Reno also opposed IGRA and won.[46] The organization faced similar hostility again and again in the 1980s and '90s. This repeated opposition to the gay rodeo was sometimes framed around the issue of money but almost always was steeped in homophobia and a fear of AIDS. (The fight against gay rodeo and its defensive plans are discussed in greater detail in chapter 3, which examines the impact of the AIDS crisis.)

In 1988, the finals rodeo lost to these outside forces and was canceled. IGRA had to invoke its contingency plan. The rule book stated that even without a finals rodeo, awards would still be given for all-around cowboy and cowgirl. For the ghost rodeo of 1988, for which a program already had been printed, those awards were determined by the standings from the regional rodeos.[47]

This was a defining incident for IGRA. Even though the lawsuits and negative publicity in 1988 could have torn the organization apart, it became a moment that united the organization, and IGRA grew explosively after this contentious public event. Indeed, it was about to enter its golden years as gay rodeo rapidly expanded over the next decade. In 1988 alone, two new associations joined IGRA: the Oregon Gay Rodeo Association and the Cowboy State Rodeo Association (Wyoming). The following year there were two more groups: Big Sky (Montana) and Utah, which was a reorganization of the earlier Golden

Spikes Gay Rodeo Association from 1979. As the GSGRA acronym was already taken by the California association, the Utah group became the Utah Gay Rodeo Association. The organization still paid homage to its earlier days as the Golden Spikes by giving out the Golden Spike Awards for "favorite cowboy, dancer, best refluff, best dressed male, best dressed female, and many more."[48]

The following decade was one of incredible growth for IGRA. In 1990 alone, four new associations joined: Northwest (Washington, Oregon, and Idaho), North Star (Minnesota and Wisconsin), Tri-State (Ohio, Indiana, and Kentucky), and Diamond State (Arkansas).[49] IGRA also fielded interest from outside the US, with an invitation to the Gay Oz Expo Rodeo in Australia.[50] In 1991 two new associations formed in locations further from traditional rodeo states: Atlantic States (Maryland, Virginia, and DC) and Southeast (Georgia). IGRA also added three rodeos to the circuit that year, bring the total to ten annually. In just two more years, that number more than doubled, to twenty-one.

To accommodate this fast growth, IGRA already had divided into geographical groupings, to better organize the association and ease the travel burden on participants. There was intense discussion at the 1988–89 IGRA convention and in membership mailings on how to better handle this growth. By that time, there were more than five hundred competitors, and if they all ended up at the same rodeo, it would take almost twenty-three days to have a full competition. A decision had to be made to make the rodeos more manageable. Proposals included dropping the camp or roping event categories, eliminating specific events like chute dogging, limiting everyone to only one event per rodeo, or raising entry fees. For each, a corresponding concern was raised. For instance, if chute dogging was cut, there would be no entry-level event for the roughstock category, and if entry fees were raised, it might discourage participation at a time when the organization wanted to grow.[51] In the end, IGRA elected to split the associations into three divisions in 1991, with a fourth made in 1994. This alleviated the pressure on each rodeo and the finals, as now members would compete within their assigned division and advance to the finals from there.[52]

FROM BOOM TO BUST IN THE 2000s

The growth of the 1980s and early '90s continued, although at a slower pace, for another decade before a serious decline began in the number of associations and eventually in the number of rodeos offered. Part of the problem likely lay in the splitting of existing groups and the emergence of associations in areas without rural, ranching populations to sustain a rodeo organization. For instance, a Michigan group was formed in 1994. In 1998 it added Ohio and southwestern Ontario, but in 1999 it reverted to a Michigan-only group. Other new groups

ANNUAL IGRA MEMBERSHIP, 1993–2018

YEAR	IGRA MEMBERSHIP	PERCENTAGE CHANGE
1993	2,817	n/a
1994	3,077	+9.23%
1995	2,891	-6.04%
1996	2,802	-3.08%
1997	2,641	-5.75%
1998	2,493	-5.60%
1999	2,862	+14.80%
2000	2,361	-17.51%
2001	2,428	+2.84%*
2002	2,490	+2.55%*
2006	3,446	+38.39%*
2007	3,376	-2.03%*
2008	2,775*	-17.80*
2009	2,719	-2.00%
2010	2,258	-16.95%*
2011	2,292*	+1.5%
2012	1,982*	-13.52%*
2013	1,685	-15%
2014	n/a	n/a
2015	n/a	n/a
2016	n/a	n/a
2017	n/a	n/a
2018	1,250	-25.81%* (2013–18)

Note: Numbers with * were calculated by the authors, not provided by IGRA.

established the late 1990s and early 2000s folded entirely within just a few years. A Pennsylvania group formed in 1995, and in 1999 became PONY, to include Ohio and New York. Even that expansion did not garner enough members, and the entire group dissolved in 2007.[53]

Between 2006 and 2014, twelve associations folded, although at least one of those was quickly reestablished. By 2013, IGRA had more defunct associations (thirty-one) than ones still in operation (twenty-eight). IGRA rodeos faced a similar contraction. At its peak, the organization hosted more than twenty annual rodeos, with the number doubling between 1991 and 1994.[54] This rapid expansion ceased in 1996, which was the first year to see cancelations instead of additions to the circuit, and the number of annual rodeos has fallen steadily since 2008. That year, IGRA hosted twenty rodeos, and only thirteen were scheduled in 2012, the fewest the organization had held in twenty years. Over the next decade, from 2012 to 2020, the number of rodeos varied annually but never returned to the golden years of the 1990s, and more than ten additional associations dissolved. The table shows the dramatic change in gay rodeo's popularity, from its high point in the mid-1990s to the prepandemic years of the late 2010s. Since the COVID-19 pandemic, gay rodeo has contracted even further.

In the 1970s, '80s, and '90s, queer sporting culture, along with ideals of "western heritage," made up an integral aspect of gay rodeo, just one of the gay sporting events that emerged in this era. The North American Gay Amateur Athletic Alliance Open Division formed in 1977 to promote softball among LGBTQ+ communities, and the International Gay Bowling Organization formed in 1980. Two years later, Tom Waddell held the first Gay Games. Waddell had competed in the 1968 Summer Olympics and used sport to hide behind a cloak of athletic heterosexuality. By the early 1980s, he wanted a safe and celebratory space for queer athletes to compete as themselves, much as Phil Ragsdale did for more western-aligned, rodeo-oriented queer people.[55] These junctures of shared interest with other gay organizations, including dance, politics, and athletics, helped draw in both dedicated members and causal attendees and kept widening the space of gay rodeo. Just as gay rodeoers participated in community AIDS fundraisers and volunteered at Pride parades, the Gay Games and gay rodeo also converged at times. Members of the Colorado branch of IGRA competed in equestrian events at the 1990 Gay Games III in Vancouver, and gay rodeo became an official affiliate event at Gay Games IX in Cleveland.⁵⁶

For many gay participants, rodeo was the hub of a much larger wheel of gay life and activities. For some, it was intimately connected to gay country-western bars like Charlie's, and for others it provided an escape from the urban gay bar lifestyle. As John King explained in 1987, "A lot of gay people who grow up in rural communities come to the big city, get caught up in the bar scene and then we lose our identity. The gay rodeo is a place for us to reclaim our heritage and be ourselves. It's a place where we fit in."⁵⁷ However, even for people unfamiliar with ranching and riding, the gay rodeo was designed to be a place where they could find a home.

IGRA provided a safe community for LGBTQ+ people to engage as spectators and to explore rodeo as participants. The amateur status of the association allowed for this, as did the conscious design of the rodeo to include entry-level events, like chute dogging and roping on foot, where no riding ability was needed. Those interested could also participate in each of the four IGRA categories without a horse, opening the rodeo to a broader economic base. While gay rodeoers going back to Phil Ragsdale often wished to be viewed as legitimate participants in cowboy culture, they also argued that they were creating spaces for nonprofessionals "to escape the day to day pressures of life and to have some fun without fear of getting hit in the head with a horse shoe by people who don't approve." When hounded by the mainstream press for not being a "real" rodeo, one Canadian association asked, "Why must we justify our right to participate?"⁵⁸ Beyond a refusal to justify its existence, IGRA actively reached out to amateurs and novices by offering "rodeo schools" before its events so that anyone could compete, not just watch, at their very first rodeo.⁵⁹

The gay rodeo also created a safe space for its competitors by attempting to protect their anonymity. By competing publicly, participants announced their sexuality and could face legal, professional, and personal losses. Because of this, the Reno rodeos and IGRA developed a system designed to hide the identities of participants. Aliases, photography bans, and a limited media presence all helped maintain the confidentiality of people who desired it. This protection was important to some competitors and allowed them to participate as themselves in rodeo for the first time. A rider on the professional circuit who competed in the 1981 Reno rodeo explained that, by using an assumed name, "out here I get to be myself," even if anonymously. Yet a newspaper article aptly noted that this freedom was temporary: "The next week he'd go back to a regular rodeo, using his real name and his fake identity."[60] By allowing these silences to exist, gay rodeo created a safe space for social engagement and competition, and the programs, newsletters, and other ephemera using aliases, hidden names, and initials serve as a reminder of the discrimination and violence that queer people faced.

In the twenty-first century, there has been a substantial transformation in attitudes toward the gay population, but as LGBTQ+ people increasingly have gained legal rights and societal acceptance, many of their separate spaces have disappeared. As one participant explained, it is possible to meet someone gay at the local coffee shop today. The gay rodeo is no longer one of the few places where these connections can be made.[61] As IGRA grapples with the closure of its member associations and fewer events, gay rodeo has reached a turning point in other ways as well, increasingly asking questions about race and gender and interrogating its own policies of inclusion.

Over the past four decades, IGRA leadership has tended to be white cisgender gay men or lesbians who had a vision for the organization. Most of them worked in unrelated industries, such as medicine, construction, travel, and forestry. Others were involved in a number of horse-riding activities and felt compelled to offer leadership and direction in both their state associations and at the national level. In general, despite the exhausting amount of commitment that leadership roles required, once a person became involved in IGRA to that extent, they tended to remain at least tangentially engaged, which at times has led to frustration among younger members, as some of the founders still dictate the shape of the organization.

The product of a particular historical moment that generated an interest in traditional masculinity, a boom in country-western chic, and the LGBTQ+ equal rights movement, gay rodeo increasingly emphasized the "serious" business of rodeo as it moved from an offshoot event of the Imperial Court to an association in its own right. As it struggled to find a new sense of purpose after the peak of the HIV/AIDS epidemic, IGRA entered the twenty-first century trying to reinvent itself amid declining numbers of participants and rodeos. The global pandemic of COVID-19 only amplified this struggle to grow membership and survive in today's world.

Oral History Vignette
BRUCE ROBY, RODEO JUDGE

I grew up in southern Idaho—Gooding and Fairfield. So, very rural, but we were always the town kids. You know, in the summer you work on the farm, but my rodeo experience really was very limited. When the rodeo came to town, of course, we went as a family to watch. But I didn't ride horses, didn't participate in any of that.

I had spent a lot of years struggling with me, being who I am and what I am. And there was a traveling salesman came through for a travel school, and I thought, "That's where the gay people are. I need a job in travel so I can meet other people like me." So I spent a summer in travel school and got a job with United Airlines in Los Angeles. So, I went from a town with two thousand people to millions of people everywhere.

That little town up in the mountains of Idaho was to me homophobe central. The worst thing you could ever call somebody—'course "gay" wasn't in the vocabulary when I was in school—it was a fag . . . there's a horrible fear every time I heard that word. I was scared to death that it may come my way.

Even in college, I thought, "Okay, when I go to college, the world is gonna open up a little bit." Oh no. I was in a fraternity at the University of Idaho and was constantly scared to death that somebody's going to find out. To me, it was like, if I move to the city, I'm anonymous. Nobody knows me, nobody cares. Sadly, I think it's still that way for a lot of rural America. It starts at home, and unless your family is open and supportive as you're growing up, you'll never believe your community is either. So you have to run.

Once I left Idaho, in Los Angeles, you don't really see rodeo. But I lived on the edge of West Hollywood, and I had seen signs for this gay rodeo thing. I'd seen them for two or three years. But I thought, you know, pink pansies, purple horses. I don't know about this gay rodeo thing; I grew up with real rodeo; I'm not interested. And some friends were coming to town for the rodeo and needed a place to say. I said, "Well, you can stay at my house. I'm working all weekend, so make yourself at home." They said, "Well, you gotta come with us." I was like, "Ehhh, I don't think it's my thing."

Well, they got me to go with them to the dance at the Burbank Hilton on Friday night. Three thousand people at this dance, men and women. And it's men, it's like regular guys. It's a different subset of the gay community. It's not necessarily the very flamboyant. They are just regular people that happen to be gay, and that's kind of where I really wanted to find life. I called in sick the next day and went to the rodeo. I called in sick the next day and went back. It was like I found a life.

And three months later, I happened to be interviewing for a job up here in the Bay Area the same weekend as the Bay Area rodeo. Walking in the gate, I heard people talking, "Gosh, we're gonna have to get a few more volunteers 'cause we are gonna need help with this." I was like, "I'll help. Tell me what you need to have done, and if I don't know, I'll tell ya." And I've been volunteering now eighteen years.

The dances were the busiest part of the whole rodeo weekend, even at the grounds. There's this giant tent with this giant dance floor, and there's these men dancing with men, women dancing with women, and it's... country dancing, but it's ballroom style. It's the most amazing thing you ever saw.

In the last ten years, the dancing has stepped away. The contestants were getting older. The younger people don't have the same need in the gay community that we had twenty, thirty, forty years ago. So we are our own worst enemy. We got the acceptance we've been dying for.

Chapter 2

"HOOKIN' UP" AT THE GAY RODEO

Normative Masculinity, Queer Sexuality, and the Authentic Cowboy

The National Reno Gay Rodeo and later IGRA rodeos were open equally to male and female competitors, but they were rooted in ideas of normative masculinity that dictated certain forms of gender performance for cowboys and pushed cowgirls to the fringes. From its origins, the gay rodeo arena was meant to be a home for traditional masculinity and for queer cowboys to find a place to compete and showcase their natural virility. To do this, it invoked a narrow, gendered framework—one that did not visually disrupt the masculine cowboy of the mainstream rodeo and instead embraced it. This was a place where men could demonstrate they were not the effeminate stereotype. In so doing, the circuit helped to redefine what it meant to be gay by allowing men to be both gay and masculine, but it also was a place that catered to and shaped a desire for a particular form of masculinity. Accordingly, it fed into larger misogynist and racially problematic understandings of cowboy identity.

Chapter 1 explained the important role that the rural West and the image of the cowboy played in forming American notions of masculinity. In the 1970s and '80s, this ideal again took hold of the American imagination—and American fashions—as part of a remasculinization that swept the country as white, middle-class American men wanted to (re)assert their masculinity in heterosocial spaces. Historian Susan Jeffords explains that this was tied to the larger emasculation of the American image, and especially of the American male, due to the failure of the Vietnam War. Jeffords says this sense of imperiled heterosexuality and traditional masculinity was amplified by the mainstreaming of disco, which some straight men saw as promoting a denigrated form of masculinity that was overly glamorous.[1] As a counter to disco's hyperstylized and inauthentic masculinity, the cowboy became a model of a more traditional—and often white—version in this era. The image of the cowboy, along with its corresponding western-wear craze, spread through straight and gay communities alike. For gay men, the vision of the cowboy was particularly powerful, because it allowed them to assert their masculinity in a way that aligned with heteronormative standards of gender presentation.

However, while gay rodeo clung to the traditional masculinity of the cowboy, the sexual culture of rodeo created a complication for its normative desires of gay rodeo and the gay cowboy. As IGRA contestant Chuck Browning acknowledged, "At any rodeo, gay or straight, it tends to be about people hookin' up!"[2] Cowboy masculinity was often connected to the sexual prowess of male riders. Cowboys proved their masculinity at straight rodeos through their own (hetero)sexual virility, buckle bunnies brought sex to cowboys on the circuit, and rodeo programs promoted hypermasculine, muscle-bound male imagery and hyperfeminine, sexualized women.[3]

Gay rodeo similarly embraced a culture that used sexual imagery and endorsed sexual activity, but in this arena, the sex was outspokenly queer in nature, though it was a queerness that almost always was designed specifically for gay men, not lesbian participants. Gay rodeo programs were explicit in their focus on the male body, with seminaked, chiseled men rather than the bikini-clad or rhinestone-covered women of straight rodeo. Advertisements promoted gay bars as hook-up locations, used male nudity to promote everything from chiropractors to bowling alleys, and encouraged sex at bathhouses. This was a space very clearly meant for gay men to be (homo)sexually active while they simultaneously performed normative masculinity. In so doing, they adopted some of the same oppressive gender understandings that characterized straight society, but by refusing to conform to all heteronormative standards, the gay cowboy also created a disruptive environment that queered the rodeo and cowboy masculinity.

This chapter follows the development of gay masculinity in the twentieth century, with the adoption of the muscular, leather-bound masculine ideal in some gay male communities. The western cowboy became an extension of this model of authentic masculinity and a sexual ideal for these men. Beyond the image of the cowboy, the creation of gay rodeo permitted rural, ranching gay men to compete publicly as queer identified. It also allowed the growing group of LGBTQ+ country-western enthusiasts in the 1970s and '80s to adopt the cowboy identity. Yet this was not a fully inclusive environment. Tension existed within the gay country-western rodeo community over claims of authenticity and rights to participation. Queer cowfolx struggled with debates over who and what was authentically western and what forms of masculinity were acceptable within their rodeos. This focus on masculinity and gay male sex often failed to attract lesbian participants, an issue discussed more deeply in chapter 6. Similarly, despite the inclusion of drag queens and camp events, male gay rodeo participants favored heteronormative presentations of masculinity and perceived other identities as threats to their claims to be authentic cowboys. Even so, their adoption of traditional markers of virility did not always lead to acceptance from mainstream society or from straight rodeo communities. Like in straight rodeo, cowboys in gay rodeo engaged in sex and used sexual imagery to promote their circuit to contestants and spectators. However, its camp events, nude and sexually suggestive advertisements and imagery, and public promotion of gay male sex set gay rodeo apart from its straight counterpart and pushed against mainstream American understandings of the traditional cowboy image.

GAY MASCULINITY AND THE COWBOY IDEAL

Prior to the 1970s and '80s, the United States had cyclically experienced masculinity crises, with a major one occurring at the turn of the twentieth century. The supposed threats of urbanization, industrialization, and immigration led to a physical culture movement that encouraged playing sports and developing a muscular body, in order to replace the more natural male musculature believed to have been present in preindustrial life. Fitness and physique magazines promoted this lifestyle and provided visual examples of the ideal male body, yet these publications soon found an audience with a different interest. The men within their pages became sexualized and were used for arousal by gay male readers. By the 1930s, gay men were regular consumers of these physique magazines, and in the 1950s and '60s, the periodicals more purposefully targeted a gay audience. In response, the American government identified them as pornographic material designed for gay men and launched attacks against them. Only after obscenity laws were overturned in the 1960s could the physique magazines become more open about their pursuit of a gay market and more explicitly sexual in their imagery.[4]

The bodybuilding, muscular masculinity of the physique magazines initially depicted the classical Grecian male figure or the all-American bodybuilder (see figure 5). It is no surprise that in their use of classic figures of Western civilization, like those of ancient Greece, these publications most frequently used white male models. Black men and other men of color were underrepresented and, when included, were depicted differently than white men. In her study of physique magazines from 1955 to 1960, Tracy D. Morgan reports that Black, Indigenous, and other men of color often appeared with props that promoted white domination and perpetuated problematic, racist stereotypes of these men.[5]

After WWII and films like *The Wild One* (1953) and *Rebel Without a Cause* (1955), the physique magazines began to promote a different kind of muscular masculinity, one that was still white but now emphasized leather, motorcycles, and working-class culture.[6] The sexually explicit drawings by Tom of Finland helped to usher in this new leather world for gay men. In his work, and later works by other artists, masculinity was the highest ideal, and, for maybe the first time, gay men could see themselves depicted as bikers, soldiers, sailors, loggers, construction workers, and cowboys (see figure 6). These were archetypes identified as having an inherent or authentic masculinity. In Tom's work, men could be masculine and gay, and these working-class muscular (white) men engaged in explicitly queer sex with others like themselves.[7] This was markedly different from the presentation of gay men as the effeminate pansies or swishes of earlier years.

From the late nineteenth to mid-twentieth centuries, American society saw male gayness as a female desire, in which the person

FIGURE 5. *Cover of* Trim, *1960. This magazine front cover features a young, lithe, and white male model exhibiting the Grecian bodybuilding ideal of the mid-twentieth century. His loincloth with a visible bulge of the genitalia suggests the growing homoerotic nature of these publications. Manuscripts and Archives Division, New York Public Library. "Trim," New York Public Library Digital Collections. 1960–05.*

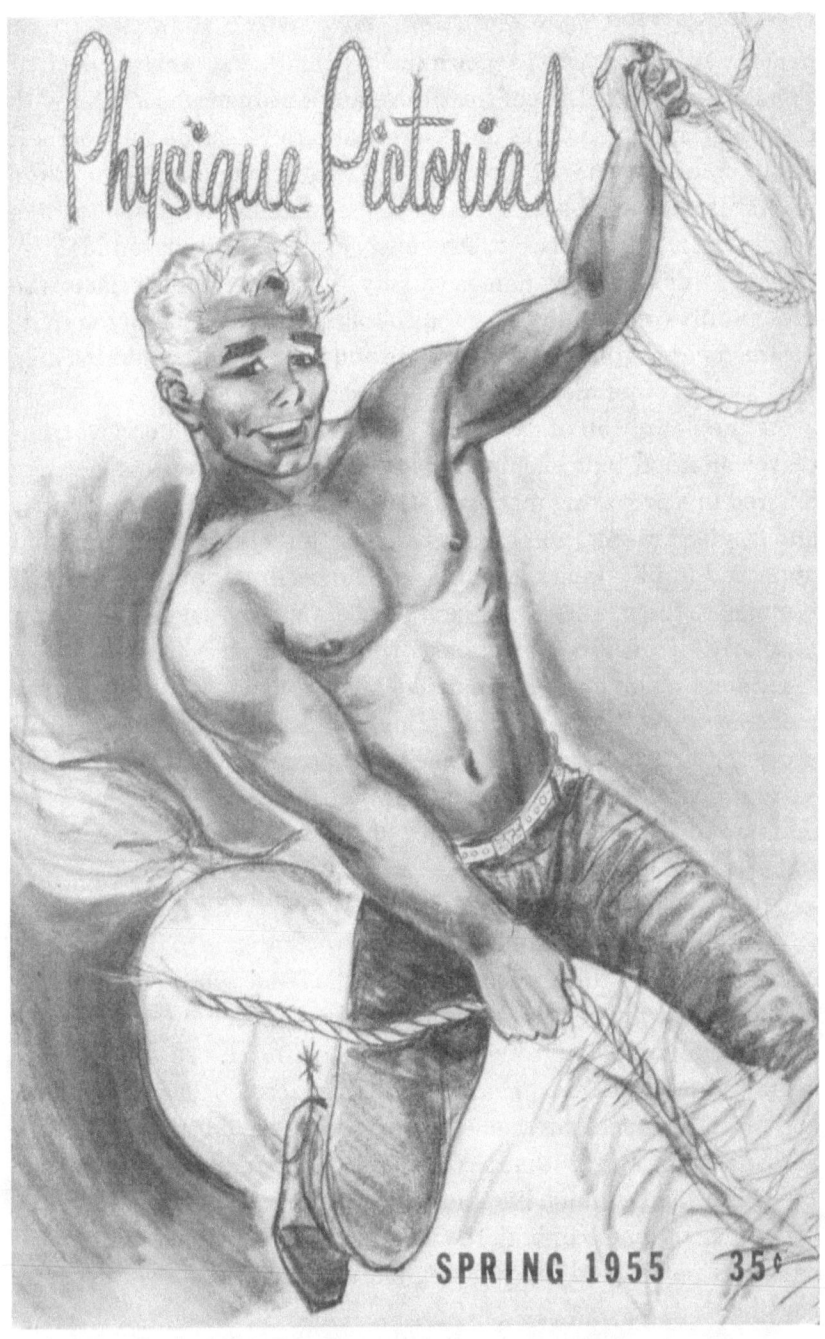

FIGURE 6. *Cover of* Physique Pictorial, *1955. This cover used a figure that was less traditionally nude for bodybuilding purposes but who was increasingly seen as a desirable model of masculinity by some gay men: the cowboy. Manuscripts and Archives Division, New York Public Library. "Physique Pictorial," New York Public Library Digital Collections. 1955.*

penetrated during sex was seen as passive and, accordingly, was identified as homosexual. In contrast, the masculine men who had sex with these feminine-presenting men were seen as straight, because of their sexual role and gender presentation. Art historian Micha Ramakers calls this a gender-based identity that equated a "feminine" role to gay men. In the mid-twentieth century, a sexuality-based identity replaced this view. In it, homosexuality for gay men could exist on the masculinity continuum rather than being seen as a female or feminine desire, meaning that both effeminate and masculine-presenting men who desired other men could now be considered gay.[8]

As the definition of gay men expanded, the physique magazines played an important role in not just presenting images that gay men desired but providing models on which to base their own identity and gender presentation. The urban working-class masculinity that appeared in physique magazines, popular films, and gay-oriented films led to the rise of gay motorcycle clubs and the gay leather scene. Similarly, the regular appearance of cowboy imagery in these magazines and on film made him a model of desirable masculinity for gay men. Several soft-core gay porn films from Kris Studio, led by homoerotic photographer Chuck Renslow, featured gay cowboys in the early 1960s, as did Andy Warhol's *Lonesome Cowboys* and the more mainstream *Midnight Cowboy* in 1968 and 1969, respectively.[9] It is important to note that this erotic world of the physique magazines and gay pornography was largely white. White bodies were presented as desirable and were created for a white audience to consume. As Morgan explains, this sometimes led to the fetishization of nonwhite men when they were depicted in these erotic spaces, but it also led to their sexual exclusion from them.[10] Gay life in the 1970s saw reality begin to match the imagined masculine spaces of these magazines and films. Bars decorated in leather and western motifs proliferated across the country, with areas designed for dancing and cruising.[11] But these spaces, much like the gay rodeo that soon followed, replicated the whiteness of both the mythologized cowboy of the American imagination and the working-class leather image of the erotic gay press.

Gay men were attracted to these masculine presentations in the mid- to late twentieth century because, for some, adopting a masculine identity was a way to survive and pass as a straight person in a homophobic society. As Cold War–era hunts for communists in the 1950s and '60s expanded to include gay men and women, many LGBTQ+ people were forced to pass as straight in order to keep their homes and jobs. Normative gender conformity became a way to hide their sexual nonconformity. For those in the nascent homophile movements, this meant an adoption of white-collar, middle-class respectability, while others turned to the blue-collar muscular masculinity presented in the physique magazines and movies. Both of these forms aligned with societal expectations for men, and gay men who conformed to heteronormative gender standards came to see themselves as distinct from more effeminate gay men. Gay men who either could not or would not present a traditional masculinity increasingly were seen as a degrading stereotype and a dangerous threat to other, more masculine-presenting, gay men.[12]

While some gay men purposefully and consciously adopted a masculine identity, its allure for others was that it allowed a broader spectrum of men to identify this way. More men could be seen as gay and could see themselves as gay, because no longer were they automatically defined as feminine.[13] The emergence of the bear identity among gay men in 1970s and '80s further expanded the conceptions of blue-collar, muscular masculinity to one defined as more natural, as opposed to the more artificial leather masculinity.[14] Men from rural or ranching backgrounds saw an avenue through muscular masculinity (and especially the "scruffy" bear version) for their own self-expression as queer, and gay rodeo became a place for them not to present an adopted identity but to express who they already were: gay, masculine cowboys. As Jason Hays, president of the Atlantic States Gay Rodeo Association in the late 1990s, who was raised in Northern California, explained, "The best thing about being a gay cowboy is that I am finally true to who I am. I am true to me being gay. And I am true to me being a cowboy. I don't make any apologies for being both at the same time."[15] Thom Sloan, another IGRA member, grew up on a rural farm in a rodeo family. Even though he initially tried to reject the western lifestyle when he left home, finding gay rodeo in 1991 allowed him to reclaim that part of his identity. As he said, "There's an element of rodeo that's part of my heritage. It connects me to my family in a special way."[16] These men already had a masculine identity and a gay identity. IGRA and the figure of the cowboy simply allowed them to embody both of these in a way that society rarely allowed.

A conventionally masculine gay body challenged notions of gay male inferiority and heteronormative male superiority, and this was particularly true at one of the bastions of traditional masculinity: the rodeo arena.[17] In the midst of a public debate over the gay rodeo in Reno in 1981, local resident Mary McHale demonstrated this entrenched perspective in a letter she wrote to the newspaper, complaining, "What on earth do gays have to do with a rodeo?" She continued, "A 'displaced male' dressed as a woman, or someone pathetically trying to imitate women, hardly does anything to the true meaning of rodeo, except to pervert it as they are perverted." McHale only saw space for one type of person in rodeo. In addition to denying all feminine people legitimate access to it, McHale also identified gay men as innately inferior to what she identified as the "true male," who she believed were the only ones with the "strength and endurance" to participate in a real rodeo.[18] Over a decade later, IGRA leadership received a spate of hateful emails similarly questioning the ability of gay people to participate in rodeo. Said one, "This is the biggest disgrace to rodeo and cowboys worldwide. I can't believe you fudgepackers think you can ride bulls when you [can't] even ride women.... YOU GODDAMN FAGS CAN'T LEAVE ANYTHING ALONE CAN YOU. Rodeo is a sport for men and now you are bastardizing it with this sick bullshit. BURN IN HELL FAGS."[19] By claiming a masculine identity and staging their own rodeo, gay men undermined these long-held hierarchies of identity and power, unsettling straight people like Mary McHale in the 1980s and the anonymous harassers years later.

    Just as the embrace of these forms of masculinity by gay men encountered the hegemonic hierarchies of power from a heterosexual society, gay men also established their own pecking order of masculinity and gender presentation among LGBTQ+ people. It led adherents of both middle-class masculinity in the homophile movement and working-class-inspired masculinity in the leather and country-western movements to engage in their own dismissal of and disdain for effeminate gay men. In doing so, they created their own hierarchies of masculinity within the gay world and replicated the same hostility directed at all gay people by straight society.[20] For instance, the homophile organization ONE, Inc., tried to create a Homosexual Bill of Rights in 1961 and asked readers of its magazine to write in with suggestions. One respondent suggested that the gay community should "STAMP OUT QUEENS!" Others said, "Attempts should be made to educate and possibly eliminate the public 'swish'" and "The 'normal' homo resents these jerks as much as the heterosexual does, I believe."[21] For these respondents, their position as more masculine-presenting men undoubtedly placed them above more effeminate gay men and legitimized the disdain directed at that group.

Similar debates existed in gay rodeo, where the royalty contests featuring drag queens and events like wild cow milking queered traditional ideas of rodeo masculinity. Wild cow milking also has appeared in some straight competitions, most commonly in ranch rodeos, which focus on ranch-related jobs, but it took a new and rebellious form in early gay rodeos. The Reno rodeo explained the rules in 1979 as "lesbian ropes, drag mugs, guy milks."[22] Rodeo organizer Phil Ragsdale included these rules after the second Reno rodeo, when he received a letter from self-styled "Macho Cowboys" who said "they would participate IF I would eliminate all the Lesbians and Drags." Even though Ragsdale wanted gay rodeo to be a place for gay men to be(come) manly, he also believed it should be an inclusive place. So in response, he introduced his version of wild cow milking, which required cowboys to work with lesbians and drag participants together as a team. To further stymie the "Macho Cowboys," he also reiterated that all were welcome at his rodeos: "Male, Female or Drag, or as I say, 'Regardless of your persuasion.'" Even when the wild drag race replaced wild cow milking in 1987, the new event still required a male, female, and drag participant.[23] Camp events like this, along with the royalty contest, continued to create tensions over appropriate masculine identity in gay rodeo.

Two decades after the initial conflict with the "Macho Cowboys," this same tension continued to simmer in gay rodeo between masculine-presenting male competitors and the camp events and drag queen presence. An audience survey at the 1997 IGRA finals rodeo revealed that respondents celebrated the "professional cowboys and cowgirls" but believed the professionalism was marred by the royalty contest with its drag queens. One person plainly stated, "Get rid of the drag queens."[24] In another disavowal of rodeo drag queens that same year, a disgruntled Golden State member criticized what he called "people in silly sashes and on power trips," referring to the drag queen royalty winners. He continued, "Too bad, because this was one chance for gays to show they can do more than just do drag and be hairdressers. I guess rodeo is too masculine a sport for most of the gay community to handle."[25] The leadership responded by reminding this individual about the important role of royalty drag queens, the primary fundraisers and workhorses of gay rodeo. Like Ragsdale had two decades earlier, GSGRA leadership in 1997 stood in support of alternative gender presentations, sarcastically saying, "Anyone who is not masculine should not be involved.... Maybe we could enact a basic membership requirement that you must be as butch as [the complaining individual] in order to join an IGRA organization."[26]

The tension over gender presentation and acceptable masculinity did not just appear on the fringes of gay rodeo, from malcontents. The first Reno rodeos ushered in this very same conflict through their design. While Ragsdale welcomed everyone to his rodeos, "regardless of your persuasion," he also intended to counter societal stereotypes about effeminate gay men. Ragsdale explained that he wanted gay rodeo to "show that the gays aren't strictly stereotyped as limp wrists."[27] He wanted it to be a place where gay men could experience the rodeo as spectators or engage in the competition as real cowboys and, accordingly, as real, masculine men. Many male contestants throughout the 1970s, '80s, and '90s participated with a similar goal. In a statement remarkably similar to Ragsdale's twenty years earlier, a male competitor in bull riding, bareback bronc riding, and calf roping said in 1999, "I don't want them to think it's a bunch of sissies running around." He needed to be taken seriously and to be seen as an authentic, traditional cowboy. To do this, he explained, "We are true to the Western spirit. We are cowboys and cowgirls even though we have a different private lifestyle."[28] For him, gayness and masculinity could coexist, but femininity proved dangerous.

Just as feminine gay men threatened the possibility of masculinity for other gay men, the rise of the "gay clone" in the 1970s and '80s urban bar scene exacerbated the tensions over who claimed the cowboy identity and how: by means of a true or inherent masculinity versus a temporary adoption of it. Martin Levine first identified the gay clone as a subculture that emphasized an adherence to a traditional, masculine gender presentation. He described the clone as wearing tight Levi's jeans and a plaid flannel shirt over a white T-shirt, with a pumped-up body and thick mustache or beard (see figure 7). This fashion uniform comprised just one part of the clone's identity. According to Levine, it was "a specific constellation of sociosexual, affective, and behavioral patterns that emerged among some gay men in the urban centers of gay American life." The (usually white) gay

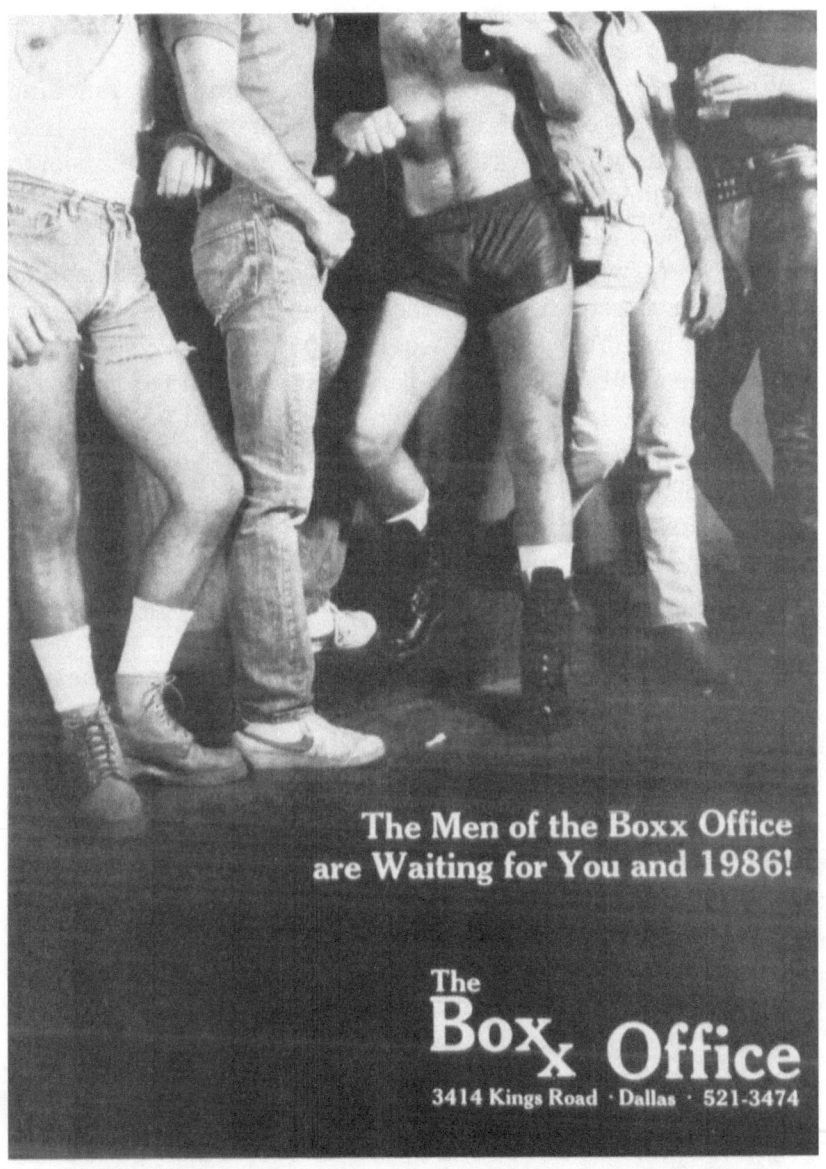

FIGURE 7. *TGRA Rodeo Program*, ad for The Boxx Office, 1985. *This ad for the Dallas-based gay bar uses the gay clone as both a selling point and an almost ironic statement about gay male fashion. Several versions of the clone can be seen here, including the cowboy second to the right. Courtesy of the Autry Museum of the American West.*

clones "butched it up" by dressing like macho, working-class men, engaging in anonymous sex and recreational drugs and partying at the many post-Stonewall gay bars.[29]

While gay rodeos attracted participants from rural, ranching backgrounds, they often were held in urban centers and purposefully included events accessible to rodeo "virgins." This opened the door to gay cowboy clones, who temporarily adopted or play-acted the part of the macho cowboy. This threatened the country-western ideals of those who saw themselves as true cowboys and created another tension over masculinity in gay rodeo—now one that was not just a debate over heteronormative masculinity (vs. effeminacy) but about authentic masculinity versus the performative version of "wannabe cowboys." Many IGRA members determinedly tried to prove they came from an appropriately rural, western background, thus differentiating themselves from the gay clones of the period. In 1980, during the National Reno Gay Rodeo, *In Touch for Men* asked one contestant, "You're a real cowboy, huh?" The man responded, "In the realest sense of the word, yes. A cowboy is a man who works with horses and cows." The magazine then asked what his response was to "pretend cowboys." He expressed his frustration at the idea of "tricking" people. He explained, "They're not being themselves. . . . If I see a San Francisco businessman in a cowboy outfit, I think he should dress and act like a business person. . . . I'd like them to appreciate me for who I am, and me to appreciate them for who they are." This gay cowboy saw his identity as grounded in his work with horses and cows, and yet he also believed dress and occupation were intimately related. When asked how to spot a faker, he quickly noted, "The way they walk, the way they dress and the way they put their hat down." All of these telltale signs privileged bodily presentation over employment, lifestyle, or personality traits. "Fake cowboys just don't move right. They wear Lees, Wranglers or some of those other form fitted jeans that are coming out. Cowboys wear one brand: Levi Strauss."[30] For this man, despite his initial definition of a cowboy as a profession, performing authentic cowboyness depended on knowing which clothing brands were "real" cowboy gear.

However, even when gay men came from an appropriately rural, ranching background and dressed in supposedly authentic western wear, gay rodeo continued to be seen as something different, dangerous, and subversive to traditional American conceptions of the rodeo and the cowboy. As the organizer of the first gay rodeo in California explained in 1985, "People can't participate in the regular rodeo circuit and be openly gay because of blatant discrimination. It's the macho image that's offended by a man who can roughride and be gay."[31] Mary McHale's earlier comments about the Reno rodeo echoed these same beliefs. She expressed shock and disgust about gay rodeo, because she did not believe gay men were capable of adequately tackling the masculine, physical feat of rodeo. Some competitors on the straight rodeo circuit refused to even believe gay riders could exist. Craig Butterfield, a straight rider on the professional circuit in the 1990s, said, "I think it's a pile of bullshit. Well, I've rodeoed for 25 years and I don't think I've ever come across a queer cowboy at a real rodeo."[32] Butterfield simultaneously denied the possibility that the cowboy could be gay and questioned the legitimacy of gay rodeo by comparing it to a "real rodeo," which to him meant a straight one. Because of doubts like this, gay rodeo struggled to balance its amateur status in order to broaden its appeal and attract new contestants with its desire for respectability, which it pursued by modeling itself on the professional circuit.

Phil Ragsdale created a more laid-back rodeo scene in the 1970s, and the media, straight and gay alike, often discussed these early events in a sensationalized manner, treating them as a kind of odd, sexy circus. The Reno rodeos could be disorganized; focused on fun and camp; featured seminaked, good-looking men; and attracted national celebrities like Joan Rivers. But competitors also were starved for opportunities to compete in a safe and welcoming place, and many yearned for a more serious environment. In a letter to Ragsdale, Wayne Jakino demonstrated this desire when he announced the formation of the Colorado Gay Rodeo Association in 1982, saying he would like to further "the professionalism of gay rodeos and the enjoyment of our members and rodeo fans alike."[33] This pull between a professional-style, serious competition and a fun, campy, amateur event continued to circle gay rodeo for the following decades.

Texas and some of the other associations in more western, rodeo-centric environments, wanted to offer competitive, serious rodeos. From its start, the Texas group explained its purpose was "to raise money for worthwhile organizations by holding an annual rodeo." Some of the associations even faced criticism for being too singularly focused on their rodeos. For instance, Colorado feared in 1995 that the weight they placed on their rodeo led them "to be isolated from the rest of Denver's Gay Community." Some associations similarly criticized the Arizona group for being too rodeo focused, too competitive, and too professional.[34] At its core, this debate between an amateur and fun, campy rodeo versus one with a professional, serious focus reflected the same concerns that the "Macho Cowboys" in the 1970s and the IGRA survey respondents in the 1990s had about royalty drag queens. This was not just about masculinity but about respectability from the rodeo world, the country-western world, and American society writ large. For some IGRA associations, such as Texas, Colorado, and Arizona, focusing on their rodeo offerings was the path to respectability, but it also occurred through the overall organization of IGRA, which intentionally modeled itself on professional rodeo.

IGRA aligned its events with many of those on the professional, high school, and college rodeo circuits. The organization also looked to professional rodeo as it attempted to expand, created internal competition brackets, and countered animal rights protest groups. IGRA developed a detailed and extensive rule book, governing board and committee structure, and review, complaint, and fining system. It ran a tight ship, and the wider rodeo community occasionally recognized IGRA for this. Even stock contractors who usually supplied straight rodeos with animals sometimes noted their preference for gay rodeos, because of the organization and professionalism on that circuit. Acknowledging their desire for greater acceptance, IGRA invited representatives from the Professional Rodeo Cowboys Association (PRCA) and International Professional Rodeo Association (IPRA) circuits to attend a gay rodeo in 1995, though only IPRA accepted. Reflecting on the visit afterward, IGRA said, "We introduced Pro-Rodeo to Gay Rodeo and we all survived without injury to body or spirit and came away with a better appreciation for each other."[35] Though disappointed that PRCA refused the invitation, IGRA was grateful that at least part of the professional circuit was willing to accept gay rodeo.

Some of the practices that set gay rodeo apart from the professional circuit, even those like the use of aliases to protect competitors' anonymity, were critiqued by IGRA members and leaders as threats to their circuit's ability to be "respectable" and "professional." Certain members regularly defined "professional" as "straight-acting" within the rodeo. For instance, one member of the IGRA board of directors recommended in 1996 that the organization require aliases to be people's names, not something like "Panda Bear," an alias in use at the time. He believed that "this type of name is not in keeping with our sport, [as] it suggests we are like professional wrestling.... A person's name would also show we are as serious about our sport as our colleagues in Pro-Rodeo competition."[36] Despite being critiqued for their own apparent unprofessionalism, Panda Bear had their own concerns about professional behavior, asking the IGRA board, "When did we forget why we started IGRA in the first place? Yes it was a time of good clean cowboy fun, a hate free place where gays could compete without the hassle of the straight world. But then we got into the mode of party-time." Panda continued, "I am asking you to please rethink your position on why you are putting on this rodeo. Is it just to have fun or are you thinking about all contestants and spectators?"[37] Though they had different critiques regarding what they saw as a lack of professionalism in gay rodeo, both Panda Bear and the board member who criticized Panda's alias were similarly concerned with respectability and public perception, which for them meant offering a rodeo that resembled straight, mainstream rodeos and shedding the aspects of gay rodeo that set it apart.

Despite this desire for respectability in the rodeo world, which some associations pursued by offering a professional-style rodeo, not all associations agreed. The Illinois group (ILGRA) promoted the amateur nature of its rodeos. ILGRA's mission identified the group as "a non-profit organization of men and women dedicated to raising funds for community related charities through functions preceding and including an annual *amateur* rodeo" (emphasis added).[38] IGRA associations like those in Michigan (MIGRA) and California (PCGRA) also focused on encouraging rodeo participation within the LGBTQ+ community rather than offering a serious rodeo intended just for experienced riders. MIGRA's intended to foster "the sport of Rodeo and Country Western Lifestyle" within the gay community, while PCGRA explained its purpose as helping gay men and women become "proficient in rodeo related sporting events."[39] Some associations, including those in Arkansas (DSRA), Georgia (SEGRA), Nebraska and Iowa (HGRA), and Pennsylvania, Ohio, and New York (PONY), sometimes hosted rodeos, but their missions placed the promotion of the country-western lifestyle at the center of their purpose.

Even at the national level, IGRA recognized that, while called the International Gay *Rodeo* Association (emphasis added), not all member associations could support a rodeo, and so the leadership decided that a country-western focus was more important than offering a rodeo. In 1998, the IGRA board replaced the informal practice of permitting associations to be members without staging a rodeo with a more explicit statement in the bylaws.[40] As a result, IGRA and many of its member associations promoted the country-western lifestyle to nonrural LGBTQ+ people and encouraged them adopt that identity. However, by opening up like this, IGRA also made room for the gay clone who was more interested in adopting the guise of the cowboy, such as the New Mexico–based art gallery owner with a "buttoned-up exterior" who competed in camp events and was a self-identified "cowboy wannabe," rather than creating a space that was only for the authentic cowboy.[41]

Despite the tensions within gay rodeo over creating an authentically western space, both the "cowboy wannabes" and the rural participants proved to be disruptive to the mainstream conception of the rodeo and the American vision of the cowboy as an icon of masculinity. An anonymous email to IGRA in 1997 asked, "Tell me why you have to have a association messing up one of the natural things of the US." Another claimed, "I hate to be so blunt, but y'all are a disgrace to any rodeo association, let alone the United States of America."[42] As these emails, along with the negative reactions by riders on the professional circuit and by community members like Mary McHale from Reno, demonstrate, gay men who conformed to heteronormative standards of masculinity and participated in the macho world of the rodeo proved deeply unsettling to straight society. To find acceptance and be taken seriously as rodeoers, IGRA contestants strove for professionalism but had to balance that with a conflicting desire to create a safe space for queer cowfolx, one that permitted amateur competition, campy fun, and—yes—sex.

SEX AT THE RODEO

In addition to an appropriately rural, ranching background and an adoption of the right kind of western wear, the discussion about who or what made for an authentically masculine cowboy also connected to sex. Even though IGRA contestant Chuck Browning accurately noted that all rodeos, straight and gay alike, were about "hookin' up," sex at the gay rodeo led to uneasy tensions between the gay and straight communities and among gay rodeo participants.

As the voice of gay rodeo, the queer country-western magazine *Roundup* tried to present itself as a serious rodeo magazine. In 1995, when a reader wrote in requesting more shirtless cowboy images, the magazine explained that no "gratuitous shots of cowboys" would be featured on its pages because "cowboys, cowgirls and the Western lifestyle are inherently sexy ... Besides, cowboys are even sexier in full gear!"[43] With its focus on clothed, and therefore "authentic," cowboys, *Roundup* attempted to differentiate itself from more skin-focused country-western erotic magazines, such as *Bronc* and *Bunkhouse* (the latter branded itself as "The International Magazine of the Western-Leather Scene"). Even other gay adult magazines, such as *Blueboy, Mandate, Numbers,* and *Honcho,* sometimes featured nude, seminude, and clone-styled cowboys in their issues in the 1980s and '90s.[44] But *Roundup* was in the business of promoting the real deal, not the play-acting gay clones or the stylized faux-cowboys of porn and erotica. IGRA and *Roundup* both wanted to present a model of authenticity and professionalism to queer cowfolx and the larger rodeo community, as a way to be taken seriously as masculine gay men and as rodeo cowboys.

Despite the concern articulated in *Roundup* about faux erotic cowboys, sex was present at the gay rodeo. It was a place where men could demonstrate their normative masculinity, but its same-sex intimacy, along with its inclusion of drag queens and camp events, conflicted with society's understanding of a form of masculinity traditionally defined as heterosexual. In his study of self-identified "masculine, straight-acting" gay men, Jay Clarkson explains that even the presentation of hegemonic masculinity cannot allow gay men to overcome the marginalization they face because of their non-normative sexuality. No matter how masculine they are, gay men will still never occupy all of the same social spaces as heterosexual men.[45] This was certainly true of gay rodeo. While various groups of queer cowfolx created rodeos for themselves that were directly modeled on professional rodeo, they never wanted these to be *straight* rodeos or intended to hide their sexuality at them. In contrast, gay rodeos were designed to be places they could celebrate both a cowboy identity and their queer identity. This was most obvious in the camp events, royalty contests, and sexual imagery in rodeo programs, the latter of which will be discussed in this chapter; camp and royalty are the focus of chapter 4.

Gay rodeo emerged in the 1970s in a post-Stonewall environment, when LGBTQ+ people, especially gay men, celebrated their identity and sexuality in a public way like never before. While many gay rodeo competitors came from rural backgrounds, most had moved to more urban environments, and gay rodeo associations were based in cities such as Reno, San Francisco, Denver, and Dallas.[46] Yet even in these places, along with the smaller communities that sometimes hosted gay rodeos, queer people encountered opposition to their presence. Phil Ragsdale faced a conservative climate in Reno, and the state of Nevada still deemed homosexual acts to be illegal in the 1970s and '80s. He made some attempts to balance his desire for a normative masculine rodeo with the longing that competitors and spectators had for a place of sexual celebration and openness. The program for the third annual Reno rodeo in 1979 included a welcome from Ragsdale but also instructions: "We do ask that dress and actions not be obscene or [lewd]."[47] The following year, Ragsdale made an even more explicit statement. He began by reminding contestants and spectators that all were welcome at his rodeo, saying it was for "ALL Gay people first, Charity second and ANYONE who wants to sit [alongside] of us and have a good time. When I say ALL GAY PEOPLE, I mean just that, regardless of YOUR OWN SEXUAL PERSUASION." However, Ragsdale also cautioned everyone on their actions: "This is a weekend whereby we can all get together for FUN. Bringing with us our sexual preference, BUT leaving our sex at home. No sexual misconduct will be tolerated during this weekend."[48] This statement appeared in all of the following Reno programs. It was a carefully crafted request, a declaration even, from Ragsdale that aimed to promote his gay rodeo as a place of respectability and acceptability for a straight, conservative community and a political landscape openly hostile to LGBTQ+ rights.

Ragsdale tried to walk a careful line between promoting gay rodeo as a place of sexual freedom and celebration and toeing the line of respectability politics in the conservative West. This occasionally allowed the Reno event to fly under the mainstream radar, but Ragsdale could not always hide—and did not always want to hide—the "gay" part of his rodeo. Sometimes gay rodeo simply warned away straight people and other times denied them access altogether. For instance, a mainstream newspaper article covering the 1981 Reno rodeo described the scene by saying, "Most gays were in couples—some holding hands, stroking shoulders or clutching waists in open but understated gestures of affection. A sign outside the rodeo grounds warned 'straights' that if such behavior bothered them, they'd best stay away." In case these displays of same-sex affection proved too much for the straight readers of the *Nevada State Journal*, the journalist reassured them: "But blatant homosexual displays appeared rare."⁴⁹ When even this tempering of heterosexual fears about same-sex affection, sex, and love seemed to be too revealing, gay rodeo at various times in the 1970s, '80s, and '90s refused admission to members of the straight press and avoided news articles in the straight media.

While the mainstream press and straight audiences shied away from some parts of gay rodeo, writers from LGBTQ+ publications told a different, much sexier, and more sexual tale of life there. At the same seemingly staid Reno rodeos described above by the *Nevada State Journal* and *Reno Evening Gazette*, a journalist for a gay publication wrote, "Before I left Reno I promised myself I'd return next year. It's a great deal of fun and the bodies [cannot] be believed. What with the heat and all, no one seems to wear a shirt for long."⁵⁰ Another journalist, this time for *The Advocate*, wrote a similarly glowing report of the skin on display: "It wasn't what the men wore that made them the most sexy, sensual, sensational, spectacular aggregation of male pulchritude these dazzled eyes ever beheld. Oceans of lotion creamed biceps, pecs, shoulders, legs and physiognomies already tanned to perfection."⁵¹ For these journalists and their readers, the attraction of the gay rodeo was the muscular nakedness and hints of homosexual arousal (see figure 8). This promotion of sexual desire certainly aligned with heteronormative masculinity, but gay rodeo's objectification of men and the male body ran counter to the appropriate object of desire at straight rodeos: the normative, feminine female body.

Beyond its presentation in the LGBTQ+ press, this overtly masculine and sexual display of men also appeared in the rodeo programs. The same programs that warned contestants and spectators away from sex at the rodeo also featured advertisements for gay bars and bathhouses. Sometimes the ads were merely suggestive, but others included graphic imagery and explicit mentions of cruising and sex. Despite the homemade feel of early Reno programs (sometimes using handwritten ads), local gay bars, bathhouses, and even one lesbian bar used seminude imagery and sexual activity to attract rodeo clientele. By 1980 the Reno programs had grown more explicit, with images of fully nude men and ads for the nitrite drug commonly called poppers, used by some gay men at clubs and during sex.⁵²

FIGURE 8. *National Reno Gay Rodeo, circa 1980s. Much like the gay clones in figure 7, the mostly male spectators at the Reno rodeos adopted an eroticized, more nude version of western work wear. They wore cowboy hats, jeans, and belt buckles, but the shirts often came off in the sun. Courtesy of ONE Archives at the USC Libraries, Ken Dickmann Collection.*

Through the 1980s, 1990s, and into the 2000s, gay rodeo continued to oscillate between a desire for respectability and putting sex on display. The ads and imagery in programs in the 1970s and '80s may appear shockingly sexual, but they would have been nothing unusual for the era. Nude (female) models were still common in mainstream magazines like *Vogue* into the 1970s; however, as straight-oriented magazines showed less and less skin in the later twentieth century, the gay press continued to openly celebrate nude bodies.[53] Gay rodeo instead followed a more conservative trend in the 1980s and '90s before returning to more sexually charged imagery in the 2000s. This transition may have occurred for several reasons, primarily tied to a desire for professionalism and mainstream respectability, along with the growing AIDS crisis.

More than in any other period, gay rodeo in the 1990s was concerned with its professional appearance. It achieved its greatest popularity in the early and mid-1990s, with almost three thousand members in twenty-two associations, four competitive divisions, and twenty-two rodeos annually.⁵⁴ In 1997, IGRA founder Wayne Jakino wrote to all IGRA members about ways to improve the gay rodeo circuit, and he identified PRCA as a point of comparison and model of success. However, this potential move to a more professional-style rodeo was met with concern from members. The Texas association gathered responses from its group; these uniformly questioned the comparison to PRCA and wanted IGRA to remain amateur. As one respondent explained, "The PRCA fulfills this area [of a high-stakes, professional rodeo]. We are not competing against PRCA for people, we are adding 1500+ people to the rodeo lifestyle. Isn't this why IGRA exists."⁵⁵ Though IGRA never adopted a model that more closely aligned its competition practices with PRCA, gay rodeo programs in the 1990s looked more like mainstream, professional ones, with images of boots, hats, chaps, and other trappings of a western identity or presentations of cowboys—and sometimes even of cowgirls—riding stoically or competing with a serious focus.

This interest in professional rodeo and respect from the western rodeo world is only part of the reason gay rodeo programs transformed and became more conservative in the 1990s. The AIDS crisis also quickly, deeply, and dramatically impacted gay rodeo. Chapter 3 examines how AIDS affected contestants on a personal level and how the epidemic caused gay rodeo to adjust its fundraising and activist focus. However, AIDS also led gay rodeo to change its public presentation in its programs. Staging a sexually conservative rodeo modeled on the professional circuit demonstrated to an increasingly hostile public that LGBTQ+ people were no different than straight people and that their rodeo was a "normal" one. Just as homophile groups in the 1950s and '60s adopted heteronormative gender presentations and middle-class lifestyles to normalize themselves, so too did queer communities during the AIDS epidemic. They attempted to prove they were just like straight people and therefore deserved to live. This included a move to "clean up" the predominant view that gay men were hypersexualized.⁵⁶ Gay rodeo was not immune to this impulse and actively presented its events as places with a family atmosphere that intended to break stereotypes about the gay community.⁵⁷ But this proved to be complicated, because many male participants still wanted to use their involvement to show their adherence to hegemonic masculinity. They now had to carefully balance a gender performance that confirmed they were masculine enough to be taken seriously as manly cowboys but not so masculine that they were perceived as sex-crazed deviants.

Additionally, this shift in presentation also was emblematic of the abrupt end to the celebration and sexual freedom of the post-Stonewall 1970s and early '80s. Because of AIDS, gay men were increasingly limited not just in how publicly they could celebrate their sexuality but in how they could have sex safely, and the rodeo programs reflected this. From the late 1980s into the 1990s, advertisements for bathhouses and erotic massage were replaced by warnings about AIDS, information about gay-friendly doctors, and memorial statements about friends lost to the disease. Through these publications, gay rodeo attempted to educate and influence the behavior of its own members and that of spectators with information about AIDS, safe sex, and healthcare providers friendly to LGBTQ+ clientele.

Like other gay rodeo programs in the early 1980s, the 1985 Los Angeles rodeo program promoted unrestrained (homo)sexual freedom. An ad for the Camp David bathhouse depicted a mostly nude man under the tagline, "the only sure bet in Las Vegas." Another ad for the country-western gay bar Rawhide featured a drawing of a naked man riding a bucking horse to sexual bliss (see figure 9).

These explicit images of sexual activity contrast sharply with the much tamer ads in the 1990 and '91 Los Angeles programs, in which the Rawhide ad now used a fully clothed cowboy who only yielded a glimpse of skin under an unbuttoned shirt, and bathhouses promoted themselves as "a fun place ... a safe place ... a clean place ... a healthy place to come." Similarly, the 1990 Denver program included a bathhouse ad that said, "It's OK to have fun!" but with the reminder, "when you play it safe." While these changes only hinted at the AIDS crisis, its impact was made more explicit elsewhere in the programs. The grand marshal in 1991 was the AIDS coordinator for the city, and the program opened with a full-page ad from AIDS Project Los Angeles, which featured a decidedly unsexy photograph of Lucy and Ethel from the *I Love Lucy* show, asking readers to "be a buddy to someone with AIDS."[58] From the early 1980s to the early '90s, the ads and imagery in rodeo programs changed from an overt and public celebration of gay male sex to cautionary tales and more conservative depictions.

However, even at the height of the AIDS crisis, sex never disappeared entirely from gay rodeo. This was not a refusal to acknowledge

FIGURE 9. *GSGRA LA Rodeo Program, ad for Rawhide, 1985. This sexually explicit ad directly linked the cowboy image with sexual activity. The word* rawhide *connoted both movie and* TV *Westerns and the raw, condom-free sexual activity that was quickly disappearing by 1985 with the explosion of the* AIDS *epidemic. Courtesy of the Autry Museum of the American West.*

the epidemic or the dangers facing many LGBTQ+ people in the 1980s and '90s. Gay rodeo, like other queer organizations in that era, focused on keeping people safe not with the elimination of sex, as conservative religious and political leaders desired, but with guidance and medical information. For instance, the Denver program from 1990 offered sex advice from the Colorado AIDS Project, which sponsored an ad that said gay men know a lot about "safer sex" and condoms but that "once in a while someone may 'slip.'"[59] Rather than chastisement, the ad offered encouragement and support to help gay men overcome feelings of guilt and anxiety around sex.

By offering this support and by continuing to sometimes include "sexy" ads and images, gay rodeo, along with other LGBTQ+ groups, helped to protect its own community. Gay sex clubs and bathhouses worked similarly. Many gay organizations regularly identified these institutions as places that promoted some of the safest sex, because of greater regulation, the availability of condoms, and the encouragement to engage in sexual activities that did not have high HIV transmission risks (see figure 10). When Los Angeles identified the baths as health hazards, ACT UP wrote a position paper in 1988 defending them and explaining how they were not the problem. Despite evidence otherwise, the moralizing messages of religious conservatives in the 1980s and '90s condemned all gay male sexuality as bad and dangerous.[60] In the face of this opposition, the appearance in gay rodeo programs of nudity, sexual arousal, sex advice, and bars and baths that continued to promote sexual encounters helped show gay men how to have sex safely and helped to make sex something positive again.

The inclusion of sexual imagery also played an important role in the mental and psychological survival of gay men in the 1980s and '90s. Activist Douglas Crimp in the 1980s and scholar José Esteban Muñoz in the 1990s both wrote about the importance of a queer imaginary during the AIDS epidemic.[61] Images like those in gay rodeo programs allowed queer cowfolx to imagine a reality that was safe from disease, permitted a re-eroticization of gay life, and saw an end to homophobic and discriminatory legislation. However, for some gay men, the queer imaginary felt too distant and without promise. In the tragic shadow of the AIDS era, some gay men resisted the emergence of a safe sex regime in the late 1980s and '90s by turning toward "barebacking," or the practice of intentionally unprotected sex. In gay cowboy culture, the risk of the rodeo and risk of unprotected sex became enmeshed. As sexuality scholar Thomas Linneman notes, "Making sex safer, by definition, reduces the risk involved in the sexual activity, thus demasculinizing it." He connected the name "barebacking" to the "days of the risk-taking, masculine frontier cowboy."[62] Gay cowboy erotica celebrated this risk-taking mentality in both the

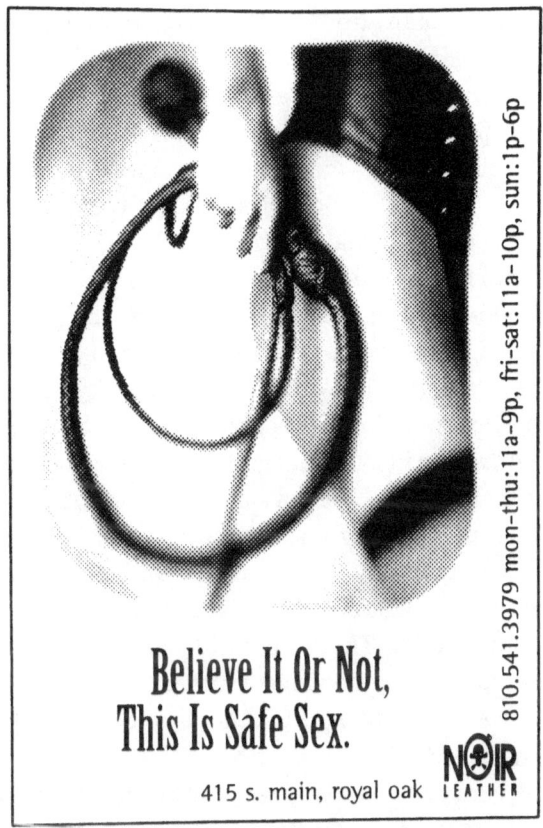

FIGURE 10. *MIGRA Rodeo Program, "Believe it or not, this is safe sex," 1995. Although S/M play was deemed problematic by much of American society, this advertisement reminds gay rodeoers that it often was a safe form of sexual activity during the AIDS crisis. Courtesy of the Autry Museum of the American West.*

arena and the bedroom with stories focused on gay rodeo riders: "In every town, no matter how big or how small, Justin Longacre always found a good ride. Sometimes it was a horse named Diablo, Crazy Eight, or Snake Eyes, and sometimes it was a man named Brogan, or Charles, or Thad. Justin didn't care which it was because he always rode bareback. He lived to take risks. It was the cowboy way."[63] The beauty and sexual potency of risk gave life meaning to many men. One bull rider asserted, "If there is such a thing as risk-free living, it certainly doesn't sound like much fun."[64] The hypersexual and hypermasculine image of the cowboy revolted against the conservative sexual politics of the era as men attempted to navigate the AIDS crisis. While it is unclear how many IGRA members actually practiced sexual barebacking at this time—and the idea certainly ran contrary to the messaging about safe sex—the tension between proper sexual behavior and the wild fantasies of cowboy enthusiasts were palpable.

With the retraction of a vibrant sexual culture in the 1980s and early '90s, the return to sexual positivity in the queer community was not a straightforward path. In the late 1990s and 2000s, the crisis point of the epidemic began to ebb. AIDS hospices closed and bathhouses reopened.[65] Yet even as the LGBTQ+ community commenced the slow path of embracing sex and their sexuality again, hesitation and shame still existed. Gay rights activist and author Larry Kramer wrote in *The Advocate* in 1997 that gay culture was too focused on sex and blamed that for AIDS: "We have our sexuality, and we have made a culture out of our sexuality, and that culture has killed us. I want to say again: We have made sex the cornerstone of gay liberation and gay culture, and it has killed us." This was just one of many moralizing articles that appeared in *The Advocate* in the late '90s. These, along with other outspoken gay neoconservative pieces, criticized everything sexual, from the return of bathhouses to lessened fears about sex among gay men.[66]

Despite the concerns raised by some in the queer community, gay rodeo began to embrace a more sexual and outwardly queer identity than it had for the previous decade. Through its programs, it presented itself as a place where gay men could reclaim their sexuality, celebrate their masculine bodies, and publicly state their sexual desires. The majority of rodeo programs still adhered to traditional western rodeo standards, but shirtless men, crotch shots, and backside views of cowboy butts reappeared in the late 1990s and 2000s. Program covers also celebrated gay pride with rainbows and same-sex affection. Rainbow imagery increased from appearances on nine program covers in the 1990s to fourteen in the 2000s. The use of sexual imagery expanded even more dramatically, from nine times in the 1990s to twenty-one in the 2000s. IGRA rodeo registration brochures also became more provocative. Fifty-four percent of the brochures from 2000 and 2001 included (homo)sexy or rainbow imagery, and this increased to 69 percent between 2003 and 2005. Even some of those with traditional imagery included taglines that hinted at sex, such as "Cowboys, cowgirls, and so much more ... something for everyone" in Tulsa in 2003 and "Buck off to Calgary!" that same year. The Chicago rodeo that year more boldly hinted at the gender play available in the royalty and camp competitions and perhaps referenced the openness of gay rodeo to trans contestants with the tagline "Where cowgirls can be cowboys and vice versa."[67] While most of the imagery highlighted relationships between men, some of these programs also hinted at a sexual life for lesbians. By doing this, gay rodeo not only returned to a celebration of sex but became more inclusive and welcoming in who it permitted to be sexual.

This pull between the (homo)sexual and the traditional, heterosexual-style rodeo could be seen publicly in the media presentation of the gay rodeo and in the way in which it presented itself to the public through its programs. But it also appeared in the more private, internal messaging of association newsletters and how contestants saw gay rodeo and the purpose and value it served for them on a personal level. For some contestants and spectators, gay rodeo was about sex and a good time, but for others it offered a respite from the gay party scene.

Even in the sexually charged era of the early 1980s, gay rodeo was more conservative in comparison to other parts of gay social life. One competitor described IGRA in 1985, saying, "It isn't any of the sleazy part of being gay. It's wholesome and it's a daytime event."[68] Similarly, someone who requested information in 1997 explained their interest by saying they were "very excited" to be involved with an organization "that I can be proud of."[69] Gay rodeo participants regularly identified feelings of depression when they first came out because they did not like the drugs, alcohol, and sex so prominent at gay bars. The Utah Gay Rodeo Association even took to its newsletter in 1990 to ensure it created a different environment, by warning its members about the dangers of drugs and reminding them that none were tolerated at UGRA functions.[70]

Despite the stated interests of many members and the actions taken by associations like Utah to differentiate their rodeos from the gay bar scenes, other times gay rodeo promoted the party scene. For instance, Phil Ragsdale asked participants to leave the sex at home, but he also included maps in the programs that identified all of the 24-hour bars and bathhouses available in Reno, along with ads that encouraged the rodeo crowd to use these facilities for sex (see figure 11).[71] Over fifteen years later, after some of the fear around HIV/AIDS had receded, IGRA

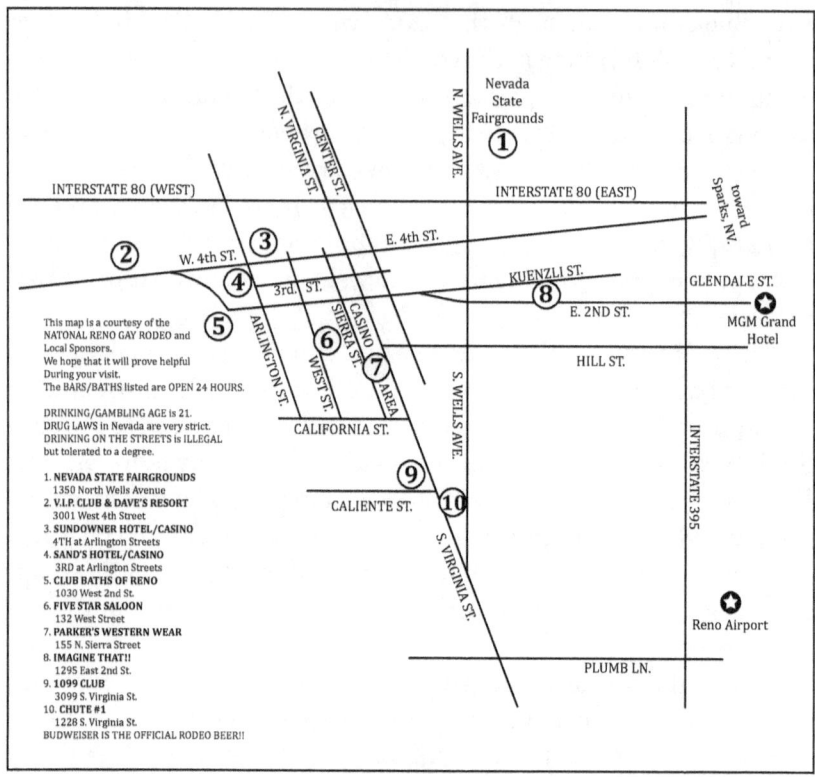

FIGURE 11. *National Reno Gay Rodeo Program, city map, 1984. Seen here is a reproduced map of the local sponsors for the 1984 Reno rodeo. The key reassures rodeoers that the bars and bathhouses on this map are open twenty-four hours and hopes this guide "will prove helpful" during their time in Reno. Map recreated by Brett Chloupek.*

offered a similar map of Las Vegas for "alternative lifestyles," and the annual convention in 1999 proudly announced, "When the work is done, we'll have our fun" at parties, receptions, and a bar crawl.[72] The Los Angeles rodeo in 2001 even went as far as to advertise itself with the tagline "Like a circuit party but with cows."[73] This shift in focus led to critiques, as some members questioned if the association had become overly focused on offering a party and not enough on the rodeo.[74]

Debates like these over the proper place of sex and fun at the rodeo are emblematic of the larger questions in gay rodeo about the pursuit of masculinity, professionalism, and respectability. Before AIDS, gay rodeo offered a place to be(come) a cowboy and celebrate sexual freedom. As the tragic years of the 1980s unfolded, gay men needed to change the public perception of their sexual activity, and they were also forced to change their sexual realities. The celebration of earlier years was replaced by messages of safety. For some gay men, this transition proved problematic, as the pursuit of hegemonic masculinity was closely connected to sex, which was now identified as increasingly deviant and problematic by both the straight and gay communities. Only with the shift in the AIDS epidemic has gay rodeo been able to return to a more carefree, sexually playful mode, but even that has been debated and critiqued by gay rodeoers, because embracing a public, queer sexuality creates a division between gay and straight rodeo. Thus, with the return to sex-positivity, gay rodeo may consequently be taken less seriously, therefore denying it the stamp of authenticity and respectability so many of its participants crave.

The blatant displays of sex and sexuality may be what (straight) outsiders first notice in gay rodeo programs, but the imagery would not surprise gay contestants and spectators, who saw more explicit articles, ads, and imagery in other gay publications of the 1980s and '90s and into the twenty-first century. Gay rodeo programs included direct references to queer sexual activity, but in most ways, the programs aligned with traditional, straight ones. They discussed the rodeo itself, often including its history and an explanation of the events as a way to welcome spectators new to the circuit and to attract more participants from these audience members. However, even with this traditional presentation, gay rodeo could not escape that it was fundamentally disruptive and dangerous to understandings of American masculinity, western identity, and notions of conservative rurality.

Thus, while organizers may have wanted to just stage a rodeo, the gay rodeo was never *just* a rodeo. It could not be. In order to have this event—even as mainstream a rodeo as possible, where gay men could shake off the "limp wrist" stereotype—they also had to fight for a space. Contestants tried to counter both social stereotypes of effeminate gay men and the derogatory and divisive image within the gay community of the clone of the 1970s and '80s by being real cowboys who participated in an organized, structured, rule-laden rodeo modeled on the professional (straight) circuit.

Yet the promotion of queer sex in its programs, along with other non-normative elements, such as drag queens, camp events, and the purported equal participation of women, as discussed in later chapters, all marked gay rodeo as different. For riders it was a serious event, but it also was a campy diversion for some spectators and was condemned by straight cowboys who believed that it made a farce of the American West and of their own straight masculinity. This created tensions within gay rodeo, as normative-presenting cowboys sometimes opposed what they identified as threats to their claims to a hegemonic masculinity. And yet the embrace by many of these same men of publicly nude male bodies and sexually explicit queer imagery and advertisements unsettled long-held understandings about cowboys and rodeo, masculinity and sexuality. In so doing, gay rodeoers have made a space for the queer cowboy to unapologetically be an authentic one.

Oral History Vignette
BRIAN HELANDER, IGRA PAST PRESIDENT

I was born in Canada, and when I was three or four, we moved to the big city—Winnipeg. My mom and dad had five kids, and my dad was a milkman, so it was not an easy life. We didn't have a car. I still to this day don't know how my mother got groceries to the house, enough for seven people, without a car. I took a job as an orderly in a nursing home they built right behind our home. That got me into the healthcare field. I went to a community college in Winnipeg, and then I moved to the United States about a year after I graduated. There was a big nursing shortage in the United States. I had a nursing license and a reason to get out of town. I got a job at Phoenix General Hospital, working night shifts in the intensive care unit. Told my mother it was just a year assignment—I'd be back, not to worry. But suddenly there was gay life in Phoenix; there wasn't any in Winnipeg. Never came back—that was forty years ago.

HIV started in 1981–1982 in that area. I was working in the ER, and one of the gay doctors came in one morning and threw down an article on the five guys that had Kaposi's sarcoma in New York and said to me, "We got a problem here." Then suddenly we started seeing guys in the

ER. Even though I was an ER nurse, I was suddenly also an HIV nurse, because I was "out" in a Catholic hospital. I was the one they called, because nobody else would go in the room. I was that guy they called down and said, "Brian, you need to come up here, because we aren't going in. You're one of them. You go in there. We're not going in."

I knew either (a) I was infected with HIV, and would shortly die, or (b) that the mode of transmission was not casual contact, because I was in casual contact with them. I was eating with them, I was shaking their hand, I was around them. This was before testing and I was healthy, so I kinda erred on the "this is not casual contact sort of thing."

I remember saying to the women who had children, my peers, my fellow nurses, "One day, you will come crawling to the gay community, to ask us how to deal with this issue, for your children." We set up the infrastructures, we set up the programs, the treatment, the outreach, the doctors who left their practices to become HIV specialists. The nurses, in large part, were gay, and we set up the infrastructure for the treatment of HIV in the 1980s. So, they did come to us. I'm still involved; it's why I'm going back to school to finish my degree in global health sciences. I want to finish this work. We're on the brink of fixing HIV. We could stop it today if we had the political will.

There were heroes, like lesbians who weren't infected by HIV but were there for the gay boys. There were heroes, like those of us who weren't infected who went into the homes of the dying and cleaned up after them and took care of them and held their hand and were with them when they died and with their partners when they died.

I can say that of probably a hundred people that I would call friends, probably three of those survived. Probably two of those were HIV positive, and they're still alive today, long-term survivors of HIV for whatever reason. One was like me and did not become infected with HIV. But I lost every friend I had. Then, suddenly, I really didn't have any friends, you know?

I think the HIV epidemic had a great impact on rodeo. If you look at pictures from the early days, the stands were packed with guys, and that audience was decimated by HIV and we've really struggled to get that audience back. They're not there. That audience, the people of my ilk, my age, the western cowboy kind of lifestyle, I'm not sure we're there anymore.

Chapter 3

"A EUPHEMISM FOR AN ORGY"

Sex, Sexuality, and the AIDS Crisis

"Sodomites, do you have AIDS yet?" asked protestors at the 1994 Seattle-area gay rodeo. Questions like this ignited opposition to gay rodeo and sparked fears for many queer cowfolx who silently asked themselves the same thing. Gay rodeo was born in the post-Stonewall excitement of the 1970s, but it came of age in the dark days of Reagan-era conservatism, the Christian Right, and the AIDS crisis. Though the legitimacy of gay rodeo already was questioned by straight competitors and adherents to the macho, heterosexual cowboy image, the AIDS crisis led to growing hostility from outside groups.

Rodeo arenas became contentious meeting grounds, further pitting gay cowboys against fearful, conservative communities and religious organizations. As their own participants received positive diagnoses and began to die, gay rodeo associations changed their messaging from sexually explicit ads to ones about the disease, healthcare, and safe sex. Gay rodeo also reconceptualized its fundraising efforts, moving from an ostensibly apolitical organization that raised money for primarily straight-identified charities, like muscular dystrophy and senior centers, to a place that could not escape the political nature of AIDS.

Using decades of rodeo ephemera, this chapter examines the opposition that targeted gay rodeo and the impact that homophobic and AIDS-based protests had on that arena. In this era, AIDS created a stronger justification for discrimination against queer groups, such as gay rodeo, but it also created a unified purpose for their existence. It brought queer people together and gave gay rodeo a greater meaning beyond the embrace of a country-western lifestyle. It formed a "culture of care" that bonded gay rodeoers to each other, their community, and a national LGBTQ+ movement.[1]

Following the Stonewall riots in 1969 and the growth of Pride events the next year, queer people saw an expansion in visibility and acceptance. In 1973 the American Psychiatric Association dropped homosexuality from its list of mental disorders with a 13-0 vote, and by 1979, twenty states had repealed their sodomy laws. There also was more support to add sexual orientation as a protected status in antidiscrimination laws.[2] However, these changes led to a corresponding conservative backlash. Opposition by spokespeople such as Anita Bryant, John Briggs, and Jerry Falwell targeted these protections, and some were repealed as soon as they were passed.[3] As these expanded rights and visibility for LGBTQ+ people competed against the growing religious conservatism in the country in the late 1970s and early '80s, medical reports of a rare disease afflicting gay men played into the hands of the Christian Right and "pro-family" supporters and posed significant difficulties for LGBTQ+ organizations, including gay rodeo.

Public awareness of AIDS grew following a June 1981 newsletter from the Centers for Disease Control (CDC) that reported on five cases of an unusual pneumonia in gay men in Los Angeles, though several years earlier, in 1979, a physician already noticed a pattern of unusual deaths among gay men.[4] Small stories ran in the *Los Angeles Times* and *San Francisco Chronicle* after the CDC report, and additional attention appeared following a July 1981 CDC report on a rare cancer in gay men in New York City, Los Angeles, and San Francisco. By the end of that year, there were 121 confirmed deaths from what soon would be known as AIDS.[5] In 1982 *Newsweek* ran several articles on AIDS, and all of the major television networks included some coverage of the growing epidemic.[6] Yet the overall media attention on such a deadly disease was limited because of the stigmatized groups connected with it—initially gay men and then intravenous drug users and Haitian immigrants. While the tragic deaths of seven Chicago residents from cyanide-laced Tylenol capsules warranted sixty news stories in two months, the deaths of three hundred people due to AIDS garnered only six news stories during all of 1982.[7]

The US government similarly ignored the growing epidemic, spending just $1 million on research in the first year. This stands in stark contrast to the $9 million spent by the CDC in 1976 on Legionnaires' disease within months of an outbreak that killed thirty-four people.[8] The federal government finally formed an Executive Task Force on AIDS in 1983, but it was made up mostly of conservative religious leaders. President Ronald Reagan did not mention the disease publicly until 1985 and only included the US Surgeon General C. Everett Koop in the task force that year.[9] There was no testing for HIV available until 1985, and until 1996, with the development of an effective antiretroviral therapy (ART), an AIDS diagnosis essentially was a death sentence.[10] By 1990 only 20 percent of those diagnosed before 1985 were still alive.[11]

Gay Americans across the country struggled to understand this disease. Specifically, for urban gay men in cities like San Francisco and New York, it initiated what Simon Watney has called "a wholesale de-sexualisation of gay culture and experience." Watney explained this to mean that the power and liberation of the 1970s was replaced in the '80s with a culture of repression, almost a return to the illegal, closeted lives gay people were forced to live in the 1950s and '60s.[12] The media and government criticized the sex lives of gay men, and religious conservatives, public health officials, and even gay organizations pushed for the closure of sexual meeting grounds, such as bathhouses and sex clubs.[13] This led cultural critic Susan Sontag to call the 1970s a period of sexual inflation and freedom while the '80s became a sexual depression.[14]

As they saw their civil rights crumble and their friends and partners die around them, LGBTQ+ community members organized to protect themselves. The Gay Men's Health Crisis formed in 1981 in New York City, the San Francisco AIDS Foundation in 1982, and AIDS Project Los Angeles that same year. While organizations like these focused on public health responses, others, such as ACT UP, established in 1987, were direct-action protest groups.[15]

Although Phil Ragsdale of the National Reno Gay Rodeo and the founders of the International Gay Rodeo Association both eschewed political messaging and involvement—instead wanting to offer participants a social activity based in the country-western lifestyle—gay rodeo could not ignore the realities of the AIDS epidemic. It faced external obstacles to its events and internal difficulties with sick and dying members. Because of this, it was forced to address the political climate around it, deal with the media in various ways, and shift its fundraising from mainstream community efforts to almost exclusively AIDS organizations and LGBTQ+ charities. Gay rodeo members keenly felt these adjustments and the traumatizing losses of the 1980s and '90s, and this era had long-lasting impacts on the development of the circuit. With the creation of lifesaving HIV medicines in the late 1990s, IGRA and its founding members struggled to readjust its fundraising efforts and ways of remembering the past while also looking to the future, remaining relevant, and embracing younger generations.

PROTESTS AND OTHER OBSTACLES BEFORE AIDS

The Christian Right espoused a belief in "family values" as a key tenet of the movement in the late 1970s. As part of a response to the growing, and increasingly successful, feminist and gay rights movements, the Christian Right connected the demise of traditional families with these issues, identified feminists and LGBTQ+ people as dangerous, and promoted the idea that opposing them would benefit all Americans.[16] Nevada, the birthplace of gay rodeo, was part of this growing movement. Dan Hansen founded Nevada's Independent American Party in 1967 and later formed the Pro-Family Christian Coalition (PFCC). The Hansen family soon became known in the state for their vitriolic, homophobic statements.[17] Even before hostility to queer people grew with the emergence of AIDS in the early 1980s, Ragsdale faced a conservative local climate in Reno and a state that made homosexual acts illegal until 1993.

In 1975 and 1976, Ragsdale worked with Reno-area officials and ranchers to secure an arena and livestock. He contracted with the Washoe County Fairgrounds and held the rodeo there throughout its tenure, from 1976 to 1984, but he found it more difficult to identify a willing stock contractor.[18] A local rancher welcomed his inquiry when Ragsdale first said he was part of a "Local Civic Group" planning a rodeo to raise money for the city's senior citizens' annual Thanksgiving Day Feed. When pushed to describe the specific group, Ragsdale admitted it was the "Reno Gay Community," and the rancher refused to be involved. After many similar rejections, Ragsdale eventually had to purchase the animals himself the day before the rodeo began.[19]

Even after some of its initial difficulties getting off the ground, the Reno rodeo received little local attention the first several years, largely by Ragsdale's own design. As he explained, "We kind of played it down because of redneck action," adding that they "don't want to create a riot" with the rodeo. The first year, the fairground manager kept it as a private event, not open to the public, and this helped it avoid publicity. By the second year, Ragsdale felt ready to share information about the gathering, and articles appeared in mainstream newspapers in San Francisco and Sacramento. Rodeo attendance increased that year to seven hundred people. The group had to eject a minister from the fairgrounds who was handing out material that claimed homosexuals were sick and needed to be cured, but Ragsdale encountered little other resistance from Nevada conservatives in 1977.[20] Instead, the first notable protests came from within the gay community, when several LGBTQ+ groups from San Francisco urged a boycott of the rodeo in 1979 to call attention to Nevada's antihomosexuality laws and the state's failure to ratify the Equal Rights Amendment.[21]

By the early 1980s, however, Ragsdale's annual rodeos became the target of repeated homophobic attacks. This opposition grew with the spread of AIDS in the mid-1980s, but earlier the hostility was based on religious and moral arguments. County Commissioner Belie Williams and Lt. Gov. Myron Leavitt made public statements in 1981 opposing Reno's gay rodeo. Williams called on the fair board to cancel its contract but was told by the state attorney's office that that could not legally happen. This failure to act raised the ire of the lieutenant governor, who made his own statement to the press: "I'm strongly opposed to queers using public property. If you give them the fairgrounds, you're condoning their lifestyle, and I don't think we should do that." Leavitt's language became even more hateful as he continued, "They call them queers because they have a screw loose. The fact of the matter is that their behavior is not normal and natural."[22] His language forced Gov. Bob List to say Leavitt was out of line in his messaging, but List acknowledged that he agreed with the spirit of Williams's and Leavitt's claims by saying the gay rodeo reflected negatively on Reno and the state.[23] Hansen also joined the fray with even more extreme language, writing to the *Reno Gazette*, "The termites of civilization have brazenly oozed out of their closet to proclaim that they have a right to maim, molest and embarrass society.... Homosexuality, like all parasites, survives by preying upon the healthy."[24] These were all malicious public statements, but they failed to have the impact that Williams, Leavitt, and Hansen had hoped.

In the summer of 1981, the first reports of unusual cancers and pneumonia in gay men began to appear in coastal urban centers, but concern had not yet reached inland cities like Reno or spread to straight communities. Because of this, the attacks in Nevada had little negative impact on gay rodeo there. Instead, Ragsdale told the *Village Voice*, a gay-friendly publication, that the political opposition had an inverse effect on the rodeo and garnered it even more support from Reno businesses, hotels, and newspapers.[25] One example of this encouragement came from local resident Robert Shaffer, who wrote to the *Reno Journal* condemning Lt. Gov. Leavitt. Leavitt had used his faith as a Latter-Day Saint to justify his stance against the rodeo. Shaffer, also LDS, called this view ignorant and harmful to gay people and said it misrepresented the church's stance on homosexuality.[26] National celebrity Joan Rivers also came to support the Reno event that year. So, rather than stop the rodeo, the attacks by government officials expanded its visibility. The National Reno Gay Rodeo drew ten thousand attendees in 1980, similar numbers 1981, and more than twenty-two thousand in 1982.[27] Yet, as AIDS continued its spread across the country, intolerance of queer people correspondingly increased, and the growing crowds in Reno soon made Ragsdale's gay rodeo a target.

THE AIDS ERA AND NEW SUCCESSES FOR THE OPPOSITION

After the expansion of the Christian Right in the 1970s, the 1980s began with a more conservative climate. AIDS provided fodder for these principles and helped to move what had been fringe beliefs into the mainstream. The growing fears around this new and terrifying disease also provided another justification to persecute LGBTQ+ people and their communities. The National Reno Gay Rodeo and later IGRA rodeos fell into the crosshairs of this more focused, outspoken, and increasingly popular opposition. Gay rodeo often won, but the antigay crusaders sometimes came out victorious.

Even when gay rodeos were not canceled, the growing resistance that they faced forced them to change their public presentation. The Reno protests in 1981 failed to garner much support, but the local landscape had begun to change by 1983. That year, several groups organized a strong front against the National Reno Gay Rodeo and worked relentlessly to cancel it. The public messaging now centered around fears of AIDS, but the hostility continued to be based in fundamentalist, religious morality and homophobia. While the debate divided Reno, many residents sided with the rodeo and continued to publicly offer their support.

The emergence of AIDS made this ongoing support of gay rodeo more important than ever. Just a four-hour drive from San Francisco, Reno was close to one of the epicenters of the growing epidemic, and local media carefully charted its course. In 1981, California reported 45 cases and 18 deaths. This expanded to 182 cases and 63 deaths in 1982. By 1983, the *Reno Gazette* reported with concern that California's cases had already doubled in just the first six months of that year, to 171 new cases and 32 new deaths.[28] While many Americans remained unfamiliar with AIDS into the mid- and late 1980s, Reno newspapers regularly included reports on the disease.[29] In 1983, the visibility of LGBTQ+ Nevadans increased with the first gay Pride event in Las Vegas, but this also brought greater opposition, as the first local AIDS case was diagnosed in Reno's Washoe County in March of that year.[30] Groups like the PFCC under Dan Hansen used these frightening developments to attack gay rodeo.

Yet rather than accept the hatred promoted by these groups, many Reno citizens chose, for the time being, to rely on medical knowledge, legal opinions, capitalist desires, and a denial of hatred writ large and side with the rodeo. In the summer of 1983, Hansen and the PFCC gathered more than three thousand signatures of people seeking to end the gay rodeo. Hansen claimed that AIDS posed a "clear and present danger" to local citizens, because the rodeo attracted thousands of gay people to the city. His attacks brought the ACLU to support the National Reno Gay Rodeo, and in late July, the two sides faced off in front of an overflow crowd at a county commissioners' meeting. The commissioners allotted each side time to debate and field audience questions. The PFCC based its argument on public health grounds, even though the CDC had already informed the commissioners that there was no health risk to the general population. The county health director agreed, and the commissioners admitted their hands were tied. Despite his earlier public opposition to gay rodeo in 1981, even Commissioner Williams said, "The law has to be honored."

The PFCC did little to support its claim about public health and offered evidence from just one health professional, a psychologist, who admitted he knew nothing about AIDS. The doctor also revealed that it was morality, rather than science or public health concerns, that were at the root of his beliefs when he said the rodeo was "an outrageous display of self-centered sexualism." Hansen made similar statements, claiming the rodeo was "nothing more than a euphemism for an orgy" and that homosexuality was "riddled with disease and full of repugnant sexual practices. We declare that to be un-American." These homophobic and scientifically unsupported remarks may have backfired and instead pushed some in the audience against Hansen's group, as newspaper articles noted more fervent audience support on the side of the rodeo. In the end, the county commissioners listened without comment and then declared they had no legal grounds to break the rodeo contract and ended the meeting.[31] However, the Pro-Family Christian Coalition refused to admit defeat and took its argument to the governor's office and the public forum of local newspapers.

After their denial in Washoe County, twenty members from the PFCC held a five-hour sit-in at the governor's office to present their petition to him instead. At this juncture, the pretense of public health and AIDS fell away entirely from their arguments. That route had been denied to them by the county commissioners, so Hansen now planned to issue a petition demanding that the governor's office uphold the state's antisodomy laws. The PFCC said that because sodomy was illegal, the rodeo should be banned, in the same way that the state would not allow a "child abusers' festival" or "drug pushers' rodeo."[32]

In addition to the public action of the PFCC and Dan Hansen, a second group, called Patriots to Normalize Reno, engaged in more devious subterfuge, using anonymous mailings and obscene phone calls. Its members focused their attack on of the horror AIDS, the supposed sexual perversion of gay people, and the protection of children and future generations. They even played into Cold War–era anxieties in their pamphlets, asking, "Would you rather see society obliterated in a nuclear war, or have a Gay Rodeo in Reno?" The group encouraged similar-minded people to publicly identify each other: "You may show your hatred for this sickism by attaching a white cloth or ribbon to your automobile antenna. Be a patriot... And may God bless straight *America!*"[33]

In the end, the attempts to cancel the rodeo failed. The governor turned the PFCC away without an audience and refused to step into the fray. Undaunted, the group threatened, "We don't plan to go away." Ragsdale doubled his security force in anticipation of problems, but no further incidents occurred. Instead, the rodeo's popularity increased, something Ragsdale credited to the free publicity from the debate. Attendance numbers that year reached thirty thousand, far surpassing all previous Reno rodeos.[34]

Even though the PFCC did not stage a protest at the 1983 National Reno Gay Rodeo itself, it continued its fight by circulating a petition again the following year, with the goal of gathering enough signatures to force a local vote. It used the same fear-mongering tactics, now claiming that homosexuals were responsible for 65 percent of all sex-related mass murders and saying "our children are threatened."[35] This time, newspapers paid little attention, and the rodeo went forward with few protests—but also with a significant drop in attendance. Ragsdale had anticipated lower numbers due to competing events in nearby California, including the summer Olympics and Democratic National Convention, but the more limited press (and lack of opposition) ironically may have played a role in this.

The steep decline to fifteen thousand attendees in 1984 dealt a crushing blow to the National Reno Gay Rodeo. Following the event, the Nevada State Fair Board announced that Ragsdale still owed $7,530 and said efforts to contact him had been unsuccessful, eventually filing a suit against him. Ultimately, it was not the homophobic attacks or panic about AIDS that ended the National Reno Gay Rodeo—attendance numbers and financial and legal troubles spelled its end.[36] Some local residents expressed their disappointment with this outcome, as one said, "especially after most of the community stood up for the right of the gay rodeo to use the fairgrounds."[37]

In the early 1980s, AIDS became a convenient excuse to try to stop gay rodeo, but it simply masked a larger right-wing agenda based in morality, religion, and homophobia. The repeated attacks against the Reno event from 1981 to 1984 all failed to stop the rodeo, but they did draw public attention to a large, queer gathering. As the AIDS epidemic reached a crisis point in the late 1980s and early '90s, the movement against LGBTQ+ people and their community activities gained momentum. This was amplified in a city like Reno, where straight people had already come to the support of gay rodeo several times. When Ragsdale's rodeo shuttered under questionable financial circumstances, the disappointment and burnout of straight Reno residents now combined with a more homophobic environment and an active AIDS presence in their community. This coalesced to form a more effective opposition to gay rodeo when it tried to return to the city in 1988.

While Ragsdale's initial rodeos grew in the excitement of the late 1970s and early '80s, when LGBTQ+ rights and visibility were expanding, IGRA formed amid the epidemic. There was just one confirmed AIDS case in Washoe County in 1983, when the homophobic attacks against the Reno rodeo were the most intense. As the disease spread, so did people's hostility to gay rodeo. By the mid-1980s, the Christian Right and, increasingly, mainstream America viewed gay men as a moral threat and a public menace. People with AIDS (PWAs) no longer were seen as victims but as those responsible for spreading the disease. Attacks on gay men increased, and the US Justice Department determined that businesses could legally discriminate against people with AIDS and employers could fire them. Even in more liberal California, a petition with seven hundred thousand signatures became a 1986 ballot initiative asking people to decide if PWAs should be put into quarantine camps (it lost 71–29).[38] The following year, polls revealed that an all-time high of 78 percent of Americans considered "homosexual relations" to be "always wrong," and many believed AIDS was a punishment for the decline in moral standards.[39]

It was in this climate that IGRA held its first finals rodeo. It took place in San Francisco in 1987, and despite the deep concern about AIDS in that city, Mayor Dianne Feinstein still sent a public letter "warmly" welcoming all of the participants and wishing them luck in the competition.[40] Though it paled in comparison to the heyday of the Reno rodeos, organizers deemed the first IGRA finals a success, with more than five thousand attendees.[41] For the second finals, IGRA planned to bring gay rodeo back to its birthplace for the first time since the last National Reno Gay Rodeo in 1984. Ragsdale had faced homophobic attacks in 1983 and legal difficulties in 1984; the 1988 IGRA finals encountered both simultaneously. This time, the situation in Reno dissolved into a brutal series of public showdowns that successfully stopped the rodeo.

A new organization unassociated with Ragsdale, the Silver State Gay Rodeo Association, part of IGRA, scheduled the finals rodeo with the University of Nevada's Lawlor Events Center. As soon as the rodeo was announced in Reno newspapers, opposition began to form. Mayor Pete Sferrazza gave weak support to the event, saying, "I'm not a gay advocate, but I don't see anything wrong with them holding a rodeo here."[42] The Nevada Families Eagle Forum and its leader, Janine Hansen, sister of Dan Hansen, identified AIDS as a public health danger. But she also repeated the same language of her brother years earlier, comparing a gay rodeo to a "drug users' rodeo or a child molesters' rodeo." She also claimed it would "promote sodomy," which she reminded people was still a felony in Nevada. Like before, the group organized a statewide mailing campaign, which urged people to ask the governor to stop the rodeo.[43] However, it was not the pro-family views alone but a contract dispute and court case that initially stopped it.

Silver State's written contract stipulated a payment structure, with part paid in advance and the remainder due after the rodeo, when the revenue from ticket, food, and beverage sales would be available. However, questions about Silver State's financial stability led Lawlor to call in all remaining expenses up front. Silver State refused, and Lawlor canceled its contract one month before the rodeo. Silver State and IGRA filed a motion to block the cancelation, but when the judge ruled against them, Silver State scrambled to make the remaining payment the following day. But in that short time, the arena had been booked for a university basketball practice and was no longer available. Believing that the university used the contract dispute as a pretense to cancel the controversial rodeo, the ACLU stepped in, saying, "This is just another form of discrimination that is going on at that university" and warned that the school may face a lawsuit in federal court.[44] Silver State and IGRA were forced to look elsewhere in the state for a venue. Many prospective locations refused, because it was a "provocative-type situation," as the county manager in Churchill County reasoned when it refused access to its fairgrounds.[45] Running out of time, Silver State accepted an offer to use a private roping arena located in another part of Churchill County. This time, the group tried to be cautious and refused to publicly announce the location until just a couple of days before the event, saying, "If the media gets the word out about it now, the local politicians have ways to stop us again."[46] IGRA's suspicions were correct, because when the district attorney learned the group had located a venue in his county, he blamed IGRA for being "sneaky" and "underhanded" and filed for a temporary restraining order.

Even though county officials carefully couched their concerns in language about traffic, parking, dust and noise control, crowds, sewage, and security, and explained they would have done the same thing for any event expected to attract more than a thousand people, the apprehensions of community members clearly were rooted elsewhere.[47] At a meeting of "concerned citizens" and county officials, locals expressed fears over AIDS and "lifestyle" rather than zoning: "We feel threatened by a group of people coming in whose philosophies are different than ours. We don't want [our] kids to see any of this. It's offending."[48] Using homophobic arguments and pointing to AIDS had failed to stop Reno's gay rodeo earlier, but as one case in 1983 became upwards of seventeen by 1988 in Washoe County alone, these tactics now were more effective.[49] With this shift in the disease landscape, and knowing he had the support of the more rural and more conservative Churchill County residents on his side, the local district attorney vowed to stop the rodeo, regardless of how the judge ruled.[50]

In the end, the judge ruled against the rodeo, and the Nevada Supreme Court denied an appeal. Since the event was canceled just one day before it was set to begin, contestants had already arrived and horses were stabled at the arena. The sheriff and highway patrol officers blocked the road and refused admittance to anyone, including rodeoers who needed to care for their animals. The police recorded the names and addresses of people who approached and videotaped everyone. Even the arena owners were guilty by association; police told them that if they entered the property, it would be an admission of their homosexuality and they would be subject to arrest. Contestants endured obscenities, and beer bottles were thrown at them. One female resident plainly stated her views, saying, "I'm glad it was canceled, and I hope they never come back. I just don't approve of their lifestyle, and I don't care anything about them. Period."[51] Following the cancelation of the 1988 finals rodeo, for which a program already had been printed (see figure 12), gay rodeo continued to find an inhospitable home in Nevada for many more years. One was not held in the state again until 1996, this time in Las Vegas, and it was not until 2004, twenty years after the last National Reno Gay Rodeo, that it returned to Reno.[52]

Even though the canceled 1988 rodeo corresponded with the increasing trepidation about AIDS, there was not a complete correla-

FIGURE 12. *IGRA Finals Rodeo program cover, 1988. The 1988 IGRA finals faced dramatic legal and popular opposition and was shut down at the last minute, but the program was already printed for this rodeo that never happened. Courtesy of the Autry Museum of the American West.*

tion between the intensification of the AIDS epidemic and the success of attacks on gay rodeo. IGRA rodeos faced similar opposition into the early 1990s, but none of these protests resulted in the same kind of public hostility, legal success, or blocked events. Following the cancelation in Reno in 1988, Phoenix successfully hosted the finals event two years in a row, and in 1991 it moved to Wichita, Kansas. The state was already home to the Kansas Gay Rodeo Association (KGRA), but the group had never staged a rodeo there, much less one on the scale of the IGRA finals. The *Wichita Eagle* featured a positive news article in July, several months before the event, stating that the city would host a gay rodeo for the first time and that two thousand attendees were expected.

With an arena and host hotels already booked, KGRA member and rodeo director Linn Copeland worried the group would encounter local resistance.[53] Copeland's instinct proved correct, as the increased public awareness from the newspaper article began to stir up protest. People called the arena, threatening to never use it again "as the food and bathroom facilities would be ruined if they let us 'Diseased Homosexuals' in," explained one association in their newsletter. The arena caved to public pressure and backed out of the contract. Gay rodeoers were ready to fight back, however, and the Arizona contingent encouraged its members to take action: "Why don't we all pack a couple ACT-UP T-Shirts along with our Wranglers? If certain segments of Wichita's population don't WANT to deal with several thousand happy and polite Rodeo Fans, then perhaps they NEED to deal with several thousand cranky Activists?"[54] Arizona contestants were able to leave their activist shirts at home in the end, because the situation in Wichita was resolved quickly when the city council unanimously approved the use of an alternate space. Even though IGRA told its members, "We foresee no further problems," the association played it safe by requesting no additional media coverage and refusing to issue press permits.[55] While it was able to move forward with the rodeo, the incident cost IGRA thousands of dollars and created fear and frustration among members.

Threats like this against gay rodeo were pivotal incidents for IGRA. Participants have passed down their memories of the homophobic attacks and abrupt cancelation of the 1988 Reno rodeo to each new generation of riders, drawing strength from their own negative experiences. These events stood as reminders of the hostility they still faced. For instance, when the Colorado Gay Rodeo Association wrote to its members about the events, it reminded members that Colorado was not all that different from Nevada. It had faced similar difficulties in staging the first Denver rodeo in 1983, were turned away by eight arenas, and easily could have encountered a legal injunction that would have prevented the rodeo. It concluded by noting that members lived in a fragile world and that "[w]e cannot afford to lay down and take this kind of treatment."[56] Colorado was sadly correct in its assessment, as IGRA rodeos continued to be threatened into the early 1990s, but gay rodeo took CGRA's advice on protecting itself and adjusted its tactics to survive in the AIDS era.

AIDS-PHOBIA AND GAY RODEO'S MEDIA PRESENCE

As AIDS reshaped the opposition to gay rodeo, organizers had to adopt new media tactics. While morality-based scare tactics had not been successful, trepidation about the disease increased people's willingness to agitate against the rodeo. In Los Angeles, for instance, attendees had rarely encountered resistance until 1993, when organizers said the growing fear of AIDS led to "regional phobia" and increased public anxiety about the event, prompting IGRA to respond in new ways.[57] At the same time, while the spread of AIDS led to more public criticism of queer organizations like IGRA, it also created an even greater need for gay rodeo, and especially its fundraising efforts, to be successful. As a result, IGRA developed media practices to shield itself from potential protests and protect its charitable work.

Even though the 1991 finals rodeo had found a new location in Wichita, it came at a significant cost. The new site required the installation of temporary animal stalls, security fences, and electrical lines. Even fire trucks had to be brought in to provide water to the animals. The original arena cost of $6,000 ballooned to $22,000 with the change in venue. Public threats created psychological trauma and limited rodeo participation, while last-minute changes to the location led to damaging drops in profits, which hurt both the gay rodeo associations and the charities they supported. As IGRA Vice President Sheryl Schelkun explained, the impact of this lost revenue hurt not only IGRA as an organization: "The tremendous monetary loss sustained by the rodeo associations affect the entire gay communities in each state. Proceeds from the rodeos are divided equally among AIDS-related organizations in each state... they were counting on this money for funding."[58]

Because of the hostile public environment in the 1980s and early '90s, IGRA—along with Phil Ragsdale—tried to be strategic in working with the media. While Ragsdale had some hesitations about the media, he also was quick to embrace it. He thanked protestors in the early 1980s for bringing his rodeo more publicity, increasing local support, and multiplying his attendance numbers. But his rodeos took place when AIDS was only a nascent threat. By the late 1980s and early '90s, it had become the hot-button issue in the country, meaning that even positive publicity was more likely to increase local opposition and hurt attendance numbers. Prior to the state's gay rodeo in 1991, the vice president of the New Mexico Gay Rodeo Association (NMGRA) explained to the *Albuquerque Tribune* that they tried to keep the rodeos low-key, with no press information provided to mainstream outlets—only to queer publications—and they required that all photos be approved in advance.[59] That same year, David Anaya, Miss Arizona Gay Rodeo Association (AGRA), explained, "The straight press too often twists our words around, tips off the homophobes to us, and ends up scaring off some of our supporters. They can't hurt us if we don't talk to them."[60] Having their voices heard in the media became a danger to gay rodeoers.

Limiting media interaction became increasingly standardized over the 1990s. AGRA hosted the IGRA finals rodeo in Phoenix again in 1992, and even though it had hosted in 1989 and 1990 without incident, the organization was wary of any media attention after the Wichita protests the previous year. AGRA shared this with its membership: "We had unwanted Media attention for the first time this Rodeo . . . Both the Republic and Gazette let it be known that they were going to do stories whether we helped them or not." The articles were positive, but the organization knew that even positive accounts could stir up controversy. AGRA wanted to avoid any kind of advance publicity, even if well intentioned, saying it was "all very nice, [but] we still would have rather done without."[61] A few months later, an Arizona royalty candidate wanted to announce an upcoming fundraiser to the media, but the AGRA board stopped it, saying the group had rules that limited communication with the "straight press."[62] Following incidents like that in Wichita in 1991 and an explosive *Jerry Springer* episode in 1993, which IGRA hoped would be an informative, positive piece about gay rodeo but instead included PRCA cowboys who attacked the existence of gay rodeo, the IGRA board of directors met in 1993 to determine a policy for media requests, with the goal of avoiding this kind of problematic publicity for the association. They designated a representative to handle all IGRA media requests but allowed local associations to continue to set their own policies and deal with local media for their regional rodeos.[63] To protect itself and its AIDS-focused beneficiaries, gay rodeo adopted a more hesitant and careful approach to the media.

The lawsuits, negative publicity, and public harassment in the 1980s and '90s could have destroyed gay rodeo, and yet it only grew in these years. The canceled 1988 finals became a moment that united IGRA, and the organization expanded rapidly over the next decade. This expansion can be credited, in part, to the growing popular interest in the country-western scene in those years, but it also was because of the greater purpose that gay rodeo now served in the LGBTQ+ community. It became a place of comfort and safety in an increasingly homophobic society and provided an important service in fundraising for local charities. As AIDS expanded and impacted LGBTQ+ communities across the country, gay rodeo hit its stride by focusing almost singularly on fighting this disease.

DEVELOPING OF A CULTURE OF CARE IN GAY RODEO

"I was not a gay man, and Boston is not New York, and I had yet to realize that *I* was under attack," wrote activist Cindy Patton in 1985 as she explained why she initially ignored AIDS.[64] But by that year, she believed it to be a larger threat and wanted to push other LGBTQ+ people to action, even if they believed AIDS was happening elsewhere or impacted other gay people.[65] Even queer people without an AIDS diagnosis were vulnerable, because the Christian Right and US government were using AIDS as a justification to limit the rights of LGBTQ+ people. For instance, spurred by AIDS-fueled homophobia, the US Supreme Court ruled in *Bowers vs. Hardwick* in 1986 that homosexual sodomy could still be outlawed and reinforced the belief that LGBTQ+ people were "unnatural and repugnant."[66] Patton was right. Even if she did not immediately perceive AIDS to be a personal threat in the early years of the epidemic, she quickly understood that all LGBTQ+ people had something to fear from the growing conservatism, hatred, and homophobia that they collectively would now face. Sociologist Deborah Gould argues that the *Hardwick* ruling, combined with the continued government failure to respond to AIDS and increasingly repressive legislation, emboldened the queer AIDS movement and led to more confrontational activism by groups like ACT UP.[67] Gould states, "The blatant homophobia of the *Hardwick* ruling shocked lesbians and gay men into a greater acknowledgement of the serious, indeed life-threatening, consequences of state-sponsored and socially sanctioned homophobia and nonrecognition."[68] The AIDS crisis and the growing threats to LGBTQ+ rights similarly spurred queer cowfolx to see the threats they all faced and to use gay rodeo—and its power in fundraising—to support each other and their communities.

Gay men in various regions reacted differently to these growing threats. Eric Rofes, founder of the Boston Lesbian and Gay Political Alliance and executive director of the Los Angeles Gay and Lesbian Community Services Center and San Francisco's Shanti Project, examined the impact of AIDS on various groups of gay men. While most of his work was with gay men in the urban areas most hard hit by the epidemic, Rofes also studied the effect of AIDS on gay men in rural areas and how they connected (or didn't) with the larger gay rights and AIDS activist movements of the 1980s and '90s. He noted significant differences: Gay men in urban areas believed they were the most impacted by the disease and the most involved in activism; in many ways, they were right, as they faced higher infection rates. However, gay men in rural areas noted that it could be more difficult and more dangerous for them to find medical and community support. The danger associated with being out and gay in many rural areas also made it difficult for gay men there to organize and host events and fundraisers.[69]

With member associations and rodeos both in coastal, hard-hit cities like Los Angeles and in rural locales less associated with the disease, such as Missouri and Arkansas, gay rodeo enveloped a broad spectrum of queer people. Both the Reno rodeo in the 1970s and IGRA-affiliated associations in the 1980s officially eschewed politics, but opposition to their rodeos, city- and statewide attacks on LGBTQ+ rights, and the AIDS crisis all forced action by gay rodeo advocates across the geographical spectrum. Their fundraising and charitable donations made bold statements, even as they assured people they remained apolitical. Avram Finkelstein, one of the founding members of the Silence=Death and Grand Fury collectives, which designed some of the most identifiable AIDS posters in the 1980s, proclaimed, "AIDS was, AIDS is, a political crisis. And silence was, silence is, packed with political meaning."[70] The US government may have remained silent for many years, but queer cowfolx refused. Though they tried to avoid public notice through a quiet media presence, they spoke loudly through their fundraising efforts and the charities they chose to support.

For the first years of the National Reno Gay Rodeo, from 1976 to 1982, the fundraising supported the wider, generally straight, community through efforts to support the Muscular Dystrophy Association (MDA), senior citizens, and children. Proceeds came from the rodeo itself, but also from the royalty competition, which began in 1977. That first year, the royalty contest raised just $214 for muscular dystrophy, but by 1981, the contests, which by then took place in eight states and nineteen cities, brought in over $35,000 for the MDA. In 1982 the Texas royalty contests alone solicited that amount, and across all gay rodeo, the royalty contests were expected to bring in $75,000.[71] This was a significant amount of money, and that year some in the gay community publicly called on the Reno rodeo to direct its attention to AIDS.

In the earliest years of the AIDS epidemic, in 1981 and 1982, a few groups and individuals began to hold fundraisers, benefits, memorial services, and candlelight vigils to raise awareness of AIDS and help those impacted, but these efforts brought in very little money. For instance, San Francisco hosted a national AIDS conference in that period but only raised $2,745 for the cause. Charles Morris, from the LGBTQ+ publication the *San Francisco Sentinel*, had been recently diagnosed with AIDS in 1982 and used his platform to call out this lack of effort—or misplaced effort, in his eyes—saying, "I think the gay community has to cut out all the bullshit fundraising and focus on AIDS. The gay rodeo in Reno raised funds for Jerry's Kids [the MDA], we're collecting money for guide dogs for the blind, but we are ignoring our own. The government is allocating only 2.2 million dollars for AIDS research, but if we put our minds to it, the gay community could raise more than that in one month."[72] Phil Ragsdale and the National Reno Gay Rodeo heeded Morris's call.

As AIDS began to spread in nearby San Francisco and as the first case was confirmed locally in Washoe County, the Reno rodeo designated "the AIDS Foundation" as its primary charity, along with "other 'worthwhile' local charities," in 1983. The royalty contests continued to support the MDA, though they too began to shift that year. Previously, the contests were required to send all funds to the MDA, but in 1983 only 50 percent of the royalty fundraising was earmarked for the MDA, and then each contest could designate a gay charity of its choice for the remainder. The majority selected the AIDS Foundation.[73] The following year, in 1984, the final Reno rodeo under Ragsdale donated 100 percent of the proceeds from the royalty contest to the AIDS Foundations in San Francisco, Sacramento, and Los Angeles.[74]

As IGRA replaced the National Reno Gay Rodeo, its member associations and finals rodeo continued to support AIDS research. For many, this interest was intensely personal and deeply felt. Roger Bergmann, a former president of IGRA, was involved since the early days of gay rodeo. He was a founding member of the Golden State Gay Rodeo Association in California and attended the first IGRA conventions in the mid-1980s. He saw the start of the AIDS crisis in one of its epicenters, San Francisco. He visited a gay bar for the first time in 1981, and almost immediately his experience of being newly out was affected by the unidentified sickness. As he explained, "It was shortly after that I picked up the gay newspaper in San Francisco, and they still didn't call it AIDS; it was just this: 'the gay disease.' Nobody knew what was causing it or anything."[75] Similarly, Bruce Roby, who worked for an airline company in Los Angeles, recalled the devastating impact of AIDS. At the height of the epidemic in the early 1990s, he said, "In our office, every week there was a memorial. Every week there was somebody out sick. There was so much going on that you were scared to death, so, you know, a lot of things didn't happen."[76] For younger generations who came of age after the 1990s, even within queer communities like that of IGRA, it can be difficult to understand the very real and traumatic experience of the American AIDS crisis in the 1980s and '90s.

Many participants in the Reno rodeos and the later IGRA ones received positive HIV and AIDS diagnoses or saw their friends and rodeo families similarly affected. David Renier said, "Back in the '80s, when I started, I had a huge amount of gay rodeo friends, and through the '80s, most of them passed away."[77] This had a lasting impact on the gay rodeo, not just in the 1980s and '90s but into the twenty-first century. As Laura, one lesbian rodeoer who participated in the earliest years of the Texas association, explained, "A lot of the guys, all the people I rodeoed with back then, they aren't here anymore. They laugh at me [today] being a dinosaur, but I'm the only one that is still alive, and it hurts my heart."[78] Frank Harrell, who participated in gay rodeo for over thirty years and who was instrumental in creating a digital archive about it, could easily have been one of these statistics. As he explained, "In 1991, I found out I had full-blown AIDS. The doctors gave me six months to live. I'm still here. At that time, that was the normal life expectancy for someone who was in my condition. I managed to make it through. Thankfully the drugs, the protease inhibitor drugs, came out just in time to save me."[79] For many gay rodeoers, the AIDS epidemic was far from tangential. They felt it closely and deeply, and their experience of gay rodeo became intimately connected to that of the epidemic.

Gay rodeo pivoted quickly to respond to this growing crisis. Programs moved from overt promotions of gay sexual freedom, expression, and enjoyment to more conservative views on gay sex, advertisements with HIV/AIDS medical advice, and "in memoriam" announcements for those who died (see figure 13). Association newsletters mailed to members similarly remembered people who had been lost. Colorado saw two founding members die of AIDS in 1986, and the association moved its charitable support from muscular dystrophy and the children's hospital to AIDS that same year. The group also established two awards to memorialize the men who died.[80]

FIGURE 13. *GSGRA Rodeo Program, In Memory of Ron DiStefano, 1988. "In memoriam" notices, like this one for Ron DiStefano, one of the founders of gay rodeo in California, appeared regularly in programs from the late 1980s into the mid-1990s. These are stark reminders of the frequent losses that gay rodeo faced because of AIDS. Courtesy of ONE Archives at the USC Libraries.*

Other associations adopted the riderless horse ceremony to recognize members who died of AIDS, and some dedicated squares on the NAMES Project AIDS Memorial Quilt to help remember in perpetuity gay rodeoers lost to the disease.[81]

In response to the death around them, the rodeo associations, like other LGBTQ+ organization in this era, felt called to help their own sick and dying members and to meet the growing needs of the wider gay community when the Reagan government and healthcare systems refused to do so.[82] Doing this work did more than help fight AIDS, however; it also provided emotional support for IGRA members, both those who were sick and dying and those who were witness to the devastation it brought. Renier, who lost many of his rodeo friends in the 1980s, explained that raising money to help with people with HIV and AIDS made gay rodeo even more compelling for him. "I love the sport," he said, "but then that was an added bonus."[83] The focus of the fundraising acted similarly on Laura in Texas: "When I first got started, they wanted me to run for Ms. TGRA, and that's when the AIDS epidemic was coming out and everybody was scared to death, and we couldn't get money. And I didn't want to do it, because there was just so much work. You had to go to fundraisers every weekend, and I was trying to make a living." However, her perspective soon changed. "My friends started dying, and I changed my mind. I said, 'What do I do?' And so I ran the first year that TGRA was formed. I ran and won Ms. TGRA. And I really wasn't doing it for the fame; I was doing it to raise money to find a cure for AIDS."[84]

Even into the early twentieth-first century, AIDS fundraising continued to be the primary driver for some gay rodeo participants. Miss Mae, a titleholder in the Missouri Gay Rodeo Association, explained in 2005 or 2006, "Sadly, each year this disease that we have been fighting for 20 years takes away some beloved member of our community. My fervent prayer is that someday I will be able to retire the pumps, wigs, and corset because a cure [for] AIDS has been found."[85] For Miss Mae, her fundraising efforts in the royalty contest—and maybe even gay rodeo has a whole—existed solely to target AIDS.

As discussed in chapter 4, the royalty branch continued to be one of the primary fundraising arms of gay rodeo. The contestants and titleholders raised significant amounts of money. Between 1982 and 1984, Texas royalty alone donated over $30,000 annually. By 1983 that money went primarily to AIDS-focused organizations.[86] Rodeo rules required that each candidate raise $500 to even qualify for the contest. So, when AGRA in Arizona had more than a dozen contestants in 1993, it meant that even just the minimum raised for local charities would be $6,000.[87] Out of personal interest in AIDS work or perhaps a reflection of the appeal these efforts had in the community, some royalty candidates far exceeded the minimum. For instance, Golden State royalty contestants in 1995 raised more than $12,000, with a single person raising $9,303 alone.[88] During two years as a titleholder, Miss AGRA David Anaya in Arizona helped raise around $30,000 and did this work specifically for AIDS and gay rights, explaining, "We really need that money in these times, and we need to get the word out to people more, and that's what Royalty is all about."[89] One the primary functions of royalty was to fundraise and support charitable work, and ostensibly the rodeo did as well, but sometimes associations conflicted with others over this purpose and were not always as effective in their efforts as the royalty contestants and titleholders.

IGRA as an organization sometimes struggled to balance its desire to host rodeos and promote the country-western lifestyle with its charitable efforts. The 1986 IGRA rule book, the first to clearly identify the object and purpose of the organization, stated, "The specific purpose of International is the fostering of national and international amateur competition and related arts and crafts, and to develop amateur athletes and activities for such competition."[90] Similarly, the first gay rodeo outside of Reno, hosted in Denver by the new Colorado association in 1983, explained that it was a charitable group but one "formed to support a segment of the community interested in a western lifestyle." CGRA did mention that it offered "support to other gay groups and organizations," yet fundraising was much less central in this statement of purpose than in some other associations, and CGRA struggled with its identity and purpose over the next couple of decades. It donated to AIDS organizations and lost two of its members to the disease in 1986 alone, but for CGRA leadership, this focus on AIDS and charity work felt like a distraction. One of the newsletters that year told members that it was time to get back to fundamentals: "Remember that we are, according to the by-laws, first and foremost a group of individuals interested in western related events." This newsletter column included no mention of fundraising as a core tenet.[91]

This is in stark contrast to other groups, such as those in California, Arizona, and Arkansas, which regularly emphasized fundraising as their primary purpose.⁹² Sometimes association members even called out the rodeo groups for failing to do enough. Colorado, with its almost single-minded focus on rodeo, was chided by one of its own members in 1995. In an open letter to the CGRA president, the member said, "In the beginning CGRA had great dreams of promoting the western lifestyle and [encouraging] support of the gay community through fundraising efforts. [Somehow] down the line I believe that CGRA lost track of their dreams." This person criticized CGRA for becoming too focused on fundraising for its own rodeo.⁹³ Even some of the gay rodeo groups most focused on AIDS work, like Arizona and Diamond State in Arkansas, were criticized by members who believed even more should be done. In 1990, a Diamond State member said, "DSRA is a charitable as well as a 'western' organization. In looking at our dollar figures for what we have given to charitable organizations this year, it does not add up to any amount to be proud of."⁹⁴ Because IGRA had a multifaceted purpose, these debates were part of the tension inherent in an organization that attempted to balance rodeos for its members with fundraising for the community. During the AIDS crisis, this balance became one of literal life and death for the queer community and for many gay rodeoers who were desperate for comfort, support, and a cure.

Even when gay rodeo associations wanted to donate to charities, staging rodeos proved to be a risky approach to fundraising. Golden State's San Francisco rodeo finally brought in a profit of $5,000 in 1995, which was donated to the San Francisco AIDS Foundation, Positive Resources, the NAMES Project AIDS Memorial Quilt, Project Open Hand, and Food for Thought, all AIDS-focused groups. However, this was the first time in three years its rodeo made enough money to pay off its bills and still have profits to donate.⁹⁵ Other groups faced similar feast-or-famine years. For instance, Atlantic States lost $5,000 in staging its 1995 rodeo but made a profit of over $20,000 two years later.⁹⁶

Despite its unpredictable donation ability, gay rodeo still raised significant amounts of money for charities. For instance, Atlantic States estimated that from its founding in 1990 to 1998, it raised more than $70,000 through its rodeo, royalty competition, and other events.⁹⁷ The recipients of donations, the broader queer community, and even government officials regularly praised gay rodeo for its significant AIDS work. Texas state representative Debra Danburg publicly recognized the work of gay rodeo in the program for TGRA's 1985 event, saying, "I am pleased to be part of this gathering and to salute the fine work you do. The non-profit organizations within the gay community provide many needed and valuable services. With your fundraising efforts, these groups are much better able to meet the community's needs."[98] AIDS service organizations were especially thankful for the donations, and gay rodeo associations frequently printed thank-you letters in their rodeo programs and organizational newsletters to remind members of the important working they were doing. An AIDS organization in religiously conservative southern Missouri said in thanks, "No other area organization; churches, civic groups, schools, or individuals, have come close to matching the support level of your organization. You are appreciated more than you can know."[99]

In addition to the work gay rodeo associations did for those with AIDS in their communities, they developed a culture of care for their own rodeoers. This included helping members suffering from AIDS and supporting each other through their own grief and anger. At the height of the epidemic, in 1992, the Tri-State Gay Rodeo Association described in its newsletter the deep impact of AIDS on the group:

> More than anything else, rodeo is about caring for each other, not only about other local rodeo members, but about responding to the pressing social needs created in the gay community by the advent of AIDS.... It comes from each individual member who has been touched in some way by AIDS, and who has not been touched? ... there is also a sobering, touching, and reverent recognition of the larger purpose at rodeo events, a mindfulness that many we have known are gone or are not well enough to celebrate. They are remembered in tributes, in ceremony, and sometimes in tears. A rodeo event is never 'a downer,' but neither is it mindless distraction. A rodeo is celebrating life, paying tribute to its painful losses, and sharing each [other's] strengths and hopes. A rodeo is giving what we can both as individuals and as a group.[100]

Reminding IGRA members about why they undertook time-consuming fundraising work was an effective way to encourage participation at their events and thus bring in more money.

But members also understood that their efforts were not just helping faceless strangers. As one association said in its newsletter,

"It's our friends we're helping."[101] This was important, personal work, but it also made remembering those who died all the more painful for gay rodeoers. When two Colorado members died of AIDS in 1986, the association acknowledged it: "We all knew that it was going to happen, but that does not change the shock that is felt by this last, and normal, part of life.... In the months ahead we are going to need each other."[102] IGRA associations all too frequently had to publish memorial statements in newsletters and rodeo programs, but even the regularity of the notifications failed to encompass all of the death. In Arizona, the board of directors said in 1991, "We've lost yet another Rodeo supporter to AIDS." But they explained that the newsletters rarely included these announcements, because it "would take up a depressing amount of space."[103] The sorrow felt by members of the association became part of the daily operations, through rodeo entries, newsletters, and advertisements (see figure 14).

Sometimes the newsletters spoke not just to the grief but to the outrage that the queer community felt. When (straight) NBA player Magic Johnson revealed his HIV status in 1991 to an upswell in public attention and support, the Arizona association decried this hypocrisy, saying, "Where has all this awareness, understanding, and funding been for the last DECADE?"[104] These varied responses demonstrate how gay rodeo participants struggled to support their own, survive themselves, and deal with their own fear, grief, and anger.

In the midst of this frustration and devastation, the associations used their newsletters and rodeo programs to educate and influence the behavior of their own members (see figure 15). For instance, one newsletter in 1987 included a press release about AIDS and a two-page article from a nurse who explained to members what AIDS was, how it was and was not spread, and how it progresses as a disease. In 1990, Diamond State used each newsletter that year to highlight a different AIDS organization working in central Arkansas. Groups also included information about regional AIDS conferences and testing locations in their states.[105] Sometimes the newsletters used humor, like when the description of an upcoming opportunity to learn how to ride horses playfully added, "When riding, let's practice just like it was sex. Play it safe getting on and getting off. Take care!"[106] Other times, they adopted a more ominous approach, such as when Missouri said, "REMEMBER: AIDS IS AN INCURABLE DISEASE! THINK ABOUT IT NOW!"[107] Notes like this stand in stark contrast to the joyful celebration of sex in the

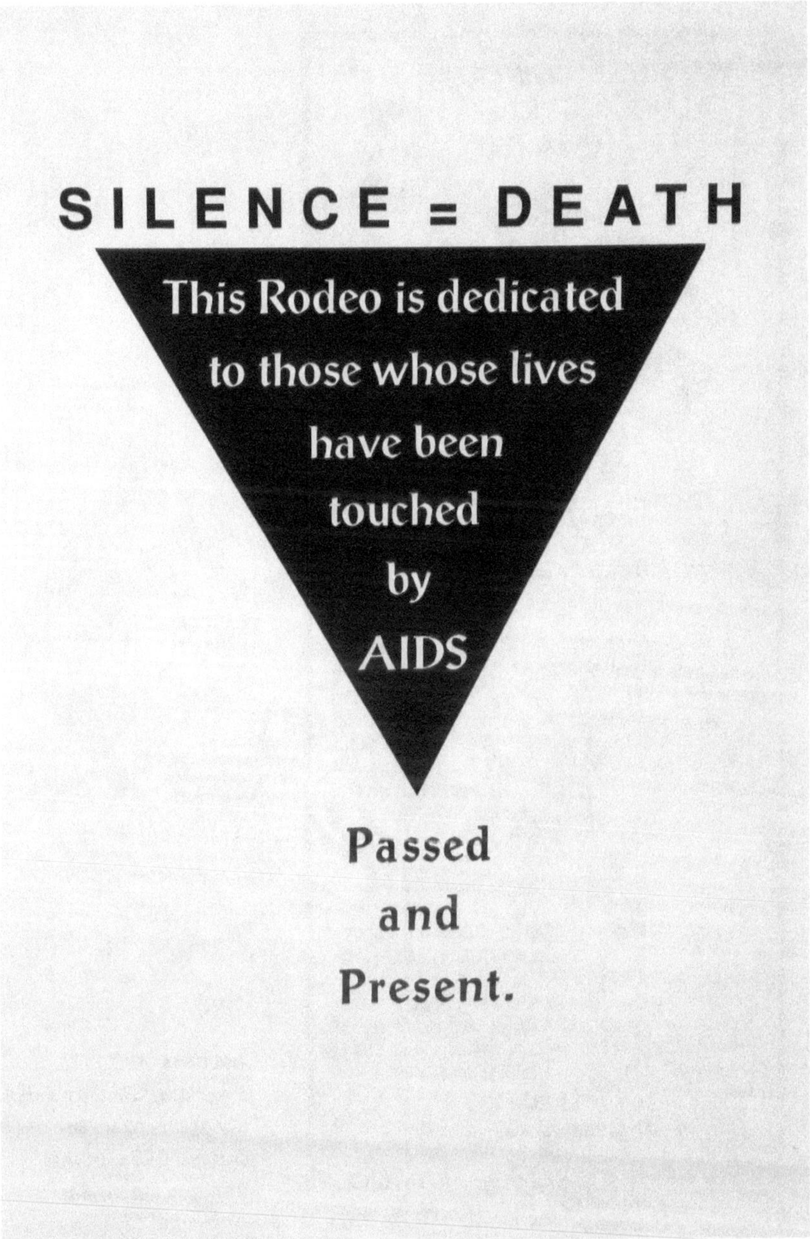

SILENCE = DEATH

This Rodeo is dedicated to those whose lives have been touched by AIDS

Passed and Present.

FIGURE 14. *NMGRA Rodeo Program, Silence = Death memorial, 1991. Gay rodeos included ceremonies to publicly recognize members who died of AIDS and sometimes, such as in the image seen here, adopted some of the symbols of AIDS activist organizations to bring attention to the disease. Courtesy of the Autry Museum of the American West.*

FIGURE 15. *ASGRA Rodeo Program*, "Real cowboys always wear their chaps!," 1992. In this announcement, the Episcopal Church organization specifically targeted gay rodeoers with its message about safe sex. Courtesy of the Autry Museum of the American West.

newsletters and programs from the 1970s and early '80s, as discussed in chapter 2.

Over the course of the 1980s and '90s, gay rodeo adjusted its fundraising efforts to meet the needs of an AIDS-stricken queer community. This was personal for many people who were driven to participate in gay rodeo not just out of a desire to connect with the country-western, rodeo lifestyle but to do something to counter the devastation that surrounded them. People united around these efforts to raise money for AIDS organizations. They developed strategies to care for sick and dying gay rodeoers, and they grappled with their own fear, pain, and frustration. As one rodeo program said early in the epidemic in 1983, "Our own need."[108] Queer cowfolx responded to this call and worked with an almost singular focus to support their own and those in their communities.

GAY RODEO AFTER THE CRISIS

Gay rodeo emerged in the 1970s out of a desire to fundraise for charity, but also to promote a queer country-western lifestyle. With the rise of AIDS in the 1980s and an increasingly hostile, homophobic environment, it adopted a culture of care to support its sick and dying members, fundraise for its own LGBTQ+ communities now under attack, and establish a safe space for all queer people. For the next decade, gay rodeo focused its fundraising efforts almost entirely on AIDS support. But then medical developments in 1996 had profound impacts on the fight against AIDS. The release of protease inhibitors and combination therapies that year meant AIDS no longer was a death sentence. Hard-hit cities saw fewer obituaries, fewer sick people in the streets, and the closure of AIDS hospices. Gay men began to celebrate the possibility of life, and elements of gay sexual culture, like bathhouses, were slowly revived. By 1997, a survey of 1,459 gay men found that one-third no longer experienced AIDS as a crisis. Yet despite this rapidly changing belief among many people, LGBTQ+ and AIDS service organizations continued into the late 1990s to maintain that the crisis was not yet over.[109] Gay rodeo, with its significant fundraising success, had these same debates within its own associations. Queer cowfolx—like other LGBTQ+ people—struggled to decide what their focus should be as AIDS moved into its next stage as a disease people lived with, rather than died from.

Many IGRA associations transitioned rather quietly in the late 1990s and early 2000s, almost without comment by their members or wider communities, away from predominantly supporting AIDS organizations. For instance, the Arizona association primarily donated to AIDS organizations up to the year 2000 but then began giving money to a more diverse group of charities, including the ASPCA (for animals) and Camp Hakuna Matata (for children), along with several of their mainstay AIDS groups. In 2002, there was a role reversal when one of the traditional AIDS beneficiaries instead provided support to AGRA by sponsoring ribbons for the annual rodeo. By 2017, the bulk of the Arizona association's support went elsewhere. It gave only $1,434 to an AIDS service organization that year, while $5,974 went to PFLAG (Parents, Families, and Friends of Lesbians and Gays).[110] An examination of rodeo programs and newsletters from twenty associations reveals that all gay rodeo associations similarly transitioned.

However, some IGRA associations struggled more with the shift in focus and used emotionally charged language to maintain members' interest in supporting AIDS efforts. While many continued to support HIV/AIDS organizations between 1996 and 2000, they often made the donations in these later years without much fanfare. In contrast, Diamond State in Arkansas used the same urgency to discuss AIDS fundraising in those years as they did at the height of the epidemic. The board told members in 1998, "Most of us don't realize how many lives we [affect] with our fund-raising for AIDS/HIV and our collection of tangible items for people living with AIDS. So if you are ever feeling down, or like life hasn't been fair to you, just look at all the good our group does. Take pride in what you are a part of. . . . Remember when you show up to any [DSRA] function, you are helping someone somewhere down the road."[111] This tactic did not always work, and so the group also used a more emotional approach, saying, "It is through your efforts, and the efforts of your fellow DSRA members, that we are able to give of our hearts to our family, friends and lovers who are surviving with HIV/AIDS."[112]

Despite these concerted efforts by the DSRA board, by the late 1990s, members appeared less willing to see AIDS as the same crisis as they did in earlier years. Only eight members showed up for AIDS Walk Arkansas in 1998 when the board had promised fifty. The newsletter expressed disappointment in a column that read, "This could have been a great time to give the AIDS/HIV community our support. I guess it was too much to assume that everyone would be willing to get up early and give up four hours of their weekend. To make matters worse, I foolishly stuck my neck out to say I could get 50 DSRA members to walk. Not even close... Please remember what we're all about."[113] By 2000, DSRA found itself in a fragile place and feared the association was on the verge of collapse. It tried to use the group's AIDS work to encourage participation and save the association, saying, "There are people out there that need the DSRA, not just a few of the DSRA, but ALL of the DSRA."[114] DSRA survived this period, but using HIV/AIDS as a call to action no longer garnered the same response as it had in years past. DSRA continued to hold small fundraisers for AIDS organizations but turned its attention to other charities, including a local women's project, a feral cat program, and canned food drives. From 2001 to 2011, DSRA newsletters rarely mentioned HIV/AIDS, and the newsletters never again included the same urgency as those from the 1990s.[115] As its members moved on from seeing AIDS as a crisis, DSRA, like all of IGRA, was forced to adjust its perspective and purpose.

This change in focus away from AIDS efforts has been trying for IGRA as the organization in the twenty-first century tries to balance the desire to remember that difficult period and those who died with a desire to find a new place in American society and attract younger members. With the release of protease inhibitors in the 1990s and pre-exposure prophylaxis (PrEP) in 2012, which can prevent HIV infection entirely, there are several generations of gay men for whom the shadow of AIDS was no longer all-consuming, but the acute years of the epidemic remain painful memories for those who lived through it. Researchers including Perry Halkitis, Dion Kagan, and Eric Rofes have studied the generational gap and conflict between gay men who experienced the epidemic and younger men who lived in a different America, one with HIV/AIDS medications and expanded LGBTQ+ rights and visibility.[116] Gay rodeo is not immune to these generational conflicts. HIV/AIDS no longer is as central in the gay rodeo, in terms of fundraising or appearances in programs, but it remains a notable focus and charitable beneficiary. This has sparked some concern among members that the epidemic has left a lingering shadow over the organization. Brian Helander, IGRA member since the mid-1990s and past president, lived through the AIDS epidemic, but he believes that the continued focus on HIV at the rodeo hurts the organization's popular appeal, even among LGBTQ+ people. As he explains, "Kids don't want to come watch that. It doesn't mean anything to them. . . . Folks don't remember; they don't care. It tends to keep people away, and we can't seem to let go of that."[117] For Helander, HIV/AIDS may no longer create the same impending doom or sense of immediacy, but it is still present as both a reality and a specter for gay rodeo into the twenty-first century.

IGRA and its members routinely present gay rodeo as a place removed from politics or activism, and while it was not traditionally activist in the same way as many of the national AIDS service organizations or direct-action protest groups in the 1980s and '90s, IGRA found a way to support its members, protect its community, and counter AIDS within a conservative, western, rural environment that was often openly hostile to the notion of gay cowboys and cowgirls. Facing the protests and working closely to care for sick rodeo friends and lovers brought queer cowfolx together in a large, active rodeo association. AIDS created significant struggles for gay rodeo, but it also acted as a point of unification of purpose for more than a decade. The AIDS crisis directed fundraising efforts and encouraged participation, and, in some ways, without it, gay rodeo has lost its footing in terms of purpose and drive.

Oral History Vignette
MARIE ANTOINETTE DU BARRY, NMGRA ROYALTY

I was born in 1980 in New Mexico. I'm the only child of an only child. My grandmother owned a bridal shop for fifty-five years, and I grew up in that bridal shop. That's where I come from, and that's who I am. That's the great beginnings of Du Barry.

I was always doing drag, I think even around five or six. Because my grandmother owned the bridal shop, I always tried on high heels. My grandma was using me for a dressmaker's dummy, because I was the right size for a flower girl. So I was constantly trying on bodices and trying on skirts and trying on hoops and stuff like that. It was very, very natural for me to just be able to slip into drag.

I think the face of drag and the face of royalty brings a lot of recognition to the rodeo, because it draws people in and says, "Well, why are they wearing crowns? What are they doing?" And when people start asking questions, then they want to join or they want to say, "Oh, I want to be a cowboy." So, it's very different. It's very different without and with royalty. I think sometimes they [the two parts of gay rodeo] are symbiotic, and they need to have each other. Sometimes it's good and sometimes it's bad, but it is what it is.

I identify as gender-fluid. I'm sort of in between; I sort of float in between being masculine and feminine. Though I live my life as a man, I am very comfortable being a woman, dressing up as a woman. I get [questions about my drag] all the time. Why do you only show your shoulders? I don't wear triple D boobs, because I don't think that's a natural thing for my body type. I think that maybe I'm a B to a C, and I don't think it's proper to have giant boobs and give other people a false impression of womanhood. Because you don't have to have giant boobs to be a beautiful woman. You don't have to have a tiny waist to be a beautiful woman.

Some people think my drag is not country enough. To me, it is country; it's just a different version of country. Somebody told me I look steampunk. Steampunk western is a perfect example of a defining moment in fashion that's western. That really is western. So, you really get these experiences of: "I don't understand you, so I'm not going to understand you. So, it's easier to not understand you, so you're not, you're not country." What the heck is country? What is the defining moment that says, "Oh, well, that's western: a cowboy hat. That's western"? There's nothing. You can pick and choose from whatever the hell you want and make it into whatever you want. So, what is it?

What is really the definer of western looks? Is it a duster? Is it all leather? Is it jeans? It's not just fashion. It's what's inside you, and sometimes it's the manners, how you take care of each other. That changes the perception of western. I come from Santa Fe, which is the end of the Santa Fe Trail. It ends with me. It ends where everybody wanted to go. Everybody was coming out to New Mexico and finding turquoise, silver, boots, and Wranglers, and concha belts. Where do you think it all came from? It came from where I come from. So, I know where I'm coming from, and I can play with it how I want to, because I am where the Santa Fe Trail ends.

I also have a Spanish background, and it's unfair to only see the Anglicized version of "western," because they were French, they were Anglo-Saxon, they were Spanish, shoot, they were buffalo soldiers, Native American peoples. What the heck is country? Well, give me what is the "right" historical western fashion—I'll stick to it. Because if you really want to get serious, go to the Native Americans.

So, most of the time, you let them have their perception of it. You love them anyway, and you accept them, because there's no reason to fight over it. If they have a defining idea of western, God bless them, let them have it. I'm not going to take it away. But maybe I've twisted their mind a little and they said, "Oh, I can do that too."

Camp is seeing things in an unordinary fashion and being able to laugh at it. The straight rodeo had been so oppressive to LGBT competitors that they needed to have something to break away from that oppression. Everybody is allowed to have their own experience, and I think you best beat back the misunderstanding and the ugliness with humor. The gay rodeo beats back that oppression with funniness, with clever funniness.

Chapter 4

"DOLLARED TO DEATH"

Gay Rodeo Queens, Camp Events, and the Labor of Inclusion

As a rodeo spectator, Chili Pepper, crowned Miss IGRA in 1993, assumed that the wild drag race would not be overly hard. You "just kind of jump on the back of an animal in costume," she thought.[1] Since the mid-1980s, this IGRA-sanctioned event has required a team of three people, with a male-identified member and a female-identified member catching and directing a steer while a third dressed in "female-style drag" mounts and rides the steer back across a demarcated line. Wild drag represents the only "camp" event in gay rodeo that officially requires playing with gender—though specifically through the performance of femininity by someone of any gender identity. After her first time as the "drag" in wild drag, however, Chili Pepper admitted she probably would not have chosen it to be her first event if she were a more experienced rodeoer. After a while, "you start realizing which events are a little bit more rough on the contestants, but it looks like so much fun."[2]

This fun has been repeatedly cited as what makes gay rodeo gay: "It's something [the audience] chuckle[s] about. They have fun watching, whether it's putting underwear on a goat or watching a guy in drag trying to get up on a steer and cross the seventy-foot line. But that's our draw, that's our draw, that's why everybody comes," said a gay rodeo participant.[3] In particular, it has been the combination of the "masculine" rodeo with the hyperfeminine performance that imbues such events with their humor and their thrill. Chili Pepper's articulation of the dangers and joys of camp events illustrates the complexities of gender, competition, and western performance for gay rodeoers at the turn of the twenty-first century.

Camp culture at the gay rodeo has encompassed two main spheres: the royalty competition, which includes formal drag performances, and rodeo camp events, which include gender play. Camp is generally marked by a self-conscious and studied performance that exaggerates its gendered, racialized, and sexualized subject.[4] As many scholars have shown, it has operated as a political tactic of resistance for marginalized communities.[5] While formal drag requires people to assume the gendered identity markers of an idealized opposite gender, including dress, mannerisms, and speech, camp is more expansive. In gay rodeo, camp has exceeded formal drag and instead, as one rodeo queen explained, required "seeing things in an unordinary fashion and being able to laugh at it." She, like many others, described the creation of these events as what defined gay rodeo as a potentially radical queer space: "I think you best beat back the misunderstanding and the ugliness with humor. So, I think the gay rodeo beats back that oppression with funniness, with clever funniness."[6] Campy humor became a way to both resist and reinforce a binary approach to gender, because gendered comedy operated to earn money and keep gay rodeo possible.

Yet IGRA solidified in the era of the urban cowboy and gay clone masculinity. Uniformed in a starched, pearl-buttoned shirt and tight-fitting Levi's, this iteration of the cowboy embodied the cultural rejection of the effeminate 1960s and the reassertion of a masculine America in the late 1970s and '80s. Ronald Reagan's film persona helped lend conservative political overtones to the era's trends of country-western music, mechanical bull riding, and western wear.[7] Through an increasingly visible network of bars, gyms, and bathhouses, cisgender gay men also rejected the "assumed effeminacy" of homosexuality.[8] The cowboy image created in mid-century westerns and fed to the baby-boomer generation represented the pinnacle of white American masculinity—taciturn, rugged, and individualistic.

Gay rodeo, often a space roped off for white masculinity, has struggled over the past forty years to balance that hypermasculine image with its mission to remain inclusive. After having suffered violence and marginalization in mainstream country-western culture, creating an inclusive community has been a stated mission and point of pride for many rodeoers: "We have never, ever turned somebody down for their race, their sexual orientation, anything."[9] Indeed, in 2000, IGRA adopted a more expansive gender policy much earlier than many other sports organizations. But as subsequent history demonstrates, it had yet to fully deal with a specifically transgender identity. This policy stated that IGRA, "hereby endorses and adopts the position that any individual member of a Member or Recognized Association is eligible to participate fully in I.G.R.A. activities under the gender classification with which the individual member identifies."[10] This statement essentially allowed competitors to select the gender category with which they identified without requiring medical documentation of surgery or hormone treatments. However, as many sport scholars have noted, most gender inclusion policies in sports still acknowledge a binary between categories.[11] In IGRA, these binaries were reinforced by the juxtaposition of the masculine cowboy with the perceived femininity of the rodeo's camp events. The story of gay rodeo became a story of binaries—and of those people who resisted that mandate to keep the association financially solvent and culturally inclusive.

As camp culture became the mechanism through which fundraising, audience engagement, and entry-level participation occurred, the idea of "inclusion" became a type of labor that was feminized and devalued, even as it was crucial to the association's survival. It is widely acknowledged that industries that demand emotional labor have long been feminized. As sociologist Arlie Russell Hochschild famously noted, "As traditionally more accomplished managers of feeling in private life, women more than men have put emotional labor on the market, and they know more about its personal costs."[12] As "diversity and inclusion" has increasingly become an organizational goal over the past several decades, studies have shown that this work, too, has been relegated to women and people of color.[13] In gay rodeo, though, the costs of inclusive labor were born by not only people who identified as women but those who performed femininity.

Rodeo camp events and the royalty competition overlap and intersect, even as they enacted gender differently. Their permeable borders allowed royalty members who participated in rodeo events to move through the stadium, helping people laugh and enjoy themselves. Through fundraising, garnering public interest, and providing entertainment, royalty members and camp event participants also provided a financial backbone for the association by doing the labor of inclusion. At the same time, the royalty competition has been rooted in a binary gender model that has often delineated between "real" and "performed" gender identities, mostly through formal drag competition. The competition has been structured to allow for gender fluidity less in terms of an identity category and more as a way for people to move between genders in competition categories (men's bronc riding/women's bronc riding or Miss/Mr.).[14] In contrast, camp events, and the wild drag race specifically, have approached gender with less rigidity and more humor, resulting in a degree of gender ambiguity in the arena. This ambiguity has aided the inclusive mission of the association by serving as both a rejection of a strict gender binary and the gateway to rodeo for many people. However, while these spaces destabilize notions of essentialized gender, the association's attachment to the white masculine cowboy of the late twentieth century, the continued enforcement of gender categories, and the humorous performance of femininity in the arena have worked to keep gay rodeo a safe haven for a particular form of masculinity. By keeping the association financially viable, camp culture both economically protected gay rodeo but, by rendering femininity as laughable, often culturally protected masculinity as well.

This chapter first traces the financial necessity of camp culture in gay rodeo and then considers the royalty competition and camp events in terms of their specific enactments of gender over the past forty years, with particular attention to how gender fluidity has functioned on the royalty stage while a broader ambiguity has been embraced in the arena. Finally, the chapter analyzes how these spaces ultimately serve to protect masculinity rooted in a specific version of the late-twentieth century cowboy.

CAMP AND CAPITAL

The creation and survival of a camp perspective in gay rodeo has helped keep the association solvent. For both royalty and camp events, money defined camp culture's role in the rodeo. This has operated through direct fundraising, drawing in broader audience members, and by doing the hard labor of making the rodeo inclusive in terms of experience, age, and gender performance.

Camp culture at gay rodeo is as old as the association itself. Phil Ragsdale first held a gay rodeo as a fundraiser for the Imperial Court System (ICS), in which he served as Reno's first emperor. As a competitive drag circuit dedicated to fundraising for the local community, the rodeo's connection to the ICS made drag performers integral to the association's founding. It provided the blueprints for both a rodeo association grounded in civic philanthropy and a royalty competition dedicated to idealized performances of gender.[15] The royalty contest held at the National Reno Gay Rodeos in the late 1970s and early '80s crowned a Mr. and Mrs. Gay Rodeo. Between the 1980s and the mid-2000s, the format of a male-identified category (Mr.), a drag queen category (Miss), and a female-identified category (Ms.) stabilized. In 2005, a MsTer, or drag king, competition was added.

Ragsdale asserted that camp culture was central to the organization, even as there were calls to expel women and drag queens from the association. He noted, "I still get complaints from within our own ranks about participation by drag queens and lesbians, but if it wasn't for the drag queens and the lesbians, there wouldn't be a gay rodeo. They were the ones who supported the event through the rough first years. There are so many ways we can be discriminatory within our own society."[16] Intimately tied to the ICS and dependent on women and drag queens from the beginning, camp culture was deeply ingrained in gay rodeo.

As IGRA grew, royalty members had two intertwined duties: to serve as public representatives and to raise money. But the demand for financial assistance has steadily increased while the right to serve as a spokesperson for the association has withered.

In the 1980s, royalty team members' main duty was to raise money for external charities, first the Muscular Dystrophy Association, then AIDS organizations as the epidemic spread, and then, after the 1990s, an array of charities, from equine rescue to hospice care. To be eligible for the international royalty competition, members had to have already raised $500 for their local associations' charity or charities of choice. As membership began to decline in the 1990s, however, IGRA itself became increasingly dependent on royalty members to fundraise for the association's operating budget. As a past Mr. and Miss titleholder explained, "IGRA relies on the royalty contest and royalty to raise money for the operations of IGRA, because we put on the world finals," the only one paid for by IGRA, instead of the local associations. "It's all based off what IGRA has . . . and what the royalty team has made."[17] By the early 2000s royalty became essential to the financial stability of the organization.

Perhaps because of these rising demands for delivering operating funds, tensions arose between royalty members and the larger association. One royalty member lamented, "Royalty is constantly asking people for money. [We] dollar people to death."[18] Titleholders have described people walking in the opposite direction when they spotted royalty at the rodeo. As Chili Pepper indicated, royalty members were supposed to elicit joy from audience members, but due to their financial obligations, they were often framed as joyless money-grubbers whose role in the association was consistently begrudged.

Alongside fundraising, IGRA expected its sash-holders to be the public face of the association, but in increasingly diminished ways, especially as AIDS created more significant opposition to the association. Initially placed on its "public relations committee," later renamed the "public relations and fund-raising committee," royalty members worked to raise the public profile of IGRA through raffles, drag performances, visits to other royal courts, and mingling with the audience during the rodeo.[19] As one royalty communication exclaimed, "Be nice to everyone, you are the perception of Gay Rodeo."[20] Due in part to an upsurge in media attention, often negative, the association began to receive as AIDS spread in the mid-1980s and early '90s, IGRA changed the name of the committee royalty chaired from "public relations" to "community outreach" as it deputized people trained in PR to speak with the media.[21] While their chief duty remained the dissemination of information, royalty were duly informed that this was to be at the community level—as cheerleaders—not as official spokespeople.

Royalty members were also increasingly required to participate in the rodeo itself. Often proud of their entertainment abilities, many chose to participate in the camp events. While gay rodeo otherwise resembled the mainstream version, with speed, roughstock, and roping competitions, camp events were explicitly framed as amateur contests in which anyone could participate. They functioned as "the open door for anybody that wants to play." As one contestant explained, "For me, that was my open door: putting panties on the goat."[22] Performed on foot, with little experience needed, camp events were a way to get newcomers into the arena and emotionally invested in the sport. They were "events where you don't have to ride a horse, you don't have to have really any skill, you just have to have the courage to step into the arena and work with somebody."[23]

Most importantly, camp events became synonymous with gay rodeo itself. As *Frontier* magazine, an LGBTQ+ publication, wrote in 1996, "Sure, they have the rough stuff events with bulls, broncs, and steers, but like any good bunch of fags and dykes, they also hold what are known as 'camp events.'"[24] Organizers of the rodeo and journalists alike often described these as what defined gay rodeo as gay and amateur. Not only did this rustle up viewer interest, but more people could also register to participate in the rodeo, thereby growing the entry fees.

Ultimately, IGRA's connection to competitive drag circuits, nondiscrimination policy, and amateur status drew people from other LGBTQ+ organizations who were searching for a place to belong. As Desirey Benavides, a titleholder from the ICS, mentioned, "I got tired of sitting around looking pretty with a gown and a crown, and I wanted to do something, I'm very hyperactive. And so I thought, 'Where can I go to, where I can still be a girl, still have fun, still move around? I'll go in the rodeo, start competing. I mean, now I compete as a girl.'"[25] Feeling constricted by standard definitions of femininity as she transitioned, Desirey sought out gay rodeo as a place where she could compete as a woman but still be active. She was never asked to provide "proof" of her gender at the rodeo, and competing in the female category was deeply satisfying for her as a trans woman.

Camp culture has financially supported gay rodeo from its birth, helped publicly mark it as a queer space, drew in spectators, worked to get new participants into the arena, and raised money for both external charities and internal operating costs. The royalty competition and camp events in the arena, however, while overlapping significantly, also used camp in different ways, creating gendered questions about the radical potential of queering the cowboy icon.

FLUIDITY ON THE ROYALTY STAGE

Unlike the rodeo itself, which, despite the camp events, remained predominantly an arena for masculinity, the royalty competition was self-consciously constructed as the place where gender fluidity could be fully expressed, at least in theory. While the royalty competition's rules have allowed for fluidity, or movement between gender categories, ideals within these categories have been linked to gendered notions of western authenticity. Specifically, gay rodeo royalty competitors have still been expected to adhere to a physical presentation of western identity that became a place to self-police normative behavior and style, rarely allowing for ambiguity. As scholars of beauty pageants have noted, these competitions "showcase values, concepts, and behavior that exist at the center of a group's sense of itself and exhibit values of morality, gender, and place."[26] For gay rodeoers in the late twentieth century, these values were deeply intertwined in the figure of the cowboy, especially as baby boomers had solidified him into America's symbol of white male strength.

Having been raised during the heyday of western television, including *Gunsmoke* and other popular shows, many gay rodeoers associated western identity with a strong sense of morality and the performance of masculinity. Rodeo volunteer Bruce Roby noted that, more than being able to ride a horse, being a cowboy meant that "you're honest, you're true."[27] This moral code was often compared to the notion of a chivalric code that marked ideas about proper manhood in an imagined European tradition. The magic of the western myth in America was an enduring image, like "the knights and ladies of the Crusades."[28] For gay rodeo royalty, the intertwined performances of gender and western identity have approached a form of mimetic performativity, or the construction of identity categories naturalized through repetition.[29] In the broadest sense, royalty members were expected to enact a country-western ideal vested in proper morality and gender presentation (see figure 16).

First and foremost, despite its subversive premise, IGRA's competition was designed to reward gendered versions of "proper" behavior. Most notably, this meant that entertainers needed to maintain their connection to country-western culture, avoid vulgarity, and physically adhere to the gender category in which they were competing. For instance, by the mid-1990s, contestants were scored on their "personal dispositions" in both the personal and public interviews. Qualifying traits included "Positive Outlook; Expressive; Respectful," while deductions were given to anyone for being "Opinionated; Pessimistic; Bias[ed]; Impolite."[30] Like other drag competitions, and the

FIGURE 16. *IGRA royalty, 2021. IGRA royalty are seen in western wear during the national anthem at the Rocky Mountain Regional Rodeo in Colorado. Photo by Alyson Roy.*

beauty pageants they invoke, IGRA consistently proscribed certain behaviors.[31] Outlandishness and disrespect were simply not tolerated. Strict inebriation disqualifications were added, as were performance space and prop requirements.[32] In 2003, an etiquette guide was created with statements like, "When you are wearing your sash, you should look nice. Clothing should be clean and pressed. If you are not wearing a hat, hair should be combed and/or styled. Exposing [your] underwear is not appropriate!" It continued, "Do not wear sash when inebriated or in a situation that will cast a negative image [on] your association. When getting smashed, remove the sash."[33] The competition therefore rewarded performers who exhibited both reserve and respect, especially since unbecoming behavior—alongside an inability to deliver financial resources—could also result in a winner being stripped of their sash. Though constraining certain behaviors was as important as proper physical presentation, the constant need to create additional rules also connotes a resistance on the part of participants to embrace these gendered assumptions of propriety.

In many ways, rodeo drag queens brought together two major performances of femininity: the mainstream drag queen and the mainstream rodeo queen. In drawing from these previously separate cultures, drag rodeo queens offered a version of hyperfemininity that complimented the hypermasculine cowboy and were both grounded in the performance of idealize white femininity. In the 1920s, mainstream rodeo queens were increasingly the daughters of local white ranchers who competed for the title through fundraising, often displacing Native American queens and rodeo cowgirls in places like Pendleton, Oregon. As neo-Victorian values took hold, women of color and women who rode roughstock lost cultural stature to young, white women dedicated to raising funds for the community. Over the century, they, as historian Joan Burbick argues, "keep alive a particular vision of the West," particularly one that aligns with white supremacy, religiosity, and political conservatism.[34] Just as mainstream drag queens must portray idealized femininity in a more general sense, mainstream rodeo queens embodied a specific version of female western identity.

At the gay rodeo, the sequins, colorful outfits, thick makeup, and hair-sprayed tresses of the average rodeo queen, alongside white country-western singers like Shania Twain and Dolly Parton, offered country-glamour inspiration for Miss contestants. As Bruce Roby explained, "When I was a young guy going to [PRCA] rodeos, there was never a bunch of tighter butts in jeans in my life, and the women had hair to heaven. I'm sorry, we got the same thing at the gay rodeo. You've got drag queens with hair to heaven, and you got men in tight pants."[35] Miss contestants were often very vocal about their skill sets. "I'm not a drag queen, I'm a rodeo queen!" 1988 Miss GSGRA Amber Westin Mills announced, while also noting she barrel-raced "in decent time, not breaking pattern, skirt hiked up around my waist, and not a hair out of place."[36] Proud of their abilities, drag queens embraced the rodeo queen as a model that provided the logic for their existence, but just like mainstream rodeo queens, their ability to fully embody the cowboy image and his abilities were often questioned.

While campy western femininity offered gay rodeoers a model for a "glamorous" entertainer outside the arena, there were concerns about drag queens' ability to adhere to strict requirements for horsemanship and western wear. In the first years of the competition, Mr. and Ms. competitors were expected to compete in "horsemanship," while Miss competitors were judged in "entertainment."[37] This split between the categories exemplified the othering of drag queens within the association: Mr. and Ms. were required to do more than just "ride around and wave"; they were believed capable of competing on "real" ranch horses.[38] As gay rodeoer Ron Neff wrote, "More likely than not the Mr. and Ms. [titles] are held by people who are active participants in the rodeo. The Miss is viewed more as a performer for all the entertainment that takes place at the rodeo."[39] As many of the Miss competitors found the rodeo through the ICS and other competitive drag or pageant organizations, other gay rodeoers sometimes doubted their abilities and questioned their role in the actual event. The Miss title therefore was framed as external to the rodeo, though deemed important to making sure people were entertained during the grand entry parade and after the competition.

Yet by the mid-1990s, IGRA members recognized that bodies and gender presentation often did not comply with idealized norms, and the association made horsemanship required for everyone. Indeed, the fluidity allowed by the competition, with some members even holding two different positions on the IGRA royalty team—as both a Mr. and Miss—demonstrated the absurdity of limiting horsemanship based on assumptions about drag queens' abilities.

Despite the rule changes, these assumptions about masculinity and horsemanship also did not dissipate over time. After 2016, to boost participation, IGRA allowed all contestants to choose between horsemanship and entertainment.[40] Many assumed that Mr. competitors would fulfill their hypermasculine horseback duties. As one rodeoer said, "The males, they would rather do horsemanship than do entertainment. Because entertaining is usually not a lot of Mr.'s fortes, so they would rather do the horsemanship."[41] This assertion proved incorrect, however, and indeed almost no competitor in any category has done horsemanship since the rule change.[42] Performing other forms of western authenticity, such as entertaining the audience with country music, was deemed sufficient to still earn the title.

Like horsemanship, competitors also were judged on "authentic" dress. During the western-wear competition, contestants were expected to "model contemporary western fashions such as could be found in [today's] western-wear catalogs or in a quality western store."[43] The rules clearly stated that Miss contestants "may not wear stage costumes for western-wear competition." This rule, which explicitly named Miss contestants as the would-be perpetrators, assumed that male-to-female drag competitors would be the most likely to introduce campy versions of the style, rejecting iterations of westernness that too clearly illuminated the show business heart of western wear. This rule also obscured how "contemporary western wear" has always been a costume, as it was developed in part by rodeo riders and Hollywood entertainers over the twentieth century.[44]

The emphasis placed on maintaining the catalog uniform of western wear crafted in the 1970s and '80s became more apparent when some queens resisted it. As former Miss New Mexico Gay Rodeo Association Marie Antoinette Du Barry stated, "What is really the definer of western looks? Is it a duster? Is it all leather? Is it jeans?"[45] Du Barry shared that she was frequently criticized for her "historical drag," such as that inspired by the French court of Louis XVI, with handstitched Mexican motifs incorporated on her skirts. She resisted being told what counted as "western." As she noted, "Women weren't wearing pants. God forbid they weren't wearing pants. They were all corseted and bustled." Particularly, she resisted the erasure of people of color: "I also have [a] Spanish background, and it's unfair to only see the Anglicized version of 'western' because . . . they were French, they were Anglo-Saxon, they were Spanish, they were—shoot, they were buffalo soldiers, Native American peoples. . . . You can pick and choose from whatever the hell you want and make it into whatever you want."[46] Embracing a more fluid interpretation of western identity markers that worked across race as well as gender and nationality, Du Barry represented a new generation in IGRA that wanted to update and push back on the "traditions" established by organization's elders.

Not only did this younger generation reject a strict version of western wear, they also at times increasingly rejected notions of static gender presentation. As new identity categories have proliferated in the past two decades, older IGRA members have struggled to adapt. For example, Chili Pepper, Miss IGRA 1993, said that she simply went by whatever pronoun matched her dress, distancing herself from the "new generation of feeling upset if someone says, 'Hey, girl, what's up?'" Chili Pepper dismissed gender fluidity as an identity, even as she lived a gender-fluid life. She also, along with several other Miss competitors, insisted that dressing in drag did not make them less male or less masculine.[47] Performing drag has often been cited as less about an innate interest in exploring femininity as a central aspect of identity and more an opportunity to fundraise.[48] Younger members, on the other hand, have been much more likely to describe themselves as floating "in between masculine and feminine."⁴⁹ Exploring gender ambiguity has indeed been a critical draw for younger members.

Royalty contests understood fluidity as a way to play with gender, but not to discard it entirely, especially as the categories of competition are based in gender identification and rules often tried to dictate the line between "reality" and "performance." In the interview and horsemanship categories, contestants were expected to dress in a gender-conforming manner. As stated in the rule book, "Miss to appear in male attire," or at times, "Miss not in face."⁵⁰ ("In face" denotes both the physical metamorphosis of drag performers and the gendered persona they inhabit.) Likewise, those competing as a MsTer must dress in "female attire."⁵¹ This emphasis on gender-conforming clothing illuminates how gender fluidity has been deemed acceptable as long as it was fully ensconced in that gender binary and, when asked, poised to shed the illusion.

These rules also make deciding competition categories excruciatingly difficult for many people. In the past decade, there have been at least two transgender men who competed under the MsTer category and were labeled as drag kings.⁵² The language of "realness" has been used consistently to delineate between categories on the royalty team, making the transitions between categories difficult even while institutionally supported.⁵³ Since the early 2000s, several competitors have changed from Miss to Ms. or from MsTer to Mr. categories. IGRA officials have acknowledged that the organization has tried to adapt: "I think now with [transgender people] and things like that, we're evolving slowly that way. . . . I have an individual that right now is a MsTer, which is a drag king. In May [he] will now be a full-fledged male. So now I have to switch 'em out of that category and put 'em in the Mr. category for when he competes, because I don't want him not to have that opportunity."⁵⁴ Officials have tried to remain supportive of contestants going through transitions, but often they simply have not had the language or experience to know how to categorize them. Becoming a "full-fledged" male, most likely a reference to a physical transition, qualified this individual to change categories from a "drag" category to a "real" category. While deeply entrenched in notions about gender and authenticity, these category changes have allowed trans people the ability to continue performing through their transitions, one not always found in other drag spaces.⁵⁵

While this western royalty pageant has increasingly adapted to a world of gender fluidity in which people could be either men or women, IGRA's competition could not fully adapt to nonbinary gender presentation. As a past sash-holder and a royalty liaison noted, "They need to choose a category." This inability to fully relinquish gender as a meaningful category was in part logistical. As was explained, it is "not that we want to force them to do that, but that's what we have. We don't have a nonbinary category."[56] With a declining membership and pool of royalty competitors, new categories still based on a strict binary have only slowly gained popularity and drawn in younger members. As seen in the embrace of masculinity in the rodeo arena, IGRA has been a place to perform gender ideals, not disregard them.

The royalty competition has represented the space in gay rodeo in which gender was most explicitly performed and fluidity celebrated. Yet this fluidity has also remained yoked to the late twentieth-century roots of the association, with binarized gender performances negotiating ideas of "realness" and "illusion." Most importantly, the ideals laid out for contestants also continue to emulate the hypermasculine cowboy and hyperfeminine rodeo queen of the late twentieth century. Notions of appropriate personal conduct, gendered assumptions about horsemanship, and concerns over western wear revealed IGRA's historically specific vision of country-western performance and, in many ways, resisted a more playful approach to gender.

AMBIGUITY IN THE RODEO ARENA

"Camp" in gay rodeo has not strictly denoted performing hyperstylized gender, but instead more broadly a sense of playfulness. Susan Sontag noted in her foundational "Notes on 'Camp'" that "the whole point of Camp is to dethrone the serious. Camp is playful, anti-serious." Camp turns the "frivolous" into the "serious." As scholars like Sara Warner have argued, frivolity has served as "an important but neglected political affect," which created "a pleasurable and empowering experience out of an event or situation that is hateful or painful."[57] Camp events both rejected the gendered assumptions about rodeo as a sphere solely for the masculine, while also continuing to play upon the inherent humor of including hyperfemininity within the arena. Similarly, in not doing "real drag," these events embraced a form of gender ambiguity otherwise not seen in IGRA's gender binary, but also anchored this ambiguity in the absurd.

While royalty competitions have often been perceived to be ancillary to the rodeo, even as they provided much needed financial support, camp events occur in the arena, in full view of a paying audience. IGRA officially sanctioned three unique camp events when it organized, drawing from both the Reno rodeo and longer rodeo traditions. Steer decorating featured one team member holding a steer by a twenty-five-foot rope while a second team member attempted to tie a ribbon on its tail. The steer had to be pulled across a line marking ten feet from the chute, the rope removed from its horns, and its tail decorated before the timer could be stopped. Goat dressing, also a timed event, required a team of contestants to race toward a small goat, lift up its hind legs, and attempt to get Jockey-style underwear onto the stubborn animal before racing back to the starting line (see figure 17). Lastly, wild drag racing involved a team of three people, including a male, a female, and a male or female member dressed in female-style drag (see figure 18). The female held the lead rope of the wild steer when it was initially released. The male had to help catch and direct the steer over the seventy-foot line, where the person in drag was waiting. The "drag" member mounted the steer's back and had to stay on until all four legs recrossed the seventy-foot line.

Unlike the royalty competition's insistence on adherence to an "authentic" image of the cowboy, organizers celebrated camp events as decidedly unauthentic to western tradition, at times obscuring these competitions' deeper western roots. The wild drag race initially began as wild cow milking, a common event at rodeos across North America. Similarly, steer decorating has been widely featured at mainstream rodeos alongside other unsanctioned events, such as chuck-wagon racing and goat tying. These events were used throughout the early and mid-twentieth century to demonstrate a cowboy's dexterity and ability to herd, as well as to provide entertainment between sanctioned events. At other rodeos, it has been the rodeo or fair queens who do these "humorous" events, with young women racing stick horses instead of real horses or trying to catch greased pigs instead of rope cattle.[58] Yet gay rodeo community members were at times insistent that these were completely unique events built out of queer culture, not a longer western tradition. As *Roundup* magazine, a gay cowboy-enthusiast publication, noted in 1996, "Camp events were created especially for the gay rodeo circuit, and they help give gay rodeos a character all their own. They're *fabulous!*"[59] Camp events were the

FIGURE 17. *Goat dressing, 2021. Cowboys and royalty contestants alike participated in the goat dressing camp event at the Rocky Mountain Regional Rodeo. Photo by Alyson Roy.*

FIGURE 18. *Wild drag race, 2002. IGRA Hall of Fame Cowboys Brian Helander (in back) and Chuck Browning (in front) stare down an uncooperative steer in the campy wild drag race in Las Vegas. Photo by Frank Harrell.*

moment when the constraints of western performance could fall away for competitors. The 1986 IGRA rule book intoned, "All contestants are required to wear long sleeve shirts, WESTERN HATS AND WESTERN BOOTS during the competition. NO ROLLED SLEEVES EXCEPT WHEN USING A WRAP DURING ROUGH STOCK EVENTS. Failure to do so will cause the contestant to be disqualified. Camp events excluded."[60] Where other competitors and even royalty members were to appear starched in their western authenticity, camp event participants were to appear playful in their queer authenticity.

As IGRA shifted to riding instead of milking the cow, in part because stock contractors would no longer need to provide lactating cows as well as steers, it took the opportunity to reject the persistent demands of cisgender gay male cowboys to exclude drag queens and lesbians from competition. Organizers kept the team-based structure of wild cow milking but stipulated that the teams must include members from across gender lines. In this way, IGRA tried to ensure inclusivity through participation, albeit in ways still grounded in a binary.[61]

Although camp events have involved theatrically embellished gender performance and an increase in cooperation across gender categories, camp has not exclusively denoted drag in the rodeo. In fact, only one of these events included a drag element, and as one gay rodeoer explained, it is not "real" drag but instead a man "just putting on a dress."[62] While the rule book excused participants in camp events from the western-wear uniform otherwise required, it did stipulate what the performance of femininity could look like: "The drag must wear female-type drag clothing and a wig."[63] Thus, even if a female was the "drag," she was required to perform prescribed forms of femininity, not masculinity. The debate about what constitutes "female" dress has continued over the decades, with a heated conversation at the 2019 annual convention concerning tutus, pantsuits, and more. In contrast to the royalty competition, which has allowed for movement between but strict adherence to gender categories, camp events have often featured men with full beards in lipstick, a wig, and colorful tights. Essentially, camp events have used markers of stereotypical femininity at times to both undermine and heighten masculine presentation.

In their mixing of masculine bodies with makeup and bright colors, camp events have to a degree mirrored the ambiguity of rodeo clowns. As sociologist D'Lane Compton notes, many participants employed drag in gay rodeo as a stand-in for clown attire, describing "a male participant in a sequined bra and underwear combo over his jeans and a brightly colored wig" as doing "the job of mainstream rodeo clowns but with a colorful and bedazzled twist."[64] For decades, rodeo clowns, often referred to as bullfighters in order to lift their masculine status and acknowledge the importance of their jobs, have used campy performance to keep roughstock riders safe. They have drawn on not only drag in their performances to evoke laughter but also blackface and other racialized performances as well. Like camp event competitors, rodeo clowns walk a line between entertaining the crowd with their antics and dealing with the potential for life-threatening injuries.

In gay rodeo, clowns have uniquely experienced the complexities of rodeo drag as both liberating and constraining in terms of gender and sexuality. One gay rodeo clown noted the change that came over him in his costume: "It requires a lot of energy to play with the crowd, and it brings out a part of me that you don't normally see. I'm a very quiet and retiring person, but under this make-up and in this costume, I can get away with anything I want." Specifically, this enjoyment and play was put into terms of anonymous sex, as he admitted: "I enjoy molesting pretty men but I'd never talk to them if it weren't for this make-up. ... Of course they like it. It embarrasses them but they don't take me seriously. I know now what it's like for people who do drag, because when I'm out there playing the audience and having a good time with them and embarrassing them to death, they don't know who I am—they know me as Bullshot, the clown, but not Dwight." When asked if he had a good sex life as a clown, he answered, "No, absolutely not. Would you fuck with someone who looks like this?"[65] In connecting clowning to camp, Bullshot acknowledged how his role encapsulated both the hypermasculine and effeminate, the serious and playful, and the sexual and desexualized, providing for an ambiguity in gender and sexual performance rarely seen elsewhere in the imagined West.

However, like the laughter induced by clowns, gay rodeo capitalized on the image of masculine cowboys in dresses attempting to execute a difficult and dangerous task to bring pleasure to the audience through humor during camp events. The sheer hilarity of this perpetuated the idea that performing femininity was still incongruous to the enactment of rodeo, thus producing laughter. When asked if a transgender woman should participate in the male or female category, former IGRA president Roger Bergmann answered ambiguously: "There's a lot of mythology surrounding cowboys and it's funny to see that some of our best cowboys are in reality the nelliest queens."[66] In attempting to illustrate how bodies and gender performance rarely affected one's ability to successfully rodeo, Bergmann used the word "funny," marking the gap between performed femininity ("the nelliest queens") and the assumed masculine space of rodeo. Importantly, in gay rodeo, male effeminacy could sometimes be acceptable but was framed in self-deprecating ways. As one association noted in its newsletter, "It was obvious the gay rodeo was in town the moment we stepped off the plane; witness the memorable sight of a cowboy throwing a 'hissy-fit.'"[67] While they attempted to break stereotypes about who could be a cowboy—an explicit IGRA goal—generalizations about femininity, gayness, and rodeo masculinity still persisted in the spaces meant to be the most inclusive.

Camp events, often performed by royalty members, were both defended (or disparaged) as the most dangerous of all, and connected to "serious" rodeo through potential injury. The wild drag race rapidly gained a reputation for producing a high number of injuries when people were dragged, stomped, and pitched off the steer's back. In 1995, the IGRA health and safety committee even recommended "the elimination and replacement of the Wild Drag Race or at least look into ways of making this event safer. (This event has the highest injury rate!)"[68] Eventually, the camp category came to be accepted as serious competition as well as good fun, in part because of these injury rates. While announcing a 2005 rodeo, the announcer stated, "Even though this is fun and a camp event, people take it *so* seriously."[69] These seemingly frivolous contests became very serious for many gay rodeoers, because they were "legitimized," for better or worse, through the potential violence people were willing to risk.

IGRA also ensured that camp events were taken seriously by giving them equal standing with other rodeo competitions, and the category makes up one of the four types of events at gay rodeos (the other categories are roughstock, speed, and roping). To qualify for the All-Around title, a contestant must have competed in three of the four categories. This system of awarding significant points for camp events required even detractors to acknowledge them as central to gay rodeo.[70] Due to their importance to the contestants' point tallies, the rules became increasingly clear and strict as to what "riding" a steer entailed or how long a ribbon must stay tied on the steer's tail.

The minutiae of these rules are still debated in the association as what constitutes worthy rodeo performance continues to change.

Camp events staged gender ambiguity as humor, marked the rodeo as gay, and kept gay rodeo amateur. They illuminated the performative tensions seen throughout all forms of rodeo, especially as drag was often a stand-in for clown attire. At the same time, the significant danger that they presented also served to legitimate them for many rodeoers who claimed to want "tradition" maintained. Their association with effeminacy, frivolity, and flamboyancy, however, could serve to mark the outer limits of gay rodeo's expansiveness, even as the association attempted to incorporate camp events as integral to the rodeo.

PROTECTING MASCULINITY

Camp culture in gay rodeo worked on several levels to invite people other than cisgender, straight men to rodeo. However, while the royalty competition adhered to the binary inherent in the country-western ideal of the 1980s and camp events embraced performed femininity as funny, both predominantly permitted male-identified people to play with gender. Ultimately, camp culture not only provided the financial support necessary to keep gay rodeo alive, it also helped protect masculinity within rodeo culture.

The royalty competition has remained a predominantly white, male sphere. In the past thirty years, male-identified contestants have consistently outnumbered female-identified ones in all categories. In total, over 370 people have competed in the male-identified categories (Mr. and Miss), while there have been only 170 in the female-identified ones (Ms. and MsTer). Rarely have Ms. contestants outnumbered Miss contestants.[71] The commitment of the IGRA royalty competition to a gender binary has helped shape the form of queer western performance as committed to masculinity. As D'Lane Compton notes, gay rodeo allowed men the ability to "demonstrate greater flexibility of femininity" by participating in dresses and participating in pole bending. Women, lesbian culture, and cisgender femininity, however, become "quite invisible."[72] Performed hyperfemininity operated more commonly as way to get a laugh and make a buck.

Toleration of performed femininity also had its malcontents, and while they never convinced IGRA to ban women and drag queens, the denigration of camp was prolific. In his experience of the gay rodeo in the late 1980s, Darrel Yates Rist described one man's negative opinion about the rodeo queens: "It makes me *sick* to see somethin' as nelly as that. I haven't got no use for it at all. People sees that kind of thing, and they think all the queers are that ways. It's enough to make you stay in a closet. Pro'ly from California anyways."[73] Similarly, another man joked, "I don't know if putting on makeup is really a sport [laughs] ... I don't think you're really fulfilling the mission of IGRA, which is to promote and preserve the Western lifestyle. Uh, obviously there were gay cowboys [during the nineteenth century], but I don't know how many of them, uh, were drag cowboys [laughs]."[74] Drag queens, intimately connected to gay rodeo from its early days, have often been written out of the image of gay rodeo even as the association benefited from their labor and commitment.

Similarly, while camp events were widely popular, members continually debated their necessity or desirability. These concerns were strong enough to induce many people to voice their displeasure on a questionnaire disseminated by IGRA in 1990. In the fifty-two completed questionnaires, forty percent of the participants stated they began their gay rodeo circuit careers in camp events. Yet almost sixty percent were in favor of de-emphasizing, limiting, or completely eliminating one or more camp events. One person claimed that these events "eliminated the real purpose of rodeo." Another gay rodeoer proclaimed, "Camp events have nothing to do with being a cowboy."[75] In 1996, the Golden State Gay Rodeo Association submitted proposed rule changes to IGRA that suggested the elimination of goat dressing, the implementation of time limits on camp events, and their removal from consideration for the All-Around title. For members of the California association, "The other 3 events are more traditional rodeo events deserving of an All Around title."[76] These comments reveal the association of the word "camp" with nontraditional, frivolous fun, especially as these events were not required to qualify for the All-Around, just one of the potential pathways for competitors.

The place of drag kings on the circuit also demonstrated the ways masculinity has been perceived as a sacred category. Unlike drag queens, who have been expected at times to lampoon femininity as a form of entertainment, drag kings often enact hypermasculinity while on stage. These performances have been referred to as "compensatory manhood acts" and included demonstrating physical prowess and at times denigrating women in displays of culturally accepted dominance.[77] Drag kings have often drawn on masculine icons, like the cowboy, as models for their portrayals.[78] Within IGRA's western pageant, kinging has provided an avenue for people to literally stage masculinity, both as a way to learn to adopt it in their everyday lives and as a way to subvert it by publicly revealing the performed nature of masculinity. Yet, as J. Halberstam noted, female masculinities, including kinging, "are framed as the rejected scraps of dominant masculinity in order that male masculinity may appear to be the real thing."[79]

In the early 2000s, Patrick "Cowboy Ram" enjoyed Washington, DC's growing drag king subculture. He believed that because of their self-conscious performance of masculinity, these drag kings would bring new vibrancy to gay rodeo's royalty competition, which had seen declining interest since the late 1990s. He saw the addition of the MsTer title as potentially transforming a "trio that could be a quartet. . . . One more body that is out there promoting [IGRA]."[80] The Atlantic States Gay Rodeo Association first incorporated drag kings in its events and then prodded the international organization to include the MsTer competition. However, even with this expansion, there have been marked regional differences in which associations are able to send participants, something based largely on local support networks and culture.[81] Though the competition was added in 2005, due to fundraising qualifications and several contestants not receiving minimum scores, IGRA had to wait until 2008 to award a MsTer title, and in the past ten years, there have been far fewer participants in the category than the other three.[82]

In the twenty-first century, much of the sporting world has policed the amount of testosterone in female bodies—despite the hormone being naturally produced by all people—as a way to protect women's sports and, by extension, reject masculinized femininity and punish any body that does not neatly fit into defined categories. IGRA similarly worried about a rapidly blurring binary. In 2008, the community outreach committee proposed rule changes to restrict people's ability to change categories by requiring "proof" of gender change, and banning gender changes from being recorded during a person's "IGRA Royalty career" instead of "reign."[83] These proposals would have taken a rule already in place, which banned someone from changing their gender identity during their reign year, and extended it to a career-long prohibition. This would mean that if a person began their royalty career in male-identified categories, they would have to continue in those categories in perpetuity. These suggested changes were in direct conflict with IGRA's larger gender policy and failed to pass. The debate revealed, however, a growing frustration among royalty about who should compete in which category, particularly as female-identified members came to have greater access to self-conscious performances of masculinity and trans people began to agitate for more inclusion. As these many debates reveal, while femininity has been widely deployed on the gay rodeo circuit, it almost always has functioned in a way to keep a particular version of cowboy masculinity protected by reifying the gender binary.

While many people embraced gay rodeo as a place for hypermasculinity, it has ultimately been the performance of femininity in both the arena and the stage that has kept the association inclusive and, indeed, alive. While these two spaces played with gender performance in different ways, with royalty embracing a degree of gender fluidity between binarized categories and camp events staging a degree of gender ambiguity for the sake of humor, they each contributed to the draw of the gay rodeo.

Perhaps the greatest use of camp in gay rodeo was not in these proscribed spaces but instead in the wider acknowledgment that everyone at this—or any—rodeo was indulging in a campy performance of an imagined past. As feminist, queer, and trans scholars have noted, the sheer act of men dressing as women has carried radical potential. Drag renders the performance of gender visible and therefore makes it vulnerable to subversion.[84] Likewise, by performing westernness in the context of a drag competition, IGRA royalty exposed all western identities as performance. Many IGRA members describe their own cowboy personas as "cowboy drag," at times calling themselves "weekend cowboys," as opposed to the "real cowboys" who own property and care for animals.[85] Yet even in their commitment to an idealized authentic cowboy, their willingness to call their own performances of masculinity drag helped render the cowboy aesthetic into a costume, subverting the association's insistence on strict binaries and the othering of camp within a larger queer country-western culture. Ultimately, in gay rodeo, campy gender performances were often used to get a laugh and make money, not to radically rewrite the history or meaning of the cowboy. However, their simple existence and importance to the survival of the association demonstrates the crucial role of gender play in late-twentieth-century queer country-western culture.

Oral History Vignette
CANDY PRATT, IGRA PAST PRESIDENT

I did grow up in the city, but my grandparents had horses and were farmers, so that's how I was always able to be around the horse world. I can tell you anything about animals, farm animals—how to take care of them, what to do to them. I can rope, I can ride, I can build anything. I can change a flat tire really fast. It just goes with being a tomboy, but then when you change it to cowgirl, I can rope well and do all the stuff it takes to work on a farm or ranch.

When I was in third grade, my parents bought me a pony, and I boarded it with a lot of other people. They had these little things called play days, which are kind of like rodeos, but they were all horse events. A lot of young kids do that for a sport, and it just developed from that. You get better and better and better, and we got more horses. Then when you're in high school, you do a little high school rodeo, and after that there's always barrel races everywhere.

I guess it was probably like 1988 in Dallas that was my first IGRA rodeo. I didn't know there was such a thing. When you grow up, you hear of Black rodeo or Indian rodeo. You don't hear white rodeo, you know—it's just rodeo. I thought, "Oh my gosh! Gay rodeo, are you kidding?" So I went and I found out. At first I just did speed events, because I didn't know how to rope and I did not know how to do any of the camp events. That was later, self-taught with some friends. It seemed like a whole lot of fun, and in the early years, there was prize money from Miller Lite, so it was fun.

We don't make money—used to we did. Years ago, there was a lot more money in gay rodeo. Miller Lite gave a lot of money, and there was more prize money. Now, if you can imagine the fuel out here and the expenses, if there's no added money, then your check is not even gonna be close. So we do it for fun. I'm fifty-five years old and have a good job. There's not a lot of twenty-year-olds that can do stuff like that. I believe the difference between straight and gay rodeo is that the straight rodeos make sure there's plenty of added prize money. That's the reason you'll see lots of young people in that.

In the early 1990s and 2000s, we came to all the California rodeos. But when the money went away, it just didn't pencil out, so we stayed around the Texas and Oklahoma area, places that we could drive to within fifteen hours. It's expensive, and you've gotta really plan things out. We have a lot of friends that all travel together. We had two trailers that traveled all the way out here, so we made it fun. All our trailers are self-contained. They have a generator, a shower, beds, everything.

I don't just compete in IGRA. I compete in other things. The draw is money. Also I try to tell [IGRA] it takes money to make money. You know, if you have $5,000 added money, you get all these extra contestants. They are going to spend money while they are there. Until the belief changes, I don't think [IGRA] will grow that much, in my personal opinion.

Chapter 5

"IT'S MILLER TIME"

Negotiating Gay Political and Consumer Identity at the Rodeo

Rodeo, at its heart, has always been about money. From rangeland competitions to the national finals rodeo, people have risked their lives to earn anything from a few coins to hundreds of thousands of dollars.[1] When asked why younger people were no longer joining IGRA, some members wrung their hands about selfish millennials who do not understand the meaning of community. For Candy Pratt, however, the answer was simple: "Years ago, there was a lot more money in gay rodeo. Miller Lite gave a lot of money." Between fuel, hotel expenses, and food, she explained, "if there's no added money, then you know your check's not even gonna be close." She continued that, as a woman in her mid-fifties, it was possible for her to absorb those costs out of dedication to the community, but "there's not a lot of twenty-year-olds that can."[2] Without added prize money provided by sponsors, she believed that young queer people would choose to participate in more lucrative mainstream circuits.

Pratt illustrates how sponsorships have been critical to the continued existence of rodeo. Over the twentieth century, rodeo professionalized into a sport while also maintaining its connection to a western identity. This made it a perfect opportunity for corporations to help construct and partake in a rugged western ideal. Western-wear companies (particularly jeans companies), as well as beer, cigarette, and truck companies, dominated advertising on national rodeo circuits in the 1980s and '90s. Rodeo historian Kristine Frediksson noted that corporate sponsorships on professional circuits topped $8 million by 1982.[3] Scholars have shown that these products were also associated with an increasingly conservative political identity as "country-western" imagery was used to promote prowar, antifeminist, and anti–civil rights stances during the 1960s and '70s, crystalized in Merle Haggard's 1969 antihippie anthem "Okie from Muskogee."[4] Nadine Hubbs notes in *Rednecks, Queers, and Country Music* that country music became synonymous with white working-class bigotry and sexism in the late 1960s, despite its often queer undertones and multiracial history.[5] As part of this growing association of country-western culture with conservative politics, the media made a concerted effort to link Ronald Reagan's "hardline" politics on the Cold War to his cowboy persona. Even Democrats denounced his penchant for "shooting from the hip," only strengthening the connections between the New Right and the cowboy icon.[6] In 1981, *U.S. News and World Report* interviewed a savvy western-wear retailer who observed, "What more could we ask than the President in a cowboy hat?"[7] The music played at rodeos, the western wear people wore, and even the Marlboro cigarettes they smoked were linked to a rapidly shifting political landscape in which rugged individualism was used to reassert white American dominance both at home and abroad. The cowboy icon was a way to sell consumer products; a white, masculine America; and rodeo performances.

Gay rodeoers were caught between two disparate movements: the mainstream LGBTQ+ rights movement and this nationalized and often politicized country-western one. While IGRA mostly attempted to avoid overt political stances, its very existence illuminated the multiple levels of debate surrounding the place of queer cowfolx, both in the American imagination and in the physical landscape. As Curt Westberg, an IGRA contestant in the 1980s described, "We weren't in there feeling this self-satisfaction about being political. We were just having a rodeo." At the same time, however, "it was political. It was a big fuck you. It was: 'No, we can do this. You can't tell us not to do this. Come try to make us not do this.'"[8] IGRA as an organization attempted to maintain at least the appearance of political neutrality, even as gay rodeo participants were spread out along the political spectrum and participated in forms of activism, from raising money for AIDS organizations to marching in Pride parades. As they fought to find a coherent political identity amid broad consumer desires and economic demands, gay rodeoers were often torn between the practical need to gain "country-western" sponsors central to their image as real cowboys and larger calls to vote with their dollar to expand their own civil rights as queer Americans. Over the decades, IGRA walked these political tightropes while carefully crafting a collective consumer identity that struggled to encapsulate members' competing desires to be understood as both country-western *and* gay when those identities were often seen at opposite ends of the political spectrum. Indeed, Pratt started participating when IGRA's first international sponsor, Miller Lite, had just signed with the association. Members then watched in horror, and fought back, as Miller became embroiled in a larger boycott of its parent company for supporting homophobic politicians.

Tracing the frictions between explicit political activity, or members' rejection of it, and the subsequent embrace of consumer citizenship by IGRA leadership, this chapter places gay rodeo in the larger national context of market-based political activism. Political statements grounded in consumption—or the refusal to consume, via boycotts—are as old as our nation. From the Boston Tea Party to the Montgomery Bus Boycott, Americans have widely embraced the idea that political rights can be gained through consumer choices. The sit-ins staged by civil rights activists in the 1950s demanded equal access to consumer services as a crucial step in gaining access to education, voting, employment, and housing opportunities.[9]

The notion of the "consumer citizen" who "voted with their dollar" solidified on both the right and the left during the 1980s. As the gay liberation movement learned tactics from civil rights activists and redeployed them around sexual identity, it contributed to a neoliberal belief that all political disputes should be settled via the free market. Indeed, much of the LGBTQ+ movement relocated itself into the marketplace, from ACT UP boycotts to the National Gay and Lesbian Task Force producing lists of friendly corporations.[10] Rooted in the writings of conservative economists like Milton and Rose Friedman, neoliberalism assured people that "no one forces you to buy. You are free to do so or go elsewhere.... You are free to choose."[11] The demand to decrease economic regulation and gut the welfare state played into the up-by-your-bootstraps message of Reagan's "tough-guy" image. For many on both the right and the left, the citizen became fully constituted through the marketplace. Within this cultural context, IGRA tried to stay connected to a broader LGBTQ+ movement that urged it to work to expand queer civil rights while also not engaging in overt politics in ways that could offend members, endanger its nonprofit status, and create dissonance with its country-western image.

IGRA's balancing act was particularly fraught, because the link between queer identity and consumerism runs even deeper than an activist tactic. John D'Emilio argued in his 1983 history of capitalism and the rise of "gay identity" that the expansion of the market economy in the late nineteenth century, which disrupted heteronormative, home-based economies and fueled urbanization, allowed for the initial organization of queer communities and the articulation of queer identities beyond same-sex desire and personal relationships.[12] Consumption of particular fashions, pictorial magazines, and fiction helped create national communities over the twentieth century, constituting a much larger "gay nation" than did participation in formal political organizations like the Mattachine Society.[13] Between the 1960s and the 1990s, a twin revolution in LGBTQ+ visibility and economic globalization resulted in an economy that was hyperspecialized and interested in selling to a niche LGBTQ+ market, particularly as the gay male segment was increasingly believed to be wealthier than its heterosexual counterparts.[14] By the 1990s, corporations actively sought queer people's business and changed hiring practices, benefits packages, and marketing strategies to earn their economic support.[15]

IGRA members participated in these consumer-based politics. The leadership often embraced forms of activism rooted in the idea of "consumer choice," which many scholars have contested simply cannot exist in a world saturated with marketing telling consumers they must buy something but providing only a small range of options. IGRA members vocally supported voting with their dollars. However, this also meant that those with more dollars had more votes, and only the issues supported or opposed by the wealthy would ever warrant a vote. As queer media scholar Amy Corey explains, "When marketplace activism stands in the place of concrete action in the public sphere, it co-opts the radical potential of LGBTQ+ activism and hinders the achievement of both civic and consumer equality."[16] As companies used LGBTQ+ organizations and events to increase their social capital, a process Eric Clarke terms "capitalist profiteering," they dictated the terms of the relationship, essentially choosing when a sponsorship was no longer valuable.[17] As IGRA leadership embraced "consumer choice" as the path to progress, their commitment to political change was subsumed within a larger commitment to a "country-western lifestyle" predicated on consumption of music, beer, fashion, and sporting events. As IGRA negotiated its public image, it was often torn between finding sponsors who fit its country-western ideal and its collective desire for a more inclusive society, alongside its own individual political beliefs.

This chapter charts the explicit political debates in IGRA, noting that even as associations strove to stay apolitical, their very existence made a political claim for expanded civil rights. As gay rodeo found itself caught between the left and the right, the leadership focused on selling the economic benefits of rodeos to cities and sponsors, while also trying to maintain relationships across the political spectrum. Similarly, IGRA encouraged members to vote with their dollars, sometimes working against several large-scale boycotts called by LGBTQ+ groups or animal rights groups, thus potentially calling into question its commitment to progressive politics. Over the late twentieth century, cultural producers, from musicians to journalists to clothing designers, helped create cultural scripts that placed queer people on the political left and country-western enthusiasts on the political right. IGRA demonstrated that these dichotomous and inflexible assumptions could not capture the reality of the lives of queer cowfolx. At the same time, its own commitment to the country-western icon, and the corporations it believed communicated that image, often contributed to the association's uneasy political identity.

TO POLITIC OR NOT TO POLITIC

As a group of people who came together because of a shared interest in country-western subculture, gay rodeoers often attempted to eschew politics altogether with statements like, "Rodeo has never been, nor will it ever be, involved in politically biased moves.... We will always (and always have) stand unbiased on every issue."[18] Yet it was impossible for members, leaders, and the meanings ascribed to rodeo itself to remain completely politically neutral, if for no other reason than because country-western identity was itself increasingly political, and a queer country-western identity even more so.

For many participants, the community they wanted to create was one that emulated the white cowboy icon of the midcentury. They wanted to be near people who valued "dedication" and "fortitude," claiming that nineteenth-century, westward Euro-American settlers upheld "ideals of strength, self-reliance, and inner pride" that "live on today embodied in what is known as the Western image." Describing itself as "not an activist or separatist group," IGRA was designed to bring together people "with a sense of Western Hospitality" to create a "positive image of gay men and women in the light of Western spirit."[19] Assuring potential members that IGRA was not a militant political group, even as its very presence was deemed political by others, current members sought to create a community that resisted monolithic stereotypes of queer people as metronormative and politically progressive. They also invested in a specific image of the hypermasculine, often nationalist, cowboy.

Gay rodeo has always faced politically charged questions, often around gender and inclusion. As discussed in several other chapters, many men questioned the place of women at the rodeo, as well as campy femininity, while other participants defended their right to participate. The explicit issue of women's rights came to the forefront when the Human Rights Commission of San Francisco wrote to Nevada's lieutenant governor, Myron Levitt, in 1981 to express outrage over the state's lack of support for the Equal Rights Amendment (ERA). A copy of this letter was sent to Phil Ragsdale and detailed support for a boycott of the state. Ragsdale's response was livid. He printed his reply in the Reno rodeo program, asking the Human Rights Commission, the National Organization for Women (NOW), and the Harvey Milk Gay Democratic Club, "if they (Pro-ERA Groups) are so hell bent on its passage here in Nevada, JUST WHERE THE HELL HAVE THEY BEEN when our legislature has been meeting?" He asserted, "I can tell you where, Sitting on their ASSES in Government paid jobs, in ratified ERA States, trying to dictate to people in unratified ERA States." Resisting the assumption of where queer people should live, he noted, "Sorry, but not all Gays want to live in ratified States." Finally, Ragsdale underscored that the ERA had become increasingly "controversial" and that it "DOES NOT have the backing of a majority of the Gay women I have personally talked to."[20] While Ragsdale was willing to support women's right to be in the rodeo arena, he bristled over what he perceived to be out-of-touch West Coast elites establishing political dictates. This willingness to denounce the ERA also epitomized the Reno rodeo's early struggles to define itself as either a place for idealized western masculinity or a place for out-and-proud campiness.

Indeed, many gay rodeoers noted that while they attended Pride parades to raise interest in the rodeo, they felt that the latter was more important for building a community that reflected their own identities. Mr. Gay Rodeo 1982 said, "To me it's better than the Gay Pride march. Don't misunderstand me, I respect the march. But this isn't political; this is what gay life is all about. The rodeo draws men closer together."[21] In 1992, at the Atlantic Stampede in Washington, DC, one participant enthused, "It gets gays out of bars and into a constructive activity. We get to share a sense of camaraderie, of teamwork, and of love." They could "celebrate what it means to be gay" but in a way that broke down "stereotypes that mainstream society pins on us. You know, it's not like we're all just a bunch of hairdressers."[22] Rodeo was imagined as a space of both celebration but also resistance to the assumed effeminacy of most urbanized queer spaces.[23] Decades later, one participant described it, saying, "This is my gay community, so to speak." While she acknowledged she went to Pride parades to promote the rodeo, she did not feel like she was the marching type, and she believed that other gay groups "don't experience what we experience." For her, a sense of "closeness" emerged from a shared love of animals and sport, which the out-and-proud politics of Pride celebrations could not replicate.[24] Yet, in its willingness to attend the parades, IGRA also contributed to a political act of queer visibility, allowing it to claim queer space while also downplaying the political implications of its participation.

Beyond just personal preference by members, rodeo associations were officially supposed to remain neutral on political issues. IGRA, and many local associations, worked hard to be designated as 501(c)(3) nonprofit organizations, and once granted that status, they were explicitly prohibited from participating in direct political campaigning. Even internal communications, such as newsletters, lacked high degrees of political engagement. Major legislative changes that affected LGBTQ+ people, from "Don't Ask, Don't Tell" to the federal legalization of marriage equality, were rarely addressed by gay rodeo associations in their written communications. Among all the associations, only ASGRA, located in Washington DC, addressed in 1993 how Bill Clinton's presidency had the potential to shift the political landscape. It wrote, "America is a beautiful collection of many faces, many beliefs, and many cultures, each free to compete amongst ourselves and enjoy the fellowship of each [other's] company." Even as it noted major potential changes for gay and lesbian Americans, it also maintained an eclectic political perspective, embracing the ability to "argue, disagree, and compromise."[25] Acknowledging the breadth of perspectives of gay rodeoers was central to the organization. One of the few mentions of the Supreme Court's overturning of the Defense of Marriage Act in 2015 was AGRA's newsletter, in which the public relations director stated that with the "outpouring of support from many large companies for the gay community I will try my hardest to reach out to them to become sponsors for this coming [year's] rodeo."[26] In this way, at least one local association acknowledged this historic moment for LGBTQ+ rights but also focused on it as an opportunity for economic positioning to gain sponsors. It sought to use a political moment to create economic stability for the organization.

Indeed, IGRA officials often walked this line very carefully. For instance, the 1988 Texas Gay Rodeo program included a letter of welcome from the Lesbian/Gay Rights Lobby of Texas. Preceded by others from TGRA officials, Austin's mayor, and the Bar Association, the letter carefully invited members to contribute financially or by contacting their legislators, without stating a formal connection to IGRA. Instead, it used vague language to gesture toward common goals: "Let's have a great time this weekend and continue working together for the betterment of the gay/lesbian community."[27] More explicitly, in 1994, Washington Citizens for Fairness sent to a letter to IGRA asking for its support in fighting discriminatory ballot initiatives in the state. The response letter noted that "although, we generally are not involved in political activities, we certainly encourage our members to become involved to the extent they desire." The letter continued, "We support your efforts and wholeheartedly agree that civil rights for any individual or group of individuals should never be limited or denied."[28] Through private letters and conversations, IGRA leaders could express their support without actually providing funds, a public statement, or other forms of tangible aid to explicitly political groups.

At times, a member's efforts on behalf of specific politicians or a notification about local legislation could appear in communications but was presented as simply informing the membership about local activity and encouraging broad participation, rather than stating that the association endorsed a particular perspective (see figure 19).[29] In 1992, for instance, AGRA posted "a political update for our 'non-political by Charter' Organization." Expressing displeasure at the Phoenix City Council, which "recently took the coward's way out, refusing to vote yes or no on the proposed anti-discrimination ordinance which would have protected sexual preference," the newsletter thanked specific members for attending and voicing their opinion at the meeting. It also went on to joke, "Due to the archaic sex laws still on the books in this State, we would also encourage all of our Homosexual Members to continue refraining from any Homosexual sex acts whatsoever, until further notice, and we thank you for your law-abiding support."[30] Associations, however, took steps to distance themselves from these discussions with disclaimers like, "THE FOLLOWING COLUMN IS INFORMATIONAL ONLY—IT DOES NOT NECESSARILY REFLECT THE OPINION OF NGRA!"[31] Despite these claims, instructions on how to make one's opinion heard often accompanied these announcements, from calling legislators to attending fundraiser events.

As these calls to fundraise indicate, economic pressure became a core tactic any time members openly discussed politics. For example, in 1992, as mentioned, AGRA members felt frustrated by the lack of decisiveness from the Phoenix City Council on adding sexual orientation to antidiscrimination statutes. They used their newsletter to call out the "turn-coat" vice-mayor, Thelda Williams, who "just last year [was] actively courting our votes, using our volunteers, our money, and holding fundraisers in our bars."[32] Williams had recently made $1,700 at a single fundraiser at gay country-western bar Charlie's, prompting the author to suggest that members write to her about a refund of their donations. As members discussed political frustrations, they bound it to their financial investments in various politicians.

Additionally, despite their protestations or machinations to not be seen as political, association members, as proud adherents of a cowboy mythology, were often caught between their own claims to belonging and the celebration of past and present colonialism. As many participants served in the military or worked as police officers,

FIGURE 19. GSGRA LA Rodeo Program, "Don't let politics impair your vision of health care reform," 1994. This ad from AIDS Project Los Angeles encouraged people to look beyond their political affiliations when deciding which health care proposal to support. For instance, the Chafee-Thomas proposal, led by two Republicans, had a clear "NO" in all categories, but so too did the Cooper-Breaux proposal, which came from two Democrats. Courtesy of the Autry Museum of the American West.

LOG CABIN CLUB OF SOUTHEAST MICHIGAN
P.O. Box 1835
Royal Oak, Michigan 48068-1835
(810) 447-2325

Michigan's Lesbian/Gay Republicans

Best wishes for a fantastic rodeo!!
Together we can win!!

FIGURE 20. *MIGRA Rodeo Program, ad for the Log Cabin Club, 1995. While progressive organizations more frequently appeared in gay rodeo programs, conservative groups, like the Log Cabin Club, which advocated for LGBTQ+ rights within the Republican Party, also demonstrated their support for gay rodeo from the 1980s and into the twenty-first century. Courtesy of the Autry Museum of the American West.*

demonstrations of nationalism were extremely important at the rodeos. Taken aback by the solemnity with which gay rodeoers sang the national anthem and prayed, a reporter in the 1990s lamented the need to prove their allegiance to a country that had largely rejected them: "Here they were—big town, cow town, redneck, white collar, liberal, Baptist—singing their allegiance with their hats over their hearts, the most denied, the most legislated against."[33]

And while the organization itself could not advocate for or against legislation, sponsorships and political booths were allowed. Log Cabin Republicans, an organization affiliated with the Republican Party that agitates for LGBTQ+ rights, have maintained a stable presence at the rodeo, with the Log Cabin Club of Southeast Michigan purchasing ad space in the 1995 Greater Motown International Rodeo's program and renting booth space at rodeos over the past several decades (see figure 20).[34] Some observers have noted that members, both men and women, have not hesitated to share their conservative viewpoints, including eschewing gun control, expounding on American exceptionalism, lamenting racial protests, and rejecting progressive economic perspectives.

Built on a racialized understanding of the cowboy image, IGRA has always been subject to the tension of urging a more inclusive future through the celebration of an exclusionary past. Often emulating a broader rodeo culture that celebrated the violent conquest of the US West and removal of Indigenous people, an uncritical embrace of the "cowboy and Indian" mythology was apparent in Native costumes at IGRA events and historical write-ups that erased Native people from the narrative of settlement.[35] Indeed, magazine articles and program introductions emphasizing the homosocial nature of cowboy culture sought to reinsert queerness into the historical West, yet they did not discuss Indigenous people, or even acknowledge the growing literature on fluidity of gender and sexuality in many Native cultures. With statements like, "The frontier code was inherently practical, civil and honorable," these narratives softened the harsh realities of racial genocide in the history of the West, even as they sought to offer more complex historical understandings of the cowboy.[36]

Already present in the 1980s and '90s, this racialized nationalism only increased in visibility at rodeos after the attacks on the World Trade Center in 2001. Nationally, country-western culture continued to be associated with prowar, white-supremacist, and nationalist stances, and often IGRA members contributed to these stereotypes. With members spread across the political spectrum, rodeo announcers and clowns often took center stage in telegraphing a wider set of beliefs to audiences. For instance, in 2016, football player Colin Kaepernick sparked a nationwide protest against police brutality toward Black Americans by kneeling during the national anthem. An IGRA rodeo announcer took exception to this protest, urging everyone to stand for the flag and anthem during the grand entry. Saying that the United States offered queer people more protections than any other nation on earth, the announcer claimed that it was every cowboy's and cowgirl's duty to honor the nation and its symbols. In these ways, some IGRA members participated in a well-established practice of pitting LGBTQ+ civil rights against the rights of other groups of Americans.

In the twenty-first century, IGRA's embrace of white cowboy masculinity and its connection to American nationalism took place in the larger context of LGBTQ+ rights being appropriated as a symbol of American superiority over Middle Eastern and Muslim people, who were cast as orientalized and homophobic others during the decades-long wars in Afghanistan and Iraq. This process was called "homonationalism" by postcolonial sociologists and media scholars.[37] As queer people's ability to function as full citizens in the United States increased in the early twenty-first century, the pressure to embrace a racialized pronationalist stance also grew, particularly for people interested in country-western culture.[38] In many ways, rodeos both fed from homonationalist rhetoric and contributed to its application within the United States. Today, it is not uncommon to see Blue Lives Matter T-shirts on rodeo participants, demonstrating that a firm commitment to socially conservative politics that inherently rejects racial justice remains among many gay rodeoers.

While participants rarely approached right-wing extremities, a general notion of what ethnomusicologist Kathryn Alexander has termed being "politely different" pervaded queer country-western culture.[39] An *In Touch for Men* interviewee at the 1980 National Reno Gay Rodeo was asked, "A lot of cowboys are right-wing, but I wonder if this applies to gay cowboys. Are you right-wing?" The contestant responded, "Sometimes I find myself in the middle. But it's a real world, and we have to start living in it." He continued, "We have to deal with it and say, I'm gay, I'm bigger and more understanding. Separatism didn't work for the Jews or the Blacks; it's not going to work for the Gays."[40] Assimilation and forms of quiet activism have often been the course set by gay rodeoers. In 1991, Roger Laughery, the president of BSGRA in Montana, wrote about how he made new friends while representing his company at a trade show, only slowly sharing with them that he identified as gay. He explained that "presenting myself first and my sexual preference second" helped him subtly persuade people to be supportive of him. Persistently providing information and avoiding overly aggressive tactics, he believed, would lead to change.[41] For many rodeoers, finding common ground, either culturally or politically, was an important part of their worldview. Quiet change, they believed, could be achieved through being politely different.

As gay rodeoers who used their own visibility to urge for expanded civil rights, IGRA members also embraced diverse political perspectives. Some viewed gay rodeo as a place beyond politics; others saw it as an avenue for progressive change, while many also saw it as a place they could safely embrace more conservative perspectives. As the larger organization tried to negotiate these tense political realities, it often looked to the marketplace for the answer. Sponsorships by specific companies could not only contribute to IGRA's cowboy image but also provide ways to leverage the collective purchasing power of gay rodeoers for political change.

SPONSORSHIPS AND IDENTITY

All rodeos need money to operate, but gay rodeo's need was both financial and existential. It needed mainstream corporate sponsors to underscore its legitimacy as a circuit. Rodeos also brought a great deal of money into the areas that hosted them. From the beginning, IGRA courted specific sponsors while host communities courted—or rejected—the rodeo's economic benefits. As economies globalized and became hyperspecialized in the 1980s and '90s, the "gay consumer" sat at the center of the emerging belief that with enough wealth, any group could be embraced by corporations, which then supported their interests through corporate policy, political donations, and marketing visibility. Corporations and local governments openly debated the economics of gay rodeos during a time when it was increasingly accepted that the LGBTQ+ consumer was wealthier, savvier, and more politically engaged than other niche markets. While many felt that supporting a gay rodeo was a political statement, others argued that it was simply an economic one.

By the early 1980s, Reno's rodeo was attracting tens of thousands of spectators, often upsetting local residents. Some complained that the rodeo got too much free publicity and that they should rename it something innocuous, without the word "gay" in the title, because they did not want "gay" events "shoved down [their] throat."[42] Others responded by calling out so-called "pro-family" groups that opposed gay rodeo in Reno: "The rodeo fans don't pose any threat to families as far as I can tell. Evidence apparently shows that AIDS isn't transmitted through ordinary contact—my family won't be engaging in sex with the gay rodeo fans. Why all the fuss? ... Any half-wit can recognize the economic benefit to individuals, families and Reno."[43] This assertion of economics over ineffective moralizing resulted in people like Maurice "Mush" Parker, manager of Parker's Western Wear, posting a banner for the National Reno Gay Rodeo in his store window. He noted that rodeo visitors "do contribute to the economy and they're excellent customers."[44] Indeed, organizers often joked that people with animals, the beer it promoted, and the places it hosted rodeos held great political meaning in these decades. Refusing to adhere to the assumptions of progressive queer urbanites and conservative, homophobic rural residents, IGRA members and their rodeos existed in a liminal space between these politicized geographies.

As IGRA gained more national notice, it drew the attention of rodeo's oldest opponent, animal advocacy organizations. Animal studies scholar Susan Nance has demonstrated how people both inside and outside of rodeo communities have been troubled by the sport's use of animals, with advocacy groups offering the most public critique.[67] Rodeo emerged at the same historical moment as animal rights groups, in the early twentieth century, and rodeoers have always fielded accusations of abuse, even as many defined themselves as animal lovers.[68] As rodeo professionalized over the twentieth century, major organizations, riders, and stock contractors became more adept at framing their relationships with animals as beneficent and familial. When asked if she thought of herself as a cowgirl, IGRA member Raeann Grow answered, "Every inch of me. I am redneck to the core." In defining what it meant to be a redneck, she said, "I've seen colts born. I've helped pull cows. I've pulled puppies.... What's it mean to be a redneck? I love my animals."[69] While it was clear that rodeoers felt a deep bond with their animals, they also articulated the difference between animal activists and themselves as one of rights and responsibilities. Randy Shulman, a gay cowboy from ASGRA, explained, "I do not think that animals have the same rights as humans. I *do* think humans have a responsibility for the safety and welfare of the animals in our care. In their housing. In their feeding. In their veterinarian care."[70] Human relationships with nonhuman animals has fundamentally shaped the practice and narrative of rodeo, with rodeoers firmly perceiving themselves as animals' caregivers. While the debate about animals in rodeo is a century old, LGBTQ+ riders were taken to task by animal rights activists not simply for their participation in the sport but because of their sexuality.

Protests by members of People for the Ethical Treatment of Animals (PETA) and other animal rights activists have been common at gay rodeos. In 1983, a flyer circulated urging people to "boycott all rodeos," calling them "one step removed from rape."[71] These calls continued throughout the 1990s and extended beyond traditional animal rights attacks on rodeo to include specific criticism of the group because of denouncing the rodeo simply provided more publicity and argued that ultimately, "Reno is a town that responds to the dollar."[45] Many locales similarly welcomed the dollars brought in by gay rodeoers, despite political objections to openly queer people in their communities.

As IGRA expanded, it became good practice to include a welcome from local politicians in rodeo programs. Notably, while they often wrote vaguely and urged rodeoers to "enjoy a few of the many historical areas of interest," these politicians rarely attended the rodeo themselves. Some people, however, were more open in their language. For instance, Colorado's lieutenant governor, Nancy Dick, wrote in 1986, "In addition to enjoying this bit of western heritage, I invite all of you to stay long enough to enjoy the natural beauty and cultural diversity which makes Colorado so special." She went on to invite participants to the "many Gay Pride activities which will be taking place throughout June." By explicitly referencing "cultural diversity" and Pride events, Dick sought to expand the groups deemed worthy to be recipients of "the special warmth of western hospitality."[46] These types of direct addresses to gay rodeoers certainly encouraged them to invest some money into the local economy.

By the early 1990s, member associations across the country were vying to host both annual conventions and finals rodeos. Application packets became more professionalized, accompanied by pamphlets marking hot tourist destinations and attractions. Hotels provided information on special rates and amenities. Gay bars wrote letters of support for the associations, offered to host events, and provided lists of commonly played songs with corresponding line dances.[47] The perception that hosting these events could be lucrative prompted an IGRA bylaws change that required a host location be decided two years in advance and rotate between divisions.[48] While organizing these events included a great deal of stress for the local association, it also provided a guaranteed economic stimulus.

Local dignitaries were willing to write welcomes and regional associations were eager to host in large part because of a growing acceptance of the so-called "pink economy." As one letter from a marketing company enthused to IGRA in 1993, "We all know that gay and lesbian customers comprise one of the most prosperous, intelligent, and loyal markets in America. But what if there was a way to effectively reach the wealthiest and most-educated gay men and women for just pennies?"[49] The assertion of queer market power found its clearest articulation in Grant Lukenbill's 1995 book, *Untold Millions: Secret Truths about Marketing to Gay and Lesbian Consumers*. In this work, Lukenbill argued that the 1980s and '90s saw a fundamental shift in corporations' valuation of the LGBTQ+ community. While they had a long history of "coding" queer imagery into their marketing schemes, they had rarely openly supported gay and lesbian consumers. Lukenbill rejoiced that "businesses are becoming stronger, more ethical, and more profitable by acknowledging and appealing to an exciting new consumer who is eager to buy but quick to see through smoke and mirrors, hollow rhetoric, and misguided marketing."[50] This perspective articulates an increasingly common-sense belief that LGBTQ+ people were more discerning consumers and that, by marketing to them, corporations would see larger profits.

Of course, this excitement over the supposed purchasing power of queer consumers was grounded in central assumptions about capitalism and democracy. As Lukenbill claimed, "The lifeblood of free enterprise comprises a great many things: capital, liberty, equal opportunity, organization independence—and perhaps, most important, visibility." As corporations sought to invest in new forms of visibility to attract niche consumers, Lukenbill and others saw the potential for creating a collective "economic and commercial identity" that surpassed a shared political identity. Through the "manipulation of compelling imagery," many hoped that this perception of economic strength could ensure political change as well. While some activists critiqued this economic approach to political organizing as ineffective and often counterproductive, since it invested in a normative version of queer life, IGRA leaders saw the economic gains they were providing, through tourism dollars and fundraising for charities, as forms of political engagement.[51]

Sponsors became the most intimate connection between IGRA and corporations. As demonstrated in chapter 2, IGRA capitalized on hypermasculine imagery that connected it to leather bars, sex shops, and bathhouses. An overwhelming majority of local sponsors for rodeos were from these enterprises and also from queer-owned businesses, from realtors and chiropractors to bowling alleys, pet shops, and print shops. While these advertisements and sponsorships guaranteed that gay rodeo was demarcated as a queer-friendly space, they did not attract casual rodeo enthusiasts. Since IGRA officially touted the "country-western lifestyle" alongside an idealized image of the traditional cowboy, it hoped to find sponsors that were less reflective of the LGBTQ+ community and more emblematic of the West.

Some board members were concerned with the close association of the rodeos with hyper(homo)sexuality. For instance, when IGRA formed a relationship with the publisher of *Roundup* magazine, former IGRA president Roger Bergmann and founding member Wayne Jakino expressed concern, because he also published "skin magazines." They negotiated so that no fully nude models or sexual personal advertisements would be included in the magazine. They were appreciative of the free advertising and the ability to write articles explaining IGRA's history and events, but they made clear that the public image of IGRA needed to steer clear of anything approaching pornography.[52]

IGRA wanted to be accepted as a legitimate rodeo, with sponsorships from large companies with a western image. In the early 1990s, it struggled to gain traction with any of these companies. Businesses like Philip Morris's Marlboro never responded to initial requests.[53] Sheplers Western Wear at first offered a $500-per-rodeo sponsorship in cities with stores, but at the following annual convention, it was reported that it, along with Wrangler and Roper, fell through, because they feared "that the straight community will not shop at their stores" if the sponsorship became too widely advertised.[54] IGRA's desire to attract mainstream sponsors was stymied by the corporations' lack of commitment early on to a niche market, let alone a political investment in LGBTQ+ civil rights.

Beer companies, however, played a more significant role in gay rodeo. They had spent a large portion of the twentieth century associating their products with masculinity, sport, and the cowboy. Like many advertisements that included homosocial settings, beer commercials often included forms of queer coding, or the inclusion of imagery that could be read as queer without an explicit commitment to LGBTQ+ communities.[55] While soliciting sponsors and vendors for the National Reno Gay Rodeo, Ragsdale reportedly had beer distributors "laugh him out of their offices." However, Joe Morrey, owner of Morrey Distributing Company, which worked with Budweiser, was happy to work with him. Within a few years, other distributors requested to sell at the rodeo, but Ragsdale refused, making Budweiser "the Official National Reno Gay Rodeo beer."[56] Relationships with local distributors, as well as parent company policies, became integral to consumer politics for IGRA members. And the retelling of these "success" stories of distributors who lost out because of their prejudiced miscalculations furthered the quest by IGRA leadership to find the "right" kind of sponsor.

For gay rodeoers in Colorado, Coors beer was a sore spot. Hispanic and African American workers initially called for a boycott of Coors in the 1960s over discriminatory employment practices and contributions to right-wing politicians. By the 1970s, San Francisco politicians, such as Harvey Milk, helped expand the boycott to LGBTQ+ activists, because Coors used polygraph testing during the hiring process, allowing them to target queer people. The boycotts would continue into the 1980s.[57]

Despite decades of reports about the company's shady employment practices, labor conditions, and political agenda, CGRA hoped members would keep an open mind, sending out announcements for "GAY DAY AT COORS." It asked, "Has all of the 'bad' press that Coors has received in the past been fair?" CGRA's board urged members to "be informed" by attending "Gay Day" at Coors, which included a free lunch, a tour of the plant, and a panel with openly gay employees and policy makers.[58] As beer vendors were essential to the rodeo, it was in the association's best interests to invest time in discovering which corporations were potentially open to an IGRA sponsorship.

Ultimately, while various liquor and beer companies provided support for local associations, it was Miller Brewing that stepped into the spotlight as the first international sponsor. In 1990, Miller had just signed on to support all IGRA-sanctioned rodeos. When Sheplers and other potential sponsors backed out, Miller upped the ante in 1992 by signing a three-year contract, for amounts in excess of $500,000. It provided a set amount of funds to help run each rodeo, usually around $4,000, and then additional sums for advertising, prize money, and promotional products, such as hats, pins, and shirts.

As a business investment, the Miller contract also outlined IGRA's reciprocal commitments. IGRA was required to host a minimum of fourteen rodeos in 1993 and sixteen in 1994. These were to include at least ten events and feature a minimum of sixty-three competitors. While these represented IGRA's goals as well, there was a stated expectation that IGRA continue to expand in membership and thereby Miller's market too. In addition, "all Rodeos shall be held in a first-class manner in accordance with the prevailing professional, ethical, humane animal treatment, and business standards, and with the utmost regard for the safety of all persons, property, the environment, and Miller's goodwill."⁵⁹ "The Rodeo Director's Checklist," a document provided to each rodeo director outlining their duties, included specific requirements for Miller Lite logos to appear on posters, award ribbons, banners, and barrel wrappers. The Miller name sometimes appeared just as largely unadorned logos but often was featured prominently on program covers (see figure 21). In addition to the stamp of the Miller name at the rodeos, directors were also required to provide free tickets to Miller representatives and allow Miller personnel participate in the awards ceremony. Importantly to IGRA's finances, the organization IGRA was allowed to seek additional sponsors, except from other "malt beverages."⁶⁰ Miller also submitted full-page advertisements for the programs. Occasionally these were generic beer ads, but more frequently they were designed for western audiences, with a rodeo theme. At times, these western ads even hinted at gay rodeo's queer audience. For instance, the "Hard Ride, Lite Finish" Miller ad with a bronc-riding cowboy read differently at a gay rodeo and titillated queer audiences in a more sexual way than it did at other rodeos.⁶¹ In 1998, the final year of IGRA's relationship with Miller, the beer company made an even bolder queer statement with a paper doll of a mostly nude gay clone who was ready for outdoor action with his blow dryer, tight shorts, snug flannel, and—of course—Miller beer (see figure 22).

Through its sponsorship of IGRA and many other LGBTQ+ organizations, Miller bought itself good press. For instance, *Gay Chicago* magazine ran an article titled, "Put Your Money Where Your Mouth Is," focusing on the role of corporations in increasing the visibility and therefore the political rights of LGBTQ+ people. The article used IGRA and Miller's relationship to narrate how organizational growth created financial pressures and necessitated corporate partnerships. As IGRA wondered who would save the day—"Levi's, Wrangler's, Coors, Miller, Bud, Jim Beam, Sheplers, Justin, *The Advocate*, Marlboro, or perhaps Chrysler?"—Miller stepped in as savior.⁶² In articles like these, Miller solidified its place as a queer-friendly corporation.

Within the narrative of the rodeo, Miller and IGRA celebrated their mutually beneficial relationship. As one letter from the company explained: "Miller Lite has been involved with I.G.R.A. almost from its inception, primarily due to the efforts by our distributors who have taken the initiative to sponsor the individual rodeos around the

FIGURE 21. *IGRA* Finals Rodeo program cover, 1993. At the finals rodeo in 1993, IGRA recognized Miller Lite as the organization's international sponsor with a subtle nod to the company. Courtesy of the Autry Museum of the American West.

country. Now that the program has grown to the national level, we very much want to continue the successful track record which has been established over the years. I think our three year commitment, combined with our ongoing promotional support, represents a strong commitment on our part to the continued growth and success of the

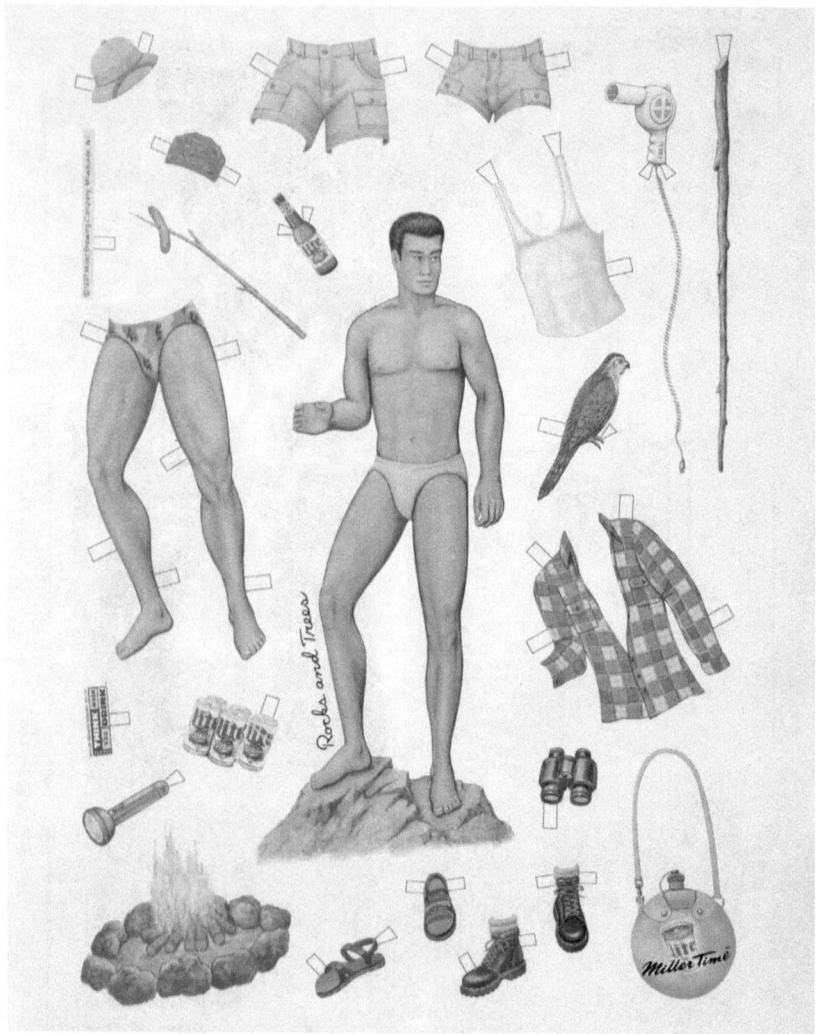

FIGURE 22. *AGRA Rodeo Program, ad for Miller Lite, 1988. In this ad, Miller Lite targets the LGBTQ+ community as beer consumers with paper dolls that include many of the accoutrements of the gay male clone. Courtesy of the Autry Museum of the American West.*

I.G.R.A. program."[63] The company's dedication to gay rodeoers was instrumental in promoting events in the mid-1990s. Indeed, without the $4,000 checks each local association received from Miller, many groups could not have hosted rodeos at all, let alone made profits to donate to their communities, often for politically important causes like AIDS research and care. In return, IGRA emphasized the benefits to Miller, beyond an existential commitment to queer visibility. By advertising with IGRA, Miller had access to IGRA's 1,600-person contestant roster, 1,500 volunteers, 1,200 supportive gay bars, and 8,000 members.

The relationship between Miller and IGRA was fairly smooth until it dissolved in the late 1990s. Indeed, it was rabidly protected by IGRA members when threatened by internal and external tensions. For instance, when Miller slapped IGRA on the wrist for allowing other beer companies to sponsor some local events, Wayne Jakino admonished rodeo directors, "At many times in IGRA's history, as a smaller organization, we were able to carefully balance two beer sponsorships at some of our rodeos but as we have gained in legitimacy and national attention this is no longer possible."[64] Protecting its sponsors became a way of protecting IGRA's own legitimacy and permanency as an organization.

As IGRA rapidly grew in the early 1990s, its ability to build a collective identity shifted into the marketplace, and the need to protect those economic relationships, even when they seemed to work against a larger LGBTQ+ political movement, became paramount. IGRA's leadership sought to find a place on a political spectrum that never imagined queer country-western enthusiasts. It was therefore often in the position of having its rodeos and sponsors—even whole states—boycotted by people who identified as politically progressive.

BEING BOYCOTTED

To explain IGRA's political balancing act, one member summarized, "We've had PETA protest us, we've had reverends protest us."[65] This is the result of both the political left and political right adopting boycotts widely during the 1980s and '90s, as each side tried to set the legislative agenda. But as sociologist Tina Fetner notes, "The boycotts from either side did little to promote policy change." Instead, they "can be seen as cultural challenges, attempts to wage symbolic battles for the sympathies of various publics." These are low-cost options organizations can make to call attention to concerning issues.[66] IGRA often found itself at the middle of debates about what it meant to be a cowboy and what it meant to be gay, through consumer boycotts that were tied to political perspectives, especially from the left. Its relationships its "gay" identity. At the Atlantic States rodeo, groups like the Eco-Dykes and PETA's Gay and Lesbian Animal Rights Caucus reportedly chanted "Don't be a mean queen" at attendees.[72] Tracy Reinman, the head of the latter group, led the charge against gay rodeo, stating, "It glorifies a time when violence against women, ethnic minorities, and gays was accepted. The way I think about it, human domination over animals is the same as human domination over other people," and "we should know about oppression."[73] In 1994, a PETA campaign delivered dozens of antirodeo letters to IGRA headquarters. A form letter stated, "Oppression comes in many guises. Gays have suffered since the earliest times. So have women and minorities. But animals are by far the most numerous of those who groan under despots, and they are by far the least able to protect or defend themselves from callous, unthinking misuse."[74] Animal rights activists used gay identity in this way as a call for understanding and action against rodeo because of shared oppression.

However, gay identity was also used as an excuse for homophobic comments. Anna Moretto handwrote at the bottom of her PETA form letter, "Gays are not to be sympathized with, they choose their lifestyle—in my opinion they are an abomination on the earth and have created all too much sickness and disease. Animals cannot choose and are to be treated humanely."[75] These protests lasted decades, with IGRA receiving over two hundred emails in 2002 asking it to ban calf roping.[76]

The tense position of advocating for one's own rights while others perceive you to be literally trampling over another living creature's right to consent proved difficult for IGRA as an organization. While many participants simply scoffed at PETA, IGRA took the critiques quite seriously. Its leaders wanted to make sure they were being as respectful as possible to animals within an entertainment setting. From its founding, IGRA prided itself on emphasizing the humane treatment of animals. PCGRA, one of the first gay rodeo groups formed in the 1980s, included the "humane treatment of livestock" as a core tenet of its mission statement.[77] As a result of the pressure exerted by PETA in the 1990s, IGRA created an animal welfare committee responsible for creating new regulations, including requiring veterinarians on-site, finding better methods to remove injured animals from the arena, and using breakaway ropes.[78] IGRA understood that being boycotted by PETA and other animal rights activists could impact its relationship with sponsors. IGRA President Roger Bergmann made sure Miller was aware of the activists' concerns, and he and the association were relieved when Miller decided to continue its sponsorship despite the bad press.

IGRA also tried to reclaim the narrative by distributing animal safety pamphlets and including direct responses to PETA in rodeo programs.[79] The public relations committee often reminded attendees and participants to be careful with their words and their images, because they did not want PETA to gain more ground in its portrayal of IGRA as abusers.[80] In the 1998 MIGRA program, the association wrote, "Most of the exaggerated accusations of abuse made toward gay rodeo are based on misinformation drawn mainly from straight, 'backwards' rodeos. None of the people disseminating this information have any [firsthand] account of abuse in a Gay Rodeo of animals. The appeal is strictly on an emotional basis."[81] While attempting to defend itself against accusations of animal cruelty, the group clearly acknowledged that some rodeos—the straight ones—could be cruel to animals. But it insisted it was different and adhered to strict rules concerning animal welfare. These arguments and actions did not fully appease organizations like PETA, because animals were still being used without their consent for entertainment purposes.

IGRA, like many organizations with experience being boycotted, did shift its tactics to try to rehabilitate its image in the eyes of the broader public. Their long-standing experience with PETA boycotts also helped train IGRA members to never simply accept boycotts against them, their states, or their sponsors as inevitable. While IGRA routinely ignored boycotts of its rodeos by the Christian Right, it explicitly addressed at least two organized by progressive groups. On November 3, 1993, Colorado passed Amendment 2, which prevented municipalities from enacting or enforcing any antidiscrimination laws protecting LGBTQ+ people and nullifying ordinances already passed, such as those in Aspen and Boulder.[82] The campaign for Amendment 2 was spearheaded by Colorado for Family Values (CFV). As noted by marketing expert Sankar Sen, the nonprofit's mission was to "'pro-actively lead and assist those opposing the militant homosexual attack on traditional values' and 'to preserve the right resist, in a civil and compassionate manner, the forced affirmation of the homosexual lifestyle.'"[83] CFV claimed to be self-funded by Coloradans concerned about an increase in "special rights" for LGBTQ+

people, but other news outlets pointed to funding from national far-right groups, such as the Christian Coalition, the Eagle Forum, and Focus on the Family.

Sue Anderson, director of Equality Colorado, helped organize the "Boycott Colorado" campaign immediately following the law's passage and helped sustain it despite legal injunctions that prevented it from ever taking effect. She explained that the boycott was designed to provide a visible deterrent to other states considering enacting similar legislation and articulate to corporations and chambers of commerce why they needed to fight against anti-LGBTQ+ measures from the start. The gay press described the boycott as "picking up speed" quickly and being a rousing success.[84] Most importantly, since the law was eventually overturned by the Supreme Court in 1995, the repercussions of these political decisions were ultimately debated within the marketplace. The law and the subsequent boycott cost the state roughly $120 million in economic sanctions. Conferences moved out of Colorado, other states and municipalities stopped buying Colorado products, and its tourism industry's image was damaged. While the estimated cost of the boycott was minor compared to the state's annual income, no one denied that the boycott hurt Colorado's cultural cachet.[85]

As CGRA was one of the most successful IGRA state associations, its leaders felt the threat to its rodeos deeply, especially as the boycott was called in defense of protecting LGBTQ+ people. IGRA received several letters in support of the boycott, scolding it for choosing to host rodeos in the state despite the boycott. One club owner stated, "Our club caters to a predominately homosexual clientele and since your state having passed anti-gay legislation, I don't feel it is correct to promote any events or businesses located in Colorado. In such a political climate, it wouldn't be very prudent of me to promote anything from your state to a homosexual audience."[86] Similarly, a wholesale jeweler from Colorado explained, "I am in total agreement with a boycott of Colorado. Mind you I am not financially set for life, but I will survive without you and your tourist dollars. The issues are too great for me to worry about my personal income."[87] Many LGBTQ+ people felt torn, as they did want to exert political pressure for change through economic means but took exception to the maligning of all Coloradoans in the press. The jeweler insisted that the Colorado electorate was not "ignorant or bigots" but instead victims of a savvy campaign that included threats of quotas, special rights, sex acts in public, and the 'Homosexual Adjenda.'" CVF manipulated people's emotions, they explained, adding, "A nationwide boycott is the only way I can see to keep this issue on the front pages." Many LGBTQ+ people felt that the best way to protect their futures was to sacrifice some income for visibility.

Simultaneously, other LGBTQ+ people expressed frustrations with having their businesses and organizations boycotted in the name of progress. As reported in the *Windy City Times*, "Some gay and lesbian groups in Colorado are resisting calls for a full-fledged boycott. The Aspen Gay and Lesbian Community said Monday that a boycott of the January Gay Ski Week in Aspen would 'give in to the so-called family values groups.'" The city of Denver overwhelmingly defeated the measure, but as one business leader noted, "One of the most liberal cities in the country will be branded with the false image of being regressive."[88] Many members from CGRA fell into this frustrated camp, prompting individuals and IGRA as an organization to mobilize against the boycott, relocating their activism away from an association with LGBTQ+ organizations and instead using the marketplace to advocate for their own self-preservation.

Gay rodeoers' frustration with how to deal with the Christian Right's attempts to pass restrictive legislation grew during the 1990s as these efforts spread. In the Pacific Northwest, there was a struggle to maintain its IGRA association (NWGRA) when the Seattle-area rodeo faced threats of violence.[89] As the Northwest became home to radical white-supremacist and homophobic groups like the Aryan Nations, local LGBTQ+ organizations were faced with both the mainstream Christian Right and these extremists.[90] For many gay rodeoers, however, their response to these attacks was to try to host events, not cancel them.

At the January 1993 IGRA Board of Directors meeting, founding member Wayne Jakino of Denver requested time to speak against the Colorado boycott. The minutes read, "Considerable discussion ensued regarding what, if any, type of statement should be prepared by the Board in response to possible questions from the media or general public. A couple attempts were made at wording that was not acceptable to a majority of those in attendance."[91] The issue was tabled, until President Roger Bergmann called a special session for later that night, at which a resolution was passed stating that the organization would promote a country-western lifestyle "irrespective of the outside pressure of special interest groups." Labeling the Boycott Colorado effort as a special interest group illustrated rodeoers' frustration with LGBTQ+ groups organizing against their event. However, the board was also clear that "nothing contained herein shall be construed as a political statement or position by IGRA or any of its Member Associations, each of which is free to pursue the goals of IGRA in any manner it may deem appropriate, provided said course of conduct is in compliance with applicable By-laws and Rules of Order of IGRA."[92] Members of the association were thereby given the "choice" to pursue the boycott or ignore it.

Jakino did not stop his efforts there. Throughout 1993, he spoke out about the issue to local associations, on the radio, and in letters. He wrote the Texas associations, saying, "We cannot begin to tell you how upset we are that anyone would desert us at this time."[93] He continued, "We will not be driven out of Colorado or any other state and we pray that you will be there in even greater numbers as a message to Colorado and the nation—We will fight against discrimination and for our Equal Rights!!" Both in the labeling of the boycott as a "special interest group" and in the assertion of "equal rights" over "special rights," Jakino and other IGRA members reiterated the idea that the people who called for the boycott were extremists who limited LGBTQ+ people's rights instead of expanding them. As Jakino explained, "The Colorado side of affairs is rarely heard, and when it is, it is always those views of a few militants in Denver."[94] The "few militants in Denver" represented a good portion of the multifaceted LGBTQ+ community in the state and around the nation, but IGRA argued that it only harmed the association and limited consumer choice. Mostly, it wanted consumers to choose to come to one of its most popular rodeos and to understand that opting not to would hurt an LGBTQ+ group rather than make a point to conservative politicians. While the boycott eventually petered out and the amendment never took effect, IGRA's approach to rejecting the boycott and actively fighting it demonstrated its commitment to a market-based collective identity.

Indeed, the tactics used by Jakino and other IGRA members in the mid-1990s were originally deployed to protect their financial relationship with their only international sponsor, Miller Lite. In 1990, the Washington, DC, chapter of ACT UP called for a national boycott of Philip Morris's Marlboro cigarettes because of the company's support for Senator Jesse Helms, a Republican from North Carolina, who began his career as an aide in campaigns for staunch segregationists during the 1950s. As a senator, he spent much of his time in the 1980s and '90s opposing AIDS research, treatment, and education. In 1988, while attempting to block a beneficial AIDS bill, Helms stated, "There is not one single case of AIDS in this country that cannot be traced in origin to sodomy."[95] He was also a solid supporter of the tobacco industry. Previously, Philip Morris provided Helms with about $200,000 in donations to his Citizenship Center in North Carolina.[96]

ACT UP, which formed in 1987 in New York, proclaimed that "silence equals death" and embraced a politics of speech—or more explicitly, a politics of publicly coming out and claiming a queer identity—to advocate for increased AIDS support. Its call for a boycott of Marlboro, and potentially Philip Morris, was widely supported among LGBTQ+ groups, with the Human Rights Task Force and the National Gay and Lesbian Task Force endorsing the action, despite its indirect approach to limiting Helms' political power. ACT UP/San Francisco urged for the inclusion of Miller Lite in the boycott, as it was also owned by Philip Morris and was "the beer of choice" in many gay bars, making it an easier target than Marlboro cigarettes. Indeed, Miller distributors in some areas were hard hit and expressed anger at Philip Morris, asking why the company's support for the tobacco industry was hurting their beer sales.[97] When ACT UP continued to apply pressure to the company to denounce its relationship with Helms, Philip Morris took steps to publicize its contributions to LGBTQ+ organizations, including IGRA.

As organizations, ACT UP and IGRA shared commitments around raising money for AIDS research and using public space to assert the citizenship rights of gay men and lesbians. They were also both invested in consumer activism as a core conduit for creating a shared cultural and political identity for marginalized people. As scholar Alexandra Chasin has written, "The conflation of U.S. national identity, gay national identity, and consumption is one of the striking features of the location of social protest in the marketplace."[98] Yet, key differences also existed between the groups. While silence equaled death for ACT UP, silence had often been crucial to the survival of IGRA as an organization. Overly publicizing events could lead to threats or cancelations, especially during the 1980s, as the AIDS crisis deepened. Maintaining a quietness about their activism had served gay cowfolx well in the first fifteen years of their existence, making many members leery of groups like ACT UP.

IGRA could not have been more dismayed over ACT UP's decision to boycott its only international sponsor. RJ Newby, IGRA president, spent long hours "compiling information to defuse the Miller Brewing, [Philip] Morris USA boycott."[99] Many members joined with the Colorado Tavern Guild to create and circulate a bright pink flyer titled "Freedom. Friendship. Facts," which said, "Freedom of Choice: The Colorado Tavern Guild has voted to protect our [patrons'] freedoms. The guild does not support a boycott that would limit your rights to freedom of choice of products."[100] Brand loyalty was extremely important, as the flyer explained: "Gay lifestyles and corporate politics do not normally create a basis for friendship. Any corporation choosing to place its name on the line in support of the gay community must be identified as a good friend." IGRA's need for "good" corporate friends pushed it to defend the corporation to the greatest extent possible.

As tobacco researchers have demonstrated, by creating the impulse for LGBTQ+ groups to defend Philip Morris in addition to Miller Brewing, the company gained entry into the queer market in a way that had previously not been available. While other activist groups were distinguishing between Miller Brewing and Philip Morris, the flyer circulated by IGRA instead chose to highlight that Philip Morris itself should be defended, since its "public corporate policies support Human Rights, Anti-discrimination in employment, job protection acts, and the Arts and health issues." The group asserted that the contributions given to Jesse Helms were far less than what the two companies provided to LGBTQ+ organizations. They concluded, "The Colorado Tavern Guild supports ACT UP's initiative to work to remove Jesse Helms from the Senate, but hopes the gay community will not use its supportive friends to accomplish this feat."[101] The boycott ultimately allowed Philip Morris to continue supporting conservative politicians while also rebranding itself as queer friendly.

IGRA's contribution to eroding the boycott encapsulated the organization's assertion that it was not political, even as it participated in deeply political—if at times contradictory—actions. As the IGRA president reported, gay rodeoers "made it possible to inform the general public to view this issue in a positive manner, as of today Act/up has retracted the boycott."[102] Within the context of the 1980s and '90s, consumer politics were seen as the culmination of "the power of the domestic gay and lesbian consumer dollar and all that it represents."[103] IGRA urged its members to "EXERCISE YOUR FREEDOM OF CHOICE" to support its corporate sponsors instead of other AIDS-related activist organizations. The motto for neoliberal investment in the marketplace, "freedom of choice" supports the idea that the market is an inherently political space. The efforts of IGRA to break the Miller and Colorado boycotts also illustrated the tension LGBTQ+ rodeoers felt between supporting a broad national "gay community" and fundamentally ensuring the continuation of their rodeo community. As one newsletter in 1991 noted, "Miller Brewing was the only int'l sponsor last year and is helping out even more next year.... (good thing the boycott is over with)."[104]

As IGRA worked against PETA, ACT UP, and the Boycott Colorado campaign, it articulated what IGRA members imagined to be "political." One royalty member shared her embarrassment at having done a fundraiser for ACT UP without realizing it was a "political organization." She said, "I'm not sure whether I support ACT-UP's tactics or not, but being a political organization, I didn't feel comfortable using my title to support them. Once the title is gone, who knows?!"[105] Many would argue that as a visible IGRA representative raising money for AIDS research, this royalty member was already a political actor. Yet, her normal duties were not deemed "political," while an ACT UP fundraiser passed the invisible benchmark marking it out-of-bounds. The royalty member noted she would potentially be open to supporting the organization after stepping down from her position, highlighting the tightrope walk between sanctioned politics and actions that crossed the line.

After the resolution of the boycott, IGRA and Miller Lite had a mutually beneficial relationship for almost a decade. In 1998, however, Miller Brewing decided to redesign its national sponsorship program and divide up money to local distributors in order to provide regional sponsorships. In a letter from the company, it explained that "the decision was made with a bit of a heavy heart because we've enjoyed a successful, beneficial relationship with IGRA. The sponsorship was instrumental in helping us to build brand relationships within the gay community in many cities throughout the U.S."[106] Miller had received what it wanted from gay rodeo: access to LGBTQ+ markets, protection against boycotts, and a level of brand loyalty. Unlike other sponsors, who had expressed concern over being associated with a gay organization, Miller left the circuit only when rodeos began declining in numbers. Therefore, economics and not homophobia drew away IGRA's best corporate friend, demonstrating the problems of relying on economic relationships instead of political commitments for continued investment in queer spaces. And, in the perspective of many members, the inability of IGRA leadership to secure other long-term national sponsorships only further destabilized the association and contributed to its declining numbers.

Sponsorships have remained at the center of debates about the future of gay rodeo. In the years following the end of the Miller contract, IGRA worked with several other companies to provide sponsorships, but many of these were tense relationships. For instance, while the leadership was working with both Bud Lite and Coors Lite on bids, GSGRA stated that it would opt out of or boycott any sponsorship with Coors, ensuring that Bud Lite received the sponsorship. Similarly, members of GSGRA expressed dismay over the notion of a United Airlines sponsorship because of its refusal to grant domestic partnership benefits to its employees. As one member said, "Any sponsorship by United Airlines similar to Miller Lite would KILL our community support here in the Bay Area."[107] This sponsorship was contentious in other ways, since many members bristled that the airline was only providing flight vouchers and not real money. At the same time, the rental car company Avis provided discount codes for member associations but requested it not be listed as an international sponsor.[108] As international sponsorships fell through, individual state associations had to work harder to gain regional sponsorships, adding to the stress of hosting a rodeo. In 2017, a thirty-year member of TGRA said, "In the straight rodeos, they keep getting more and more money in it. And that's bringing the straight people in. But as far as the gay rodeos, we're not getting the money."[109]

Miller was able to capitalize on IGRA's desire to partner with a rugged beer brand to gain access to LGBTQ+ markets and brand loyalty. Once it accomplished that goal, it shifted to more lucrative ventures. For the past two decades, IGRA has tried to recapture the magic of that time, but despite moments of increased visibility, it has rarely had the same financial success. As it has searched for other sponsors, similar tensions between finding businesses that signal themselves as queer friendly versus those that frame themselves as "country" or "country-western" have continued, and success with the latter has still proved elusive for gay rodeo well into the twenty-first century. In some ways, this attraction of queer businesses has helped draw in LGBTQ+ casual viewers, even as some of the aspects of the masculine, Reagan-era cowboy performance alienates many young people from joining the association. And while participants often prove to be too old and gay rodeo itself too conservative to interest younger generations, it fails to be conservative and traditional enough for the mainstream country-western audience and sponsors.

Alternately ridiculed and boycotted by both the right and left, with a membership spread across the political spectrum, IGRA as an organization struggled to articulate a clear political identity as an LGBTQ+ organization and instead often focused on economic benefits, patriotism, and the country-western lifestyle. Sponsorships not only made the rodeo economically viable but also served as avenues for identification, particularly as a way to communicate an idealized western image and a marker for success. As the IGRA secretary explained in 2003, "We are no longer the small Association we were when we began in 1985; we have grown tremendously, and have changed dramatically," adding, most importantly, "I remember the days when we had no sponsors; Associations had to raise the money they needed to produce a rodeo; and sometimes, it was not too easy to even find a rodeo facility."[110] Therefore, he argued, it was vital to adhere strictly to sponsor contracts and not antagonize financial supporters. Sponsors were vital to both the perceived legitimacy and the financial stability of the organization.

While the early 1990s are often remembered as the halcyon days of the association, with an international sponsor and booming growth, IGRA members worked hard to maintain that success, fighting against boycotts by PETA, and ACT UP, as well as Boycott Colorado, plus resisting conservative communities and the Christian Right. In doing so, they carved out a market-based politics that illuminated their collective space as too queer to be accepted by conservatives but also too connected to a specific cowboy image to truly approach radical queer political action. Instead, in their approach to being queer cowfolx—unwilling to be erased but also resistant to radical action—they in many ways rewrote the accepted political and geographical maps of the era.

IGRA as an organization has had to straddle the right and the left, because in the political context of the late twentieth and early twenty-first centuries, it did not fit easily into any imagined category—whether political or geographic. With a membership that embraced political perspectives from across the spectrum, it struck an uneasy balance of enacting politics while claiming to be apolitical. As it strove to garner sponsorships from established western corporations, it made itself less legible to people following specific scripts for queer performance. At the same time, few of those western companies could imagine a space for queer performance, with some, like Sheplers and Wrangler, refusing to sponsor the circuit. IGRA's willingness to denounce radical LGBTQ+ political groups and promote neoliberal tactics of market-based politics demonstrated its inability to fully speak to either side of a divided political spectrum. Instead, it chose to form a new and often precarious queer country-western community.

Oral History Vignette
LAURA, CHAMPION COWGIRL

I lived in Kingsville until I was about sixteen. Since I was probably twenty years old, I've been in San Antonio. I had to ride my bike about fifteen or twenty miles to my horse, and I rode my horse just about every day as a teenager. I had a miniature horse, and I outgrew it. My sister's horse was crazy, so I'd sneak in and ride it. I got caught on the crazy horse and got in trouble, but that's okay. They realized I could really ride, and I just kind of inherited horses. We didn't have much money, so I couldn't afford to go and buy a good horse. I just got what was given to me.

I quit riding because, when I moved out, I was going to high school and trying to have my own apartment. Trying to survive as a sixteen-year-old kid on your own isn't real easy. I couldn't afford a horse or anything, so I got out of it for years. Until I guess I was twenty-one, when I walked into a bar and they were talking about it.

There was a bar called OP's, Our Place, and the owner used to be a horse person. We had a lot of fun. When I first got started, they wanted me to run for Ms. TGRA. That's when the AIDS epidemic was coming out. Everybody was scared to death, and we couldn't get money.

I didn't want to be Ms. TGRA, because there was just so much work. I mean, you had to go to fundraisers every weekend, and I was trying to make a living, I was just trying to survive. Then my friends started dying, and I changed my mind. I said, "What do I do?" So I ran the first year that TGRA was formed. I ran and won Ms. TGRA. And I wasn't doing it for the fame. I was doing it to raise money to find a cure for AIDS.

I did everything at the rodeo. I did barrels, poles, break-away, team roping, wild drag, steer decorating, goat decorating. The only thing I did not do were the bareback horses and bulls. I didn't always ride steers. When I went out of state and needed money—because back then we didn't have the money we have nowadays, and you get there and pray to God you would win to get gas money to go home—so if I needed it and I didn't feel like I was going to do good, then I'd ride steers. But luckily I only had to do it a couple of times.

There was quite a few women, and what's funny is a lot of those women competing back then are still in there competing. We are old and crippled and need a ladder to get on a horse, but by God, they are still doing it, and I'm proud of them. A lot of times, I was traveling by myself, but sometimes with friends. It was whoever I could grab in the truck to go with me. My wife, poor thing, she's a city girl. She didn't realize what she was getting into. They were warned or they said, "Don't get with her, she's a cowgirl." She's always with me. Now we can hit the rodeos we want to go to.

It's been a rough thirty-three years. Trust me. I just wish we knew of a way to get the kids involved to build this organization up. A lot of people, we are getting old. Of course, when the young whippersnappers come in and beat them, we're mad, because they came in and beat them. But on the other hand, you're glad, because you're getting fresh people in here. And we're actually getting straight people; they are starting to come and ride in rodeos. We need the young kids to come in and fight the good battle, and they need to remember why we're doing this. It's for a good cause, and not all our money goes to AIDS anymore. A lot of it goes to all kinds of different things—human health services, cancer places, and homeless shelters.

Chapter 6

"FOR ALL GAY PEOPLE"

Outreach, Acceptance, and the Boundaries of Inclusion

"You don't have to be gay to compete, you just have to be of legal age," proclaimed the International Gay Rodeo Association in 2022.¹ Openness like this was nothing new for IGRA. From its inception, gay rodeo framed itself differently than other western rodeos. Rather than promoting a single vision of the American West or being designed for just one group of people, gay rodeo positioned itself as an inclusive organization. In the early days of the Reno rodeos, Phil Ragsdale explained that he wanted his events to be a place "for ALL GAY PEOPLE."² Ragsdale fought for women and drag events in the 1970s and '80s, and IGRA and its member associations continued his approach. Upon its formation in 1990, the Southeast Gay Rodeo Association (SEGRA), based in Georgia, designed an organizational statement similar to Ragsdale's stance, saying that the group was for "the entire Community barring all prejudice."³ This message became more expansive as IGRA moved into the twenty-first century and adopted a policy of "total nondiscrimination" and opened gay rodeo to people outside of a queer identity.⁴ However, while the circuit pursued an inclusive approach and crafted welcoming statements, its membership rarely reflected the wider diversity it supported.

The statements from SEGRA in 1990 and IGRA in 2022 were comprehensive in their intent, but they also were vague in who actually would be welcomed at gay rodeo. The participants and leadership have had different understandings over the years of what nondiscrimination meant and who should be included. Some based this on sexuality, much like IGRA's statement that participants did not have to be gay to be involved. For others, it is more about the diversity of sexualities along the LGBTQ+ spectrum. The Colorado association's newsletter said in 2013 that it was a rodeo family, regardless of who you were—"a Gay Man or a Lesbian, a Bi-Sexual or Trans-Gender or just Questioning yourself."[5] This proved attractive to many participants. Tamara Marks was a member of the Michigan and Heartland associations in the 1990s and 2000s. As an urban transplant, she found that gay rodeo fulfilled her longing for the country, but IGRA appealed to her also because it was one of the rare organizations in the queer community where she saw gay, straight, bisexual, and trans people come together.[6]

Sometimes the emphasis on gay rodeo's inclusivity highlighted the equal participation opportunities it offered women. Other times the focus was race, such as when an IGRA promotional flyer from the late 1990s described the organization as "without regard to race, ethnic group or sexual orientation."[7] More infrequently, this inclusion extended across the political aisle. For instance, Colorado pointedly said that the group welcomed both Democrats and Republicans. Even though the LGBTQ+ movement has most frequently identified with urban, left-leaning politics, gay rodeo also attracted a more rural and sometimes more conservative group of queer people, and the Colorado association wanted to demonstrate that gay rodeo did not care about a participant's political leanings.[8] As these varied statements suggest, each member association carefully crafted its own definition about what inclusion within IGRA would look like.

Yet an undercurrent in all of these perspectives around inclusion was the desire to expand IGRA and the country-western lifestyle. Kathy Ward, president of the Heartland association, explained that gay rodeo was special because of the "acceptance for who you are... newby, expert, questioning, straight... everyone is family."[9] As discussed in previous chapters, gay rodeo worked diligently to attract people unfamiliar with rodeo through its schools, training programs, and outreach events. However, in its celebration of the masculine cowboy, IGRA often failed to fully welcome all LGBTQ+ subcultures equally into the organization. Gay rodeo has maintained a wary relationship with effeminate gay men, the Imperial Court System, and the drag scene. In contrast, associations regularly held joint events with more masculine gay groups, such as bears and leathermen. For those who have not aligned with the white, normative gender binary, such as people of color and transgender contestants, gay rodeo has either been ineffective in adopting more inclusive practices or established problematic policies that created more harm than supportive inclusion. Specifically, gay rodeo has done little to purposefully expand its primarily white racial base, and, while it has tried to develop policies that address the evolving needs of transgender members, these conversations sometimes endorsed problematic views of trans people in sport and have led to the adoption of harmful practices. Gay rodeo has had a similarly tense relationship with female competitors, and the low number of lesbian participants fails to correlate with the position of gender equality that IGRA so proudly proclaims. In contrast, straight competitors have found a friendlier environment in gay rodeo than many of these other queer subgroups.

This chapter examines the boundaries of gay rodeo, who is allowed admission but not always welcomed, and the tensions the circuit has faced over the years as it has tried to follow its policy of inclusion but struggled to meet its ideals. Chapter 2 discussed these questions as connected to gender presentation and the desire that many gay men had to exert and prove their masculinity. Chapter 4 explained the impact that this desire had on non-normative events at gay rodeo, such as camp events and royalty contests. This chapter continues these discussions and reveals other groups that have been either welcomed in or excluded from gay rodeo. Gay subcultures of bears and leathermen who embraced forms of traditional masculinity contributed to the pursuit of "authentic" rodeo and so were approved and even pursued by gay rodeoers. The arrival of straight contestants similarly demonstrated that gay rodeo had adequately modeled itself on other western rodeos and lent an air of authenticity to its scene. In contrast, transgender people, nonwhite contestants, and lesbians contradicted normative assumptions about the rodeo and undermined efforts to create a serious, professional circuit. Gay rodeo permitted groups like these to participate but rarely made concerted efforts to attract them as new members. These unequal efforts point to the tensions that lie at the core of gay rodeo. Despite its inclusive stance and its desire to create a safe space for all queer people in a world that often refused to accept them, its need to adopt certain aspects of the traditional western rodeo ideal has meant that the gay rodeo arena has unintentionally created barriers that limit rather than support its efforts of "total non-discrimination."

EMBRACING INCLUSION AT GAY RODEO: PARTNERING WITH STRAIGHT RIDERS, LEATHERMEN, AND BEARS

Straight riders, leathermen, and bears all potentially could have had problematic relationships with gay rodeo and did not necessarily align with its charitable mission and desire to spread the country-western lifestyle. In spite of this, each of these groups has lent legitimacy to gay rodeo and so were welcomed. The inclusion of straight participants attested to the mainstream acceptance of LGBTQ+ people. More importantly, it validated the work gay rodeo had done to create a competitive arena that was taken seriously by the nonqueer rodeo world. Leathermen and bears, with their adoption of the hegemonic masculine ideal, supported the serious rodeo environment that gay riders wanted to achieve.

While gay rodeo has had a close but sometimes uncomfortable relationship with the drag community and its Imperial Court and royalty contests, as well as with clone culture and circuit boys on the party scene, it found closer partners in the more masculine bear and leather groups. Identified as husky, hairy, and "authentically" masculine, bears often sported beards and comfortable jeans that reflected a supposedly more natural masculinity with rural, working-class roots. In contrast, leathermen adopted an exaggerated hypermasculinity through black leather clothing and sexual bondage play.[10] Though all different from each other, the three gay subcultures of bears, leathermen, and cowboys similarly desired a masculine appearance, and gay cowboys were the perfect amalgamation of both bears (in their daytime, casual Wranglers) and leathermen (in boots, hats, and chaps for competitions). Working closely with these macho-styled groups supported gay rodeo's interest in expanding a country-western lifestyle rooted in hegemonic forms of masculinity and in cultivating a rodeo scene modeled on the professional circuit.

A number of IGRA associations worked closely with bear groups in their regions (see figure 23). Some sponsored bear nights, while others held joint fundraisers with local bear groups.[11] Diamond State, out of Arkansas, provided members with an expansive slate of monthly offerings, including a bear night, a Levi's/leather night, and even a women's night, at the clubhouse. More than simply trying to attract these groups to be members, the association was actively supported by each through their fundraising for the annual Little Rock rodeo. In 2002, the DSRA newsletter noted that this diversity was the association's strength, saying it was "so glad to see other aspects of our community coming together with us for our project. The leather men, the bears, the women's groups, [everyone] is stepping up to the plate and chipping in their part for the DSRA and our community."[12]

Despite an interest in reaching out to bear groups, not all associations were successful in their attempts to form these relationships. Atlantic States offered a regular trail ride for the Chesapeake Bears but struggled with attendance by its own members. When one ride attracted seventeen bears but only three ASGRA members, the association newsletter urged its members to improve their attendance.[13] Gay rodeoers may have extended a welcome mat to groups like bears, who aligned with their traditional understanding of masculine appearance, but the entire membership did not always pursue their participation actively. The involvement of groups like bears contributed to the authenticity of gay rodeo as a masculine, authentically rural realm, but the macho image of competitors was not contingent on them.

Local associations reached out to leather groups less frequently than they did to bears, but a closer—and more complicated—relationship existed between gay rodeo and the leather community. Leather bars and fetish stores advertised in rodeo programs (see figure 24), and spectators often donned leather. But sometimes the masculinity of leathermen was too performative and the sexuality too far in the fetish world for the authenticity and acceptance that many gay rodeoers craved.

Members of these two communities overlapped at gay rodeos: leathermen sat in the stands, and leather bars advertised to the cowboy competitors as potential customers. Leather groups also reached out to cowboys in other ways. For instance, both they and motorcycle clubs in the mid-Atlantic region, from Maryland to New Jersey, regularly held cowboy-leather contests in the early 1990s. Leather bars hosted Mr. Tri-State Cowboy, Mr. Baltimore Cowboy, Mr. DC

FIGURE 23. *IGRA Finals Rodeo Program, ad for The Buffalo, 1988. The Buffalo promoted itself as a "Levi-Leather" bar, but its imagery was mostly bear, showing the model's hairy face, arms, chest, and stomach. Courtesy of the Autry Museum of the American West.*

Cowboy, and Mr. Remington competitions, and gay rodeoers flocked to these events. To illustrate this, the 1992 reigning Mr. Remington was an Atlantic States member, as were the newly crowned titleholder and runner-up. These were not leather contests in disguise but truly meant to incorporate the cowboy look into the leather community,

FIGURE 24. *IGRA Finals Rodeo Program, ad for The Bum Steer, 1990. Unlike the hairy, cuddly bear at bars like The Buffalo, this bar promised gay rodeoers muscles, leather, and harnesses. Courtesy of the Autry Museum of the American West.*

with judging categories like formal wear, Wrangler wear, and "waterin' hole" attire. In this way, leathermen helped bolster the image and viability of gay rodeo and cowboy culture in an area of the country with limited ties to rodeo and ranching culture. ASGRA understood the importance of these cross-community endeavors and saw these contests as a way to grow the organization, meet more local cowboys, and work together with "our friends from the leather community."[14]

Other, more traditionally leather-only contests also sometimes extended opportunities to cowboy groups, though not always with harmonious results. The American Brotherhood contest in Boston was established to unite leather communities, and in 1993, its awards expanded to include an "American Cowboy" title. Gay rodeoers viewed the winner that first year as more of a cowboy clone or "wannabe cowboy," because he did not come from the rodeo world. In contrast, they celebrated the following year, when a cowboy who competed in gay and straight rodeos took the title.[15] Conflicting views over authenticity, like these, demonstrate the tension that could exist even between masculine gay groups like cowboys and leathermen.

Gay rodeoers often saw themselves as aligned with leathermen, and many appreciated similar black leather dress and sexual fetish wear. Yet while the leathermen are a masculine community and have had a clear presence at gay rodeos, they were not seen as legitimate or authentic cowboys. Because of this, rodeoers sometimes questioned the connection between the two communities. When IGRA sent materials to the Leather Archives & Museum, some association board members pushed back. One said it was "rather peculiar that we would think about a membership with such an organization with their focus."[16] The owner of leather bar The Cuff in Seattle also pointed to the sometimes-strained relationship between the cowboy and leather groups, saying Seattle was the "only city where the brown [cowboy leather] and black leather communities are working together, and supporting each other." With this, he bestowed the Leather Emerald Award on the Northwest Gay Rodeo Association for its close engagement with the leather world and the work that both groups did for the wider community.[17] Gay rodeoers routinely pursued relationships with other masculine-appearing gay groups that contributed to their goals. However, when those groups conflicted with these goals, such as the non-normative sexual presentation of leathermen, gay rodeoers have challenged the value of these partnerships. Gay rodeo's inclusion of straight contestants has been less fraught, as they more directly lent to its authenticity.

Rodeo programs, newsletters, and other ephemera are important reminders of the discrimination, retaliation, and violence that many queer people faced in their daily lives. With the very real fears that

LGBTQ+ people have had over their reception in the rodeo world and the communities in which their events are held, and in light of the lengths IGRA has gone to protect its members from the mainstream media, gay rodeo's inclusion of straight contestants and audience members can seem startling. Despite the concern that some members had about their visibility in straight society, gay rodeo's emphasis on openness and inclusivity made it difficult to deny access to anyone, even straight people. Further, by modeling itself on professional rodeo and given its desire to be recognized as a serious circuit with real cowboy (and cowgirl) contestants, attracting straight participants became an important marker of authenticity and acceptance.

Phil Ragsdale never specifically tried to appeal to a straight audience, but it arrived nonetheless. In 1981, the sixth year of the Reno rodeo, Ragsdale told reporters there were more straight attendees than ever before.[18] But as the AIDS crisis deepened and community-rodeo relationships became more fraught, there was little mention of straight enthusiasts in other news articles from the 1980s and early '90s. By the 2000s, however, gay rodeo's appeal to the straight community increased, and news articles and internal IGRA documents more frequently mentioned not only straight fans but also stock contractors and competitors.[19]

Some associations purposefully tried to include straight people, either to change the views they had of LGBTQ+ people or to expand gay rodeo's membership. The Sooner State Rodeo Association, one of the groups that eschewed the term "gay" in its name, described itself as a "Gay, Lesbian, Bi, Transgender, and Straight Not-For-Profit Organization dedicated to [performing] charitable duties for the surrounding area through fundraisers, horse shows, and rodeo performances."[20] The Michigan group similarly characterized its purpose as bringing together "men and women, straight and gay, who have come together to promote the sport of Rodeo and to be active members of both of our communities—gay and straight."[21] By 2014, straight people made up 18.5 percent of the Colorado association's membership and 39 percent of the most recent members. They also became active participants: IGRA estimated that 10 percent of the ninety-three competitors at the 2015 Denver rodeo were straight. In light of statistics like this, the CGRA president questioned "the whole 'Gay' tag." While many in the group were gay and proud of that identity, he wondered if removing "gay" from the association's name would "[encourage] others to join with the teachings of the Western Lifestyle and the sport of Gay Rodeo."²²

However, attempts to increase straight inclusion were not always embraced. When the Los Angeles Central chapter of GSGRA dissolved in 1995, GSGRA sent chapter members a notice asking them to still stay involved and support "the sport of Rodeo *For* the Gay Community and *In* the Gay Community."²³ While probably intended to be a statement demonstrating support for LGBTQ+ groups and activities, it was noticeably more queer-focused than the Sooner State, Michigan, and Colorado associations, all of which intentionally broadened their scope beyond the LGBTQ+ community. Even when they participated, some straight contestants questioned how welcome they really were. One straight contestant wrote IGRA in 1996 when her barrel racing belt buckle was stolen during an awards ceremony. "I don't know if they took the buckle because I'm straight and they didn't like me, but since there seems to be a lot of mixed feelings about who I am and me running with this association, I just don't know anymore."²⁴ She regularly won events and wondered if this had led to resentment. Gay rodeoer Candy Pratt acknowledged this to be a concern that she had of straight participants. She said, "I agree with the participation if they are there to support the associations and events and not to just take prize money."²⁵ Pratt approved of straight riders, but only if they understood IGRA, followed its mission, and supported its queer members.

Despite the concerns that some queer cowfolx had about straight involvement, IGRA representatives repeatedly reiterated its acceptance of straight competitors at gay rodeos, and straight contestants reported a similar reception. One Colorado member wrote a long column in the association newsletter in 1983 to express her thanks to gay rodeo, which had become a home for her during a difficult time. She said the people in CGRA "were truly my FRIENDS—with everything precious that word implies. You truly liked me, truly cared about my happiness.... You didn't love me in spite of the fact that I'm straight, and I didn't love you in spite of the fact that you're gay.... You make me so very proud that you have chosen to allow me to share in your lives."²⁶ Unlike fears that some straight contestants may just have used gay rodeo for its prizes, this CGRA member demonstrated that straight people could fully integrate into the associations, and they were welcomed when they did so.

Straight participants and audience members became involved in gay rodeo for various reasons. Many valued its openness, friendliness, and family feel. Some thought it was more organized and more professional than other western rodeos. In fact, some straight competitors saw it as no different than other rodeos. They were drawn to it despite it being gay; it was just one more place to compete and to win. In contrast, other straight participants, especially women, came to gay rodeo precisely because it was different than other rodeos; it was more welcoming of female participants and allowed for more equal involvement by women.

Many of the straight competitors, volunteers, and spectators participated in gay rodeo in the past, and continue to do so today, for reasons similar to those of queer cowfolx: they found it to be a safer, more welcoming, and more caring place. Some even competed with their entire family on the gay circuit, as one man has done with his wife, mother, brother, and sister-in-law. According to his roping partner, who is gay, "They have a blast. They like it better than other rodeos because we are a family."[27] As longtime IGRA participant Bruce Roby explained, "It only takes a short time for [straight people] to be comfortable and claim us all as their family too."[28] This close relationship developed in gay rodeo because of the care that participants directed toward each other. Gay rider David Hallwood described an incident at the Kansas City rodeo in which a straight bronc rider was knocked unconscious during the event. He awoke to a group of people who had surrounded him, blocking him off from the audience, while medical attendants examined him. Later, at the hospital, he was shocked when members of the Missouri association came to visit him.[29] The care and attention he received, even as a new IGRA member, differed dramatically from what he had experienced at (straight) western rodeos.

Another aspect of the gay rodeo that has been appealing to straight participants is their playfulness. Todd Garrett, who established the Florida association, said he found straight participants in the most surprising places: "It takes a special, open-minded straight person to be able to participate in a gay rodeo, but they usually end up being the drag in wild drag, and they love it."[30] This permission to find joy in such events is remarkable and has been true not just for competitors. Gay rodeoers have observed that spectators also routinely note the fun they have at gay rodeos and the welcome they experience there.

Said one participant, "Over the years, I've had a diverse collection of people in the audience remark to me that they feel much more comfortable at gay rodeos."[31]

This ability to welcome straight participants and audience members has also translated to the organization's work with the community of rodeo producers. Gay rodeo has always relied on straight stock contractors, producers, and arena owners to stage its events. These workers have sometimes been hesitant to associate with gay rodeo, but, for those willing to overcome the antigay prejudice within the straight rodeo world, long-term, positive relationships often developed. For instance, the stock contractor for Texas gay rodeos in the 1990s explained that he preferred the gay circuit because it had less fighting, was better organized, and had more volunteers than other western rodeos.[32] Carl and Michelle, owners of Classic Rodeo Productions in Pennsylvania even wrote a thank-you note to ASGRA for letting them be part of its 2002 event.[33] This was a far cry from the stock contractors who refused to work with Phil Ragsdale in the 1970s, when he eventually was forced to purchase his own animals for the first Reno rodeo, or the TGRA members who felt compelled to note in their 1984 newsletter that they were "fortunate to have an arena in which to stage [our] rodeo that is owned by a fair, non-prejudiced person."[34] By the 1990s, associations instead began to field interest requests from production companies, rather than having to hide their identity or feel lucky to find the rare "non-prejudiced person."[35] As American society increasingly accepted queer people in the late twentieth and early twenty-first centuries, gay rodeo has become a respected enterprise in the small and often insular rodeo community.

Just as rodeo workers and stock contractors sometimes were attracted to gay rodeo because they saw a difference—and an improvement—between it and its straight counterpart, straight women have been similarly drawn to it because it promises a different kind of environment. An IGRA member explained that at gay rodeo, "girls get to compete at some of the same stuff guys get to compete in: steer riding, bull riding, chute dogging. You don't ever see a girl throwing down a steer [in straight rodeo]. You don't see it. But in our rodeo, whatever the guys do, the girls can do it. Have at it, if you want. If you're game to do it, then do it."[36] Women in roughstock events, in particular, have found gay rodeo to be more welcoming of their participation. When several straight women competed in the 2010s in bull riding at a Texas rodeo, they contrasted the opposition they faced from straight cowboys with the opportunities and support they experienced in gay rodeo.[37] Lisa LeAnn Dalton and Elodie Huttner shared similar stories about their experiences as bronc riders in the 2000s. Though straight, they turned to gay rodeo for opportunities they were denied at other events. Huttner, for instance, had been told that bronc riding was for men and that she should barrel race instead.[38] She was able to escape these gender stereotypes and the limitations of mainstream rodeo by coming to gay rodeo, where events are open to all participants: women can participate in bull and bronc riding, while men can compete in barrel racing, sometimes outnumbering women. Thus, it was at the gay rodeo that, even as a straight woman, Huttner found an environment where she was not just permitted to compete but was cheered on and encouraged.

Even though many straight contestants and spectators have been drawn to gay rodeo because it is different, some straight contestants saw it as just another rodeo. For them, queerness has become so mainstream that an IGRA contest functions like any other western rodeo, and they, like some of the queer participants, compete in gay and straight events alike.[39] Bruce Roby explained this mainstream success: "We [LGBTQ+ people] got the acceptance we've been dying for. When you go out to the arena, there are straight people competing with us and bragging to their friend that they're competing in the gay rodeo and having a ball."[40] This is a world apart from the early gay rodeos, at the far fringes of the rodeo world, that warned straight people they would see same-sex affection if they entered the arena. The participation of straight contestants, especially those who also compete on the mainstream circuit, demonstrates gay rodeo's commitment to creating a serious, professional-styled event—and its success in doing so.

Leathermen, bears, and straight participants all invoke forms of hegemonic masculinity and the dominant gender presentations that many gay rodeoers wanted to exhibit themselves. These groups help fulfill IGRA's purpose. Accordingly, they have had the greatest amount of entrée into gay rodeo and been the recipients of the most outreach efforts. Other groups, however, threaten, rather than support, gay rodeo's mission of societal acceptance. Transgender contestants, people of color, and lesbians have found a less welcoming community in gay rodeo and rarely have been appealed to as potential members.

THE THREAT OF NONCONFORMITY AND THE BOUNDARIES OF INCLUSION

Transgender members, nonwhite competitors, and lesbian riders have had complicated relationships with gay rodeo. All three are covered in IGRA's mission of inclusion, and each group has sometimes been identified specifically as being valuable to the organization. However, the low number of participants belies the official stance of gay rodeo. Though not excluded from membership, the involvement of trans, POC, and lesbian competitors does little to support gay rodeo's goal of mainstream acceptance and gender normative presentation. Consequently, it has made limited efforts to purposefully target these groups as potential members or to fully make them at home when they do join.

Gay rodeo included camp contests and the idea of gender play from its start in the 1970s, but identity was always constructed on the binary of men and women. While all events were open to men and women, they competed separately with some variation in rules, such as women being permitted to use two hands in steer riding. Most team events, like roping and steer decorating, made no mention of gender, but others had strict requirements. As described in chapter 4, the three-person teams for wild drag race included one female-identified member dressed as a woman, one man dressed as a man, and a "drag" role that could be male or female but required a dress and wig.[41]

As trans voices and calls for rights increased, IGRA began to adjust its policies in the early twenty-first century. In 2000, the group passed a rule book policy regarding a change in gender identification. IGRA also created a sensitivity and gender issues committee, which saw significant participation at the annual convention that year. The committee discussed bathroom issues, job security, and personal safety for trans people. Because (according to ASGRA itself) Atlantic States was "at the forefront of educating the masses on transgender issues," the committee also invited a speaker from that association to "educate the cowboys and cowgirls on diversity and sensitivity." In a report to ASGRA membership about the meeting, the representative said that, based on the high turnout, IGRA clearly needed the conversation. The speaker hoped for even more interest in the future, saying, "Next year, perhaps we will have all nineteen [associations present]."[42] However, this interest failed to appear, and attendance instead dropped significantly, from eighteen to nine people.[43]

The conversation also took a more conservative turn in 2001. Committee members raised concerns that some people changed (or potentially could change) their identity every year and that "a few people are using the rule to allow for unfair competition, allowing more ability to 'win' as something else."[44] This mirrored the larger debate surrounding trans identity and rights in the sporting community, which has couched discriminatory practices under the guise of fairness.[45] Further, it demonstrates IGRA's commitment to a binary understanding of gender, in which male-identified participants compete in only men's events while female-identified participants compete only in women's events. In fact, some of these debates emerged when a cisgender female contestant wanted to compete in men's events, which she viewed as being more competitive and more lucrative.[46] IGRA's refusal to permit this, even under threat of legal action, reveals the discomfort that the association's leadership had in adjusting its traditional definitions of gender and identity, and what it perceived to be competitive fairness.

Despite the problematic practices that emerged, IGRA also developed policies to protect and supports its trans members. In the midst of its discussion about unfair competition, the sensitivity and gender issues committee acknowledged the difficulty of changing legal gender documentation and that doing so could put trans people in dangerous situations. Similarly, the health and safety committee asked the organization to be sensitive to the privacy needs of trans people. Following reports that several transgender contestants experienced identity-based discrimination at hospitals, the committee recommended that a support person accompany a trans person to the hospital if they were injured at a rodeo. In 2003, IGRA added a statement to the finals rodeo program that publicly clarified its position on gender identification: "any individual member . . . is eligible to participate fully in IGRA activities under the gender classification with which the individual member identifies."[47] The work done by IGRA has made space for trans contestants in its rodeo events and royalty competition, as discussed in chapter 4, and it has helped trans members feel welcome. Desirey Benavides expressed this sentiment, saying that no one questioned her when she transitioned and began to compete as a woman. As she explained, "it was never an issue . . . my rodeo experience has always been really good."[48]

While IGRA has devoted time to discussing the inclusion and safety of trans contestants and debating the fairness of competition rules for transgender members, the organization has spent much less time looking at issues of race. Not surprisingly, gay rodeo—much like other western rodeos—has remained mostly white. In 1987, an IGRA-wide association poll netted 108 responses, which revealed that 87 percent of respondents were white. Only 13 percent were Black, Native American, or Hispanic, along with a few who did not identify.[49] Neither IGRA nor individual associations routinely tracked their racial makeup, but members acknowledged the whiteness of the organization. Newsletters and programs made few references to racial diversity, and there was an assumed whiteness that appeared in almost all gay rodeo marketing efforts. IGRA's systematic failure to track race, the assumed whiteness of its public-facing and members-only materials, and the widespread silence on the circuit's racial inequities speaks volumes about the interests of gay rodeo.

This problem of whiteness is not just one of gay rodeo. It is endemic in much of LGBTQ+ organizing in the United States. Scholar Allan Bérubé has noted that racial categories are constructed, even without intentionality, and that this "making of whiteness" within the queer movement has important implications for how its agenda is shaped and who reaps the benefits from a queer identity. Bérubé explains that the gay rights movement has presented itself and its interests as color-blind and gender-neutral, but the reality is that it has been very white and very male. This impacts the issues on the gay rights agenda versus "supposedly nongay issues, such as homelessness, unemployment, welfare, universal health care, union organizing, affirmative action, and abortion rights."[50] Yet these very issues intimately affect many lesbians, trans people, and gay men of color. Thus, while the gay rights movement presented itself as inclusive and working toward more rights for all queer people, it has been deeply exclusionary in its organizing principles.[51]

Gay rodeo has faced a similar problem. As it pushed for what Bérubé calls the "positive image" of the gay person, it often emphasized "traditional values" in exchange for credibility and more rights for its members. This image was generally a white, middle-class, cisgender man.[52] Gay rodeoers pursued this same model of normativity and conformity. In chasing their desire for a serious, professional-style rodeo—one rooted in hegemonic, white masculinity—they unintentionally created an environment that has not welcomed nonwhite members in a manner that aligns with their organizations' inclusive mission statements.

Generally, the racial makeup of local gay rodeo associations has reflected the demographics of that region. For instance, Colorado and Texas historically had higher rates of Hispanic participation, while Michigan, with its home base in Detroit, had more Black representation on its board and royalty team than did most other associations.[53] Similarly, the Bay Area's chapter reflected the greater diversity of San Francisco, in contrast to the Sacramento chapter, where there was much less. Joe Rodriguez, a member of the Bay Area group, explained that his chapter proudly promoted its diversity, which points to its relative rarity in gay rodeo.[54] Bruce Gros, a former president of IGRA (2014–18), recognized some of these regional differences, saying:

> In our experience, I think, in IGRA, it's always been predominantly white. In the South, I don't think any of our organizations have had a lot of African American or non-Caucasian members. I think ... the Southwest is the one area where you'll see a little bit more Indigenous people participating. Rodeo is strong already there. What surprises me is [that] as strong as rodeo is in the Hispanic community, we have very little direct connection to them. We do it differently, but unless it's focused on or factored on the machismo, you know, the whole idea that men can't be gay ... culturally we haven't bridged that yet. I don't know what that it is just yet. I just note the fact, note the absence.[55]

Although the racial makeup of local associations often mirrored regional demographics, Gros noted some key exceptions to this alignment. The American South has a substantial Black population, lays claim to a notable Black ranching and rodeoing tradition, and is home to several Black rodeo circuits.[56] But despite these demographics and this history, gay rodeo has failed to attract Black riders to its organizations in the South.

Although Gros only identifies IGRA's failure to attract Black members in the South, there is a larger whitewashing of rodeo culture in gay rodeo's public image. Previous chapters discuss how this happened across the American West and at western rodeos. As women and people of color, especially African Americans, were written out of Americans' memories of the West, separate rodeos formed to offer these men and women competitive opportunities. Perhaps more importantly, however, these rodeos—such as the Black circuits, Native American rodeos, and the *charreada*—created their own supportive cultural communities. At times, gay rodeo programs demonstrated that these communities could overlap. For instance, the 1991 Los Angeles rodeo program included a full-page image of a Black cowboy in an ad for *BLK* magazine, which also said, "Where the news is colored on purpose. And that's no bull." *BLK* magazine focused more broadly on Black life and stories, but, for the gay rodeo program, it used western imagery and encouraged readers to "keep up with black lesbians and gay men across the range," hinting that there were more stories to tell about Black queer cowfolx.[57] Yet this promise went unfulfilled, not because of a failure on the part of rodeoers of color, but because gay rodeo did little to actively encourage nonwhite participation.

Despite noting an organizational failure to attract Black and Hispanic participants, Gros believed there was more racial diversity and progress in the Southwest regarding inclusivity toward Indigenous communities. In reality, this was rarely reflected in the rodeo programs or participants themselves. It was in the earliest years of gay rodeo, not in the 2010s (when Gros was president), that there was the most purposeful inclusion of Indigenous peoples. A large ad for the Nevada Indian Rodeo Association's upcoming "All Indian" rodeo appeared in the 1980 Reno program. Several years later, in 1984, the Reno program said that the Comstock association was "honored to have the Gay Indians of America participating once again this year, with their Indian Dancing, for your enjoyment," and a booth with "authentic" art.[58] These examples, albeit infrequent, still outnumbered those of the following decades, when IGRA leadership thought that successful inroads had been made with gay Native American rodeoers.

In some of the Southwestern states that are home to significant Native ranching and rodeo histories, such as Oklahoma and Arizona, there has been little acknowledgement of these communities by gay rodeo. One of the few exceptions to this was at the 2003 finals, held in Tulsa, Oklahoma. That rodeo included a powwow, and the Oklahoma Gay Rodeo Association invited a local Native American Two-Spirit organization to participate in the opening ceremonies.[59] In contrast, the Tucson and Phoenix programs from the 1980s, 1990s, and 2000s included no explicit mention of Indigenous participation and failed to attract any advertisements from Indigenous rodeo communities, despite the state being home to some of the largest and oldest Native American rodeo associations.[60]

Even with these silences, gay rodeo in the Southwest has managed to attract some Native participants who feel like they have a home in IGRA. Greg Begay, who is Navajo, moves between his identities and communities by competing on both the gay and Indigenous circuits—as he says, "just everywhere where horses take me."[61] Though he feels welcome in both arenas, each offers him something different.

This notion of gay rodeo fulfilling the desire for LGBTQ+ people for a queer community but often failing to create a home for nonwhite queer cowfolx lies at the heart of its race problem. An IGRA promotional flyer from the late 1990s described the organization as "without regard to race, ethnic group or sexual orientation," but as white and nonwhite participants alike have noted, it rarely made an effort to promote itself to communities of color. The Colorado association invited a "Ballet Mexicano" group to perform at one of its fundraisers in 1987 and promised to include them at future events, though they are not mentioned again. A couple of associations sometimes hosted Latin dance or movie nights, but it is unclear if these were meant to target Hispanic group members or just entertain white ones, much like the "Indian Dancing" at the 1984 Reno rodeo.[62] This small number of events across four decades speaks to the larger problem of diversity and inclusion in gay rodeo.

IGRA membership has dropped dramatically since the 1990s, while the American population has become more racially diverse. In the 2010s, John King, a founding member of IGRA and owner of Charlie's bar in Denver, identified this lack of outreach as a concern. As a white, gay business owner, he believed that the organization must be able to reach out to different communities, noting, for instance, the recent growth in the Colorado group among young Hispanic men. King acknowledged that the association had done little to include them in a meaningful way, explaining that "the problem is that nobody on the gay rodeo circuit is thinking about adjusting any of their rules in order to really incorporate them. They're only thinking in terms of: 'You're welcome—by the way, here are the rules,' and stamp[ing] the rules on you."[63] The organization allows anyone to participate, but it has done little to make them want to participate, thus limiting the effectiveness of IGRA's nondiscrimination policy.

This tacit inclusion that is in name only is readily apparent with regard to the Hispanic community. Given its deep roots in ranching in the Southwest and competitive *charreada* groups from California to Illinois, the Hispanic population in the US has significant cultural connections to the cowboy and the rodeo, but this has not always translated to an involvement in gay rodeo. For instance, in a state with one of the largest Hispanic populations and several active *charreada* associations, Arizona has been home to a gay rodeo association with predominantly white leadership from 1985 to 2010. In a rare instance of racial identification, the group's newsletter in 1992 teased a white member about "that cute little Hispanic boy he was hanging with" at a recent rodeo. While intended to be just playful banter, it reveals the assumed whiteness of AGRA's membership and hints at larger racial inequalities within the association. That same year, a mostly white board of directors ran AGRA, while the Hispanic royalty team was charged with the legwork of fundraising to support the organization and its charity efforts.[64] Also in the 1990s, the Arizona rodeos, along with the one in San Diego, regularly took place at charro arenas. This initially appears to be an exciting place of cross-cultural cooperation, but it led to no deeper crossover, and gay contestants sometimes complained about using the differently shaped Mexican rodeo arena.[65] IGRA's leadership, like Bruce Gros, may have scratched their heads wondering why the Hispanic population in the Southwest had not been attracted to gay rodeo, yet these moments of cultural exclusion and microaggressions are telling.

It is clear that not all LGBTQ+ people of color with ties to the rural, ranching world have found a home in gay rodeo, but neither have they openly felt welcomed by Native rodeo circuits, Black rodeo, or *charreadas*—and so they instead created other avenues to claim a sexual and racial identity. Los Angeles and the Bay Area are home to significant Hispanic populations, and both have a growing gay vaquero scene. Los Angeles has held "vaquero nights" for Hispanic queer men since the early 1990s, while the Bay Area has hosted the Mr. Gay Vaquero contest since 2000.[66] In her study of Mexican American country music fans, Nadine Hubbs explains that country music and gay vaquero nights reinforce *mexicanidad* identity, promote cultural pride, and allow for queer connections.[67] It is the ties to home and culture that draw gay vaqueros to these primarily Hispanic queer communities rather than gay rodeo, which, given its pursuit of the white, masculine ideal, has not created a space for Hispanic people to readily celebrate their own histories and identities.[68] This mirrors the formation of gay rodeo itself. White gay men who identified with specific forms of masculinity created gay rodeo to celebrate their gayness and their masculinity. Because that space has not yet made the same kind of room for nonwhite racial identities, some queer Hispanic westerners have formed their own spaces with these vaquero nights, where they can be not just gay and masculine but also Hispanic.

Even though the whiteness of gay rodeo is problematic, current IGRA members of color routinely remark that they feel welcome there. Rick Phoummany, who is Laotian American, competes in rodeos as part of the Texas association and held the 2016 Mr. TGRA title. He concedes that gay rodeo is "predominately white" but says the "loving spirit that everyone has" makes it great.[69] Joe Rodriguez, who is of Filipino descent, explains that race does not impact his participation: "Whether straight or gay, we have the throw off the labels: 'Oh, I'm Asian and therefore I cannot be this or I cannot do that.' I don't live for labels. I don't like labels, but I recognize the heritage of my name and the color of my skin and... my ethnic background, and I acknowledge that. I just also happen to be a rodeo cowboy."[70] Raised in Hawai'i, Rodriguez connects with his heritage by competing at rodeos under the name Paniolo Joe, a reference to the Hawaiian cowboys, who are called "paniolos." Desirey Benavides does something similar in the royalty contests. She usually performs to country-western music but sometimes incorporates her Mexican heritage by using mariachi music or songs by pop star Paulina Rubio.[71] And while some Hispanic cowboys created their own queer vaquero nights as a more culturally inclusive option than gay rodeo, others managed to find a home there. Historian and gay rodeoer Nicholas Villanueva explains that, at least in Colorado, there are Hispanic gay rodeo participants who use that arena to reclaim the figure of the vaquero as the authentic cowboy and to expand his identity into one that is more sexually inclusive. For them, gay rodeo has become their "Pride" festival, rather than the official Pride events in Denver, which are predominantly white and middle-class.[72]

While gay rodeo willingly reached out to similarly masculine-styled groups, such as bears and leathermen, IGRA faced a more conflicted relationship with effeminate gay men, the court and drag scenes, and participants who did not neatly fit into the normative, white gender binary. Some people of color and trans cowfolx have found gay rodeo to be an inclusive and welcoming place, but IGRA's actual policies have not always embraced these groups without question. Similarly, IGRA has done little beyond a stated policy of inclusion to attract trans and nonwhite members. As the US becomes more diverse and as LGBTQ+ people become more vocal about the rights all community members should have, John King's advice that gay rodeo needs to make itself more appealing to diverse queer communities becomes all the more important. To reach out to people of color and transgender people, IGRA will need to break out of its established patterns of silence and no longer expect that potential members will automatically align with business as usual in the organization.

THE COMPLICATED POSITION OF LESBIANS IN GAY RODEO

Unlike trans contestants and queer cowfolx of color, who only sometimes were specifically identified in IGRA statements about inclusion, lesbians were more purposefully included from the very beginning of gay rodeo. From the beginning, all events were open to men and women, although they generally were judged separately. This was in stark contrast to most western rodeos, in which cowgirls were limited to barrel racing and breakaway roping. These often are still the only events open to women, and they usually are exclusively for female competitors at the collegiate, semiprofessional, and professional levels of competition. This creates a distinctly gender-stratified environment at most western rodeos. Gay rodeo disrupts these gender norms and queers the arena by opening all events to both men and women.

And yet, where are the lesbians of gay rodeo? Their participation numbers in royalty contestants have always paled in comparison to the Mr. and Miss categories. They have rarely appeared on association boards of directors. The calls for a muscular or scruffy masculinity have refused to accommodate women, even dyke presentations of female masculinity, and rodeo programs that focus on gay male sex have made little room for female sexuality and certainly did not make lesbian members feel welcome. The stated equality of gay rodeo clearly has not led to equal participation by men and women. This section examines how gay rodeo attempted to incorporate lesbians into its design and addresses the failures of these efforts at equal participation.[73]

The year 1993 fell in the midst of gay rodeo's expansion. It was deemed the year of "lesbian chic" as kd lang graced the cover of *New York* magazine and other lesbians received central billing in *Newsweek* and *Vanity Fair*. As literary and cultural studies scholar Anne M. Ciasullo explains, lesbians had become a pop culture phenomenon and seemed to be everywhere early in the decade.[74] However, even as they became more publicly visible and consumable in the 1990s, they still continued to experience discrimination and condemnation. When Ellen DeGeneres came out on her ABC sitcom in 1997 and again in *Time* magazine, she received public support but also swift critiques. Her show was canceled the following year, in part for including too much gay content.[75] Lesbians were celebrated—but not really—in straight society, and they encountered this same kind of double-bind in queer spaces too.

Lesbians did not experience the same welcome in queer spaces as gay men did, a decades-old problem. In the early 1960s, members of the nascent homophile organizations, such as gay men in Mattachine Society and lesbians in the Daughters of Bilitis, had different concerns and viewed each other with suspicion. Gay men believed women did not face the same levels of abuse or violence, while lesbians thought that gay men's dress, public actions, and sexual lives were problematic for the queer image.[76] While there was some lesbian involvement in the gay liberation movement in the early 1970s, gay men dominated it. That decade, lesbians formed a distinctive sensibility and culture and understood being a lesbian as conferring an identity that went beyond sexual desire. The lesbian separatist movement and articles such as "F—— You, 'Brothers'! or Yet Another Woman Leaves the Gay Liberation Movement," which appeared in lesbian publication *The Ladder*, demonstrated the growing divisions between the gay and lesbian sectors of the queer community.[77]

Some lesbians separated from gay communities, organizations, and spaces as a way to construct their own identity and create a place of power for themselves, but other times, lesbians were simply not welcomed into gay spaces. Gay rodeo was open to female competitors from the beginning, but it did little to attract women or make them feel included. Sometimes, lesbians even faced an outwardly hostile environment in the rodeo arena and its companion country-western spaces. The original intentions behind gay rodeo help to illuminate some of these tensions. While gay men in the 1970s and

'80s endeavored to create a rodeo based on patriarchal understandings of the West and hegemonic masculinity, albeit one that permitted a queer sexuality, lesbians were separating from gay alliances and establishing their own rural communities. These "back-to-the-land" lesbian farmers challenged the patriarchal, masculine ideals of the American West that the men of gay rodeo so closely embraced.[78]

The Golden State Cowboys, an early rodeo enthusiast group established in the late 1960s, did not explicitly deny membership to women, but it did not identify any female members or appear to welcome them into the organization.[79] Phil Ragsdale's Reno rodeos could have developed similarly given his intention to create a space for gay men to prove their masculinity. He tried to avoid this by offering events, such as wild cow milking, later replaced with the wild drag race, that incorporated women and camp roles. Even when some male contestants refused to work on teams with "Lesbians and Drags," Ragsdale maintained that he wanted his rodeos to be a place "for ALL GAY PEOPLE."[80] He also sometimes permitted men and women to compete directly against each other, even in roughstock events like bull riding, which a woman won at the 1982 rodeo.[81]

Despite these statements affirming the right of women to participate and the recognition of women as grand marshals, such as Reno gay bar owner Pearl Wilson in 1980 and comedian Joan Rivers in 1982, few participated in the early rodeos. The gay press emphasized the sexy male bodies on display, and photographer Ken Dickmann, who documented the Reno rodeos in the 1980s, showed an almost entirely male audience (see the images in chapter 2 and this chapter). Rodeo programs targeted this male audience with frequent male nudity and by directing attendees to "where the men are" at various local bars (see chapter 2 for more on this imagery).[82] In contrast, in the six years of Reno programs that are publicly available, there are only two ads for lesbian or women-friendly bars, and just one hints at sexual activity for women (see figure 25).[83] Women's participation in the Reno rodeos reflected the makeup of the audience and representation in the programs. The 1982 rodeo illustrates just how limited this was. That year, the newly formed Colorado association trumpeted its purported success with women by bringing six female competitors to Reno. But they formed just a third of the overall group from Colorado, and even that low number made it largest state contingent of women to that point in the rodeo's history.[84]

FIGURE 25. *National Reno Gay Rodeo Program, ad for Scissors, 1979. Advertisements for men's bars always outnumbered those for lesbians. This one for Scissors is even more unusual, because it depicts two women moving toward each other for a kiss. Unlike the gay bar ads that often used sex and nudity, those for lesbian bars rarely used sexual imagery. Courtesy of ONE Archives at the USC Libraries.*

As IGRA replaced Ragsdale's leadership, representation in rodeo programs remained almost exclusively focused on the masculine cowboy, with some regional variation. From 1982 to 1989, gay rodeos took place in Denver, Phoenix, Oklahoma City, and cities across Texas and California. Their programs depicted women to varying degrees, but all fell far behind the program ads that targeted men and largely reflected the precedent set by the Reno programs.[85] Even though women held leadership positions in both the Colorado and Arizona associations, the Denver and Phoenix rodeo programs included the least representation of women. None of the Denver programs from the 1980s featured women, and no ads were directed at them. The four Phoenix rodeo programs have just slightly better representation, with ads for two lesbian bars, which appeared in just a single year. In contrast, women held similar rates of leadership positions in the Texas and California associations, but material directed at women appeared in almost every rodeo program in those two states. The Texas programs included two to four ads for lesbian bars each year, and sometimes even the gay bars used male and female imagery to attract a broader clientele. Overall, these ads were sexually tamer than those targeting men. They never included full nudity and rarely used seminude models or sexually suggestive poses. The California program advertisements also depicted women each year and used images of cowboys and cowgirls on the program covers. However, the California ads are distinctly different from those in the Texas programs. All of the Texas ads were for lesbian bars, while the California ones rarely highlighted those establishments, even though they existed in the state. Instead, the they most frequently came from the Southern California Women for Understanding, who wanted to "eradicate negative stereotypical images of lesbians by example and through positive educational programs about our concerns, lifestyles, issues and lives."[86] Just like some gay men saw rodeo as a way to exert their masculinity and counter societal stereotypes about gay men, this organization believed rodeo could similarly help lesbians, and so it sponsored a female competitor for several years in the late 1980s. But ads targeting lesbians like this were rare.

An increase in participation by women, even at the leadership level, did not always translate to their increased representation in rodeo programs. For instance, the Great Plains rodeo in the 1980s was jointly sponsored by the Oklahoma, Kansas, and Missouri associations. The latter two groups had significant female involvement on their boards, with 50 percent women on the MGRA board and 40 percent in KGRA. Two of those years, the program covers featured an equal number of men and women, and several program ads for more broadly queer-identified businesses used images of women, rather than men, to target their customer base.[87] However, there was no notable increase in the overall number of ads that specifically targeted women, and almost no lesbian-only businesses were featured. Because there was no noticeable change in rodeo programs even when more women held leadership positions, this suggests that IGRA's gender imbalance was a larger structural issue.

Gay rodeo promoted the equal participation opportunities it afforded women, but its programs included few images that would encourage lesbians to join. They depicted masculine, sexual men. This reasserted many IGRA members' desire to exert a hegemonic masculinity. The suspicion many gay rodeoers held for femininity, whether in its male, drag, or trans participants, also extended to lesbians. An IGRA poll from 1987 revealed that 89 percent of the respondents were men versus just 7 percent women.[88] A survey taken at the IGRA finals rodeo a decade later showed improvement: 71.4 percent male and 28.6 percent female respondents.[89] Almost twenty years later, however, the ratio, at least in some associations, had stayed much the same. Colorado reported 73 percent male versus 27 percent female membership rates in 2014.[90] Rodeo participation numbers directly reflected these membership rates, with female competitors often hovering around 25 percent.[91] These trends continued into the twenty-first century, and sometimes have worsened. At the 2014 rodeo in Kansas City, the gender disparity was stark. Steer riding included no women, chute dogging had only a couple of women participants, and goat dressing had no all-women teams and only a few women partnered with men. Even events that often attract more female-identified participants failed to do so that year. Fourteen men and seven women competed in pole bending, and the ratio in barrel racing was even more dramatic: twenty-eight men versus just eight women. The closest ratio was the flag race, with fifteen men and ten women.[92]

All gay rodeo events sometimes struggled to attract women competitors, as demonstrated above, but IGRA has had a particularly hard time filling the female spots in its roughstock events. IGRA reports regularly list almost equal participation in barrel racing, pole bending, and the flag race, but far fewer women in bull riding, steer riding, and bareback bronc riding.[93] Gay rodeo's failure to attract an equal number of competitors who identify as women became a cyclical problem. If more men rode, more entry fees were paid, and therefore the payout was larger for men's events. By the late 1990s and early 2000s, this became a growing concern for gay rodeo, especially as overall participation began to decline in those same years. In 1998 the IGRA board debated what to do with the award money from the women's bull riding contest at the finals rodeo. Only one female contestant qualified that year, and she failed to complete a successful ride at the finals.[94] A couple of years later, the board again discussed the failure of not only the women's roughstock events but also the women's speed events to have enough registrants to fill all of the spots at the finals rodeo.[95] Phil Ragsdale and IGRA both loudly promoted the gender equality of gay rodeo, particularly in its roughstock events, because that equal participation made gay rodeo distinct from and, in Ragsdale's eyes, better than other rodeo circuits. Yet the advertised banner of equality has rarely been pursued and never actually achieved.

Sometimes gay rodeo and the queer country-western community have been called out for their limited depiction of female and lesbian participants. A letter to the editor in *Roundup* magazine reminded readers, "Women are a big and growing part of our C&W community and should be profiled as often as possible."[96] An even more pointed critique appeared in the IGRA inbox in 1998. Kat Bertram said, "What's up?" and asked the organization, "How come all the pictures are of men?" She recommended that IGRA should be a more "equal opportunity organization and show just that. Thank You."[97]

Though queries like this led to little change in the depiction of women in program ads, gay rodeo did make some attempts to improve its female numbers. Individual associations adopted a variety of approaches in the 1980s and '90s to drive up women's membership. They sometimes recognized that events and meetings at male gay bars failed to attract lesbian members. Regarding its regular events at a local male strip club, the Minnesota association tantalizingly asked its women members, "Ladies . . . By now you probably know about the male disrobing artists. Do you want to see women doing the same thing? Let us know!"[98] Other times, groups offered events such as women's movie nights or meet-ups at lesbian bars for its female members.[99] But often the associations simply decried the lack of women's involvement or tried to shame their members into greater levels of participation. Few of these approaches resulted in more lesbian members. For instance, one of the California chapters said it wanted to see more women turn out at the rodeo but did little to make it more attractive to them, saying, "We need volunteers like you and we guarantee you'll have a wonderful time while demonstrating that the cowgirls care as much as the cowboys."[100] The Arkansas association used an even more emphatic belittlement of its women members in a particularly misguided attempt to boost their participation. It bemoaned in a 1991 newsletter that "for the third straight year NO women would agree to run for any office. There is no excuse for an organization of over 100 members (27 of whom are women) to find itself in this position."[101] Unsurprisingly, these approaches toward outreach to women failed, often because no one tried very hard to develop an environment that was truly more welcoming to women or that listened to their voices and concerns.

ASGRA was a rare exception to this. Atlantic States was one of the few associations to take a more introspective and committed approach to the lesbian dilemma. In a 1992 newsletter, the group said to its members, "ASGRA Women . . . We Miss You!" and began to solicit advice on how to improve women's involvement. One female member invited other women to help with the newsletter, fundraising, or line dancing activities. The group also offered a special training session, taught by a female member, for women to learn some of the rodeo events. It continued these endeavors for several years, and in 1994 distributed a member survey that asked for suggestions on how to attract more women members. Disappointingly, the survey results included few actionable recommendations, as most respondents left that question blank, identified social events for men, or made no distinction between the interests of men and women, listing the same events as the questions that targeted improvements for both genders. Regardless of the limited responses, the continued efforts by ASGRA did not go unnoticed, and the organization enthusiastically remarked later that year that it had seen more participation among women.[102]

Recognizing its inability to attract women, IGRA formed a women's outreach committee in 2009, ostensibly created to improve women's participation. The board minutes reveal, however, that the organization's primary concern was the overall decline in membership.

In debating this recent drop in popularity, one board member suggested that IGRA "recruit younger participants in bars and elsewhere; increase our exposure, especially our outreach to women."[103] The group was scrambling for solutions and looked to women as a potential answer. In 2010 the women's outreach committee began to meet and set out a series of goals. They wanted to understand why women's participation was low, and they put forth several ideas to increase their involvement, such as organizing events for women and contacting lesbian organizations.[104] However, by 2012, the committee admitted they had made little progress on these goals, and no future plans were forthcoming, as only eight people attended the committee meeting the following year and the group discussed no proposals.[105]

Even when women's participation increased, not all IGRA members welcomed this change. Grounded in a binary that defined people as masculine or not, IGRA often maintained a "us versus them" mentality. At times, gay rodeo both wanted and yet seemed to fear an increase in lesbian participation. For instance, following its exhortations for women to become more involved, Diamond State began to host a popular women's film night in 1995, and the following year the association saw a dramatic flip in its board makeup. From 1991, when it had zero female candidates, the board in 1996 shifted to roughly 60 percent women.[106] However, as women's participation increased, Diamond State saw a steep decline in men's participation. The female president said, "Some of you guys have been kind of scarce as of late. I hope there are no hard feelings because of there being more women board members than ever or the overwhelming participation of the women. I personally feel it would be a shame for us to become sexist at this point when we are all [supposed] to be in this together." The female DSRA leadership had to demonstrate that they were adequately maintaining male spaces. The group hosted a monthly leather/Levi's night "to give Men and Women in the community who enjoy Leather/Levi the opportunity to socialize, make contacts, and enjoy each [other's] company." To counter any fears by male members that the female presence had grown too much, the newsletter reassured the membership that the leather/Levi's nights "will remain geared towards men," something that "will only change when and if a significant number of women show they wish to participate."[107]

In 2010, the IGRA women's outreach committee was similarly concerned about protecting the image and actions of men. The minutes stated, "Women's Outreach is meant to create a space for women and does not discount men's participation. No male bashing!"[108] Women actively created policies like this, enforcing a gendered deference that protected gay rodeo as a male space. Established on a binary, gay rodeo wanted to include women, but attempts to do so were often interpreted as potentially damaging to the traditional rodeo environment that had been created, one that served its male participants so well.

It was this issue—the fear of losing their own already limited space—that sometimes made gay men react negatively to the presence of lesbians. In an interview with gay-oriented *Instinct* magazine in 2002, lesbians noted that they rarely felt welcome in gay bars.[109] While gay rodeoers often viewed their rodeo circuit and country-western gay bars as friendlier to women, lesbians still encountered misogynistic attitudes there. In their study of a gay country-western bar, Corey W. Johnson and D. M. Samdahl describe the gay men who were the regular bar crowd as expressing dislike to intense hatred of lesbians at the bar's weekly "lesbian night." Even though male patrons claimed the bar was an inclusive community where everyone, including women, was welcome, they complained that lesbians did not know how to dance, were stingy tippers, caused more fights, and invaded men's personal space. The overwhelming consensus was that gay men saw the space as belonging to them and were unhappy when lesbians outnumbered gay men.[110]

IGRA sometimes dealt with equally combative views, as demonstrated in Diamond State when women took over leadership positions. This also was sometimes felt in the gay bars frequently used as meeting places for members. In 1986 the Colorado association received a letter from the ACLU hinting at unequal treatment of male and female members. In response, CGRA denied any prejudice or inequality but admitted that women had experienced "difficulties" at Charlie's, the host bar for the association.[111] A decade later, IGRA was forced to deal with an even more explosive complaint regarding bar behavior, and it refused to address concerns regarding the mistreatment of lesbians. A female member reported that, in a postrodeo bar celebration, someone in an IGRA leadership position had confronted her, saying, "Charlie's was his bar, that F—— Lesbians were not [welcome] and that he would have me ejected permanently." She filed a formal complaint when he also threatened to withhold IGRA information and funds from her. She was rightly concerned about these threats, the language used, the discrimination involved, and the abuse of a position of power and asked for an apology from the organization and for disciplinary action to be taken. In her complaint, she invoked IGRA's commitment to "providing a place where both men and women can compete together" and said the organization had failed to do this. The IGRA ethical practices review board barely discussed the incident, even though they seemed to accept the veracity of the accusation. The committee noted that it was an "unfortunate and unprofessional altercation" but refused to formally review it due to a technicality: the complaint had not been made on an official IGRA form. In the end, the accused man remained in his position and was only warned verbally that he was expected to act in a more professional manner.[112] IGRA and its member associations repeatedly voiced concerns that they needed to protect male members from potentially overwhelming or combative lesbians, and they did little to take action when lesbians expressed concerns regarding their own mistreatment.

Despite the struggles to systematically support female and lesbian members, gay rodeoers, both men and women, repeatedly pointed out the inclusive gender environment of the circuit in the 1980s and '90s (see figure 26). As a member of the Colorado royalty team noted in 1988, "The concept of gay men, women and drags working so closely together is foreign to [a lot] of people. We don't feel that way. The rodeo associations across this great nation of [ours have] proven the bond that we have for and from our brothers and sisters."[113] IGRA associations kidded playfully with female members, just as they did with men. The Missouri group used a clever double entendre to tease one its most active female members about her involvement in the wild cow milking contest, saying, "Through the Gay Rodeo Association, many people have had their fantasies fulfilled (many in more than one way!). One of these is our own Frances. We all know she likes to play with big teats (right B.O.?) and just last August she got more teats than she could handle." By equating milking a wild cow to "handling" her partner's breasts, MGRA leadership used its newsletter to celebrate the sexuality of its lesbian members. As MGRA noted, "Gay Rodeo is not just bulls, broncs, and horses. There is something there for everyone. Cowboys and Cowgirls, dancing, Hot Cowboys, beautiful Cowgirls, parties, Hunky Cowboys, and sinsational Cowgirls."[114] In the early 2000s, the Illinois association similarly promoted "Hot Cowboys!" and "Hot Cowgirls!" at its rodeo.[115]

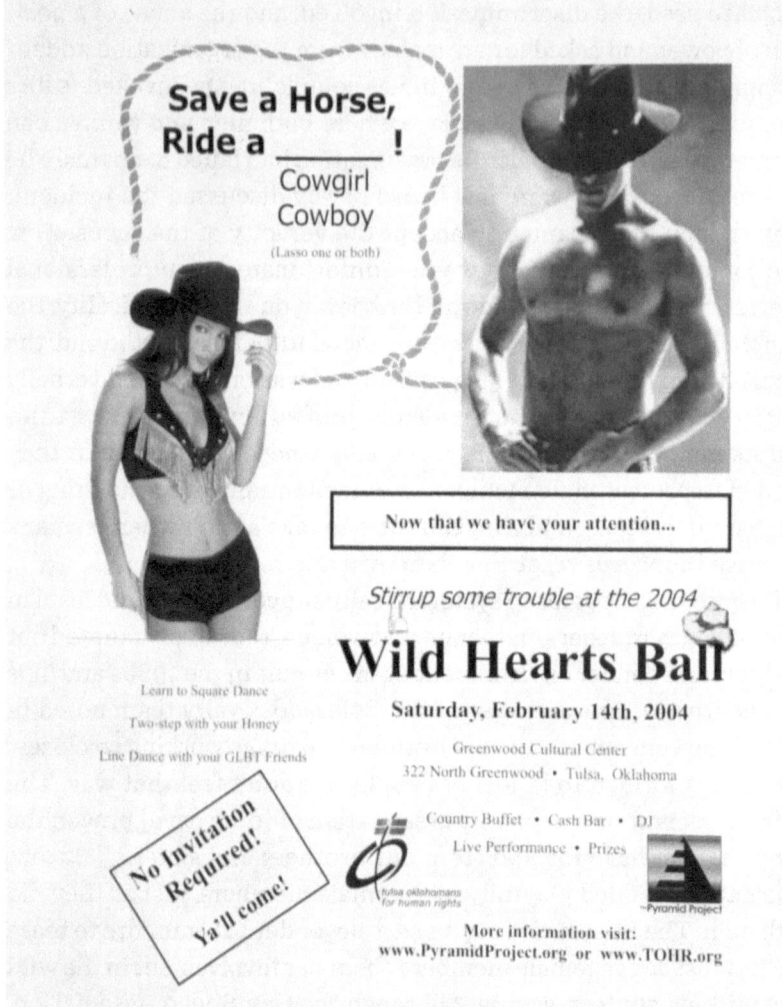

FIGURE 26. *IGRA Finals Rodeo Program, "Save a horse ride a ____!," 2003. While gay rodeo program ads more frequently focused on sex between men, the one seen here spoke to a broader audience that could include gay men, lesbians, and even straight rodeo enthusiasts. Courtesy of the Autry Museum of the American West.*

IGRA also made concerted efforts, even in the midst of the HIV/AIDS crisis, to support lesbian interests such as breast cancer research.[116] This increased after the AIDS crisis peaked in the mid-1990s, and in 1998, the Susan G. Komen Breast Cancer Foundation wrote to the IGRA president, saying, "I must applaud IGRA's commitment to recognize and address women's issues. As you know breast cancer touches so many people and is particularly prevalent in the lesbian community."[117]

Gay men and lesbians both regularly identify gay rodeo as a friendly and welcoming place and especially note the equal inclusion of women as a point of pride, something that makes it stand apart from—above even—other western rodeos. However, simply permitting women to compete in all the same events as men has not led to equal participation or equal treatment. Both the Reno rodeos and IGRA attempted to reach out to female and lesbian competitors, but much of their messaging and imagery has remained focused on gay men and actively supports a vision of America—one based in patriarchal domination and a narrow vision of traditional masculinity—that counters the goals of many lesbian movements of the 1970s, '80s, and '90s. Unless gay rodeo is willing to adjust its efforts and interests and more decisively pursue lesbian members, gay men likely will continue to comprise the majority of IGRA participants.

From the outset, most organizers of gay rodeos saw them as a place that could include everyone under the LGBTQ+ umbrella. Even though he hoped the rodeo would emphasize the masculinity of gay men, Phil Ragsdale also countered "Macho Cowboys" by including camp events, drag, and lesbians. IGRA has continued to try to make room for transgender contestants in the royalty competition and rodeo events. Gay rodeo has regularly coordinated with various gay subcultures, such as masculine-presenting groups like bears and leathermen. Even straight competitors and audience members have been welcomed. It is a place that has allowed people to be who they are and who they want to be, largely without judgmental eyes. One member with physical disabilities joined the Arkansas association in 1990, even though they could not participate in any of the rodeo events. They were drawn to the larger purpose of IGRA, saying:

> Well this rodeo association is for everyone, it's not just about riding, roping, and such. It's about the gay society having something to do. Something that's fun, entertaining, where you can meet new people, make friends, and all in all, help bring the gay community closer together.... It's rough enough

at times to be gay, but put gay and handicapped together and you feel like an outcast. Well, here is your chance. A chance to feel part of a group and a part of life. Come be with us. I'm sure you will like it. I do![118]

Members have always stressed that IGRA was a place where anyone could find a way to belong and to contribute, and this vision of the association has been long-standing. Much like the statement above from 1990, Malcolm Cook, who has a degenerative brain disease, thanked the organization in 2022 for fulfilling his dream of competing. As he explained, "I felt included, normal, seen, heard, loved. Not one person told me that I couldn't do it, every single person at the rodeo showed me support and encouragement."[119]

Without discounting the important work gay rodeo has done to welcome a diverse group of people, its mission of inclusion has proven loftier and more hopeful than the reality of who has been attracted to and included in its vision of the West. The groups that regularly found the most comfortable home in gay rodeo have been those with shared views of gender identity and who supported its goal of acceptance by the mainstream rodeo world. Straight riders, leathermen, and bears generally aligned with the white, normative ideals of this vision of the West. Deemed valuable to gay rodeo's pursuit of "authenticity," these groups have been pursued by IGRA and incorporated into its ranks, largely without question or concern.

Other groups of people failed to support these intentions and sometimes even obstructed them. Transgender people, people of color, and lesbians ran counter to the wider purpose that some people had for gay rodeo. Because of this, its stated ideals of openness and inclusion were not always the reality. The assumed whiteness that is readily apparent in its promotional materials has translated to a predominantly white membership. Though members of color feel included in gay rodeo and rarely point to moments of exclusion, racism, or discrimination, it has done little to really incorporate nonwhite queer cowfolx, and few contestants of color have identified it as their home. Some, like Hispanic gay vaqueros, have created their own, more culturally attuned environments in order to find a community that celebrates their sexual identity *and* racial identity. Other groups, like trans participants, have called for change in the rodeo arena. IGRA responded with some supportive practices, but other policies limited, rather than expanded, trans rights. Lesbian members experienced similarly problematic treatment, and gay male members frequently viewed lesbians as desirable for their numbers but troublesome when they pushed for change or threatened the status quo. This failure is especially noticeable because gay rodeo has trumpeted its policy of gender equality most loudly.

IGRA rarely has reached out to other LGBTQ+ groups with any sustained or purposeful efforts. Neither has it asked how increased participation by these groups could enhance gay rodeo, instead viewing them as simply additional bodies to buoy its numbers and continued existence. As IGRA moves into its second decade of declining numbers, the critiques by gay rodeoers like Bruce Gros and John King feel all the more prescient. Only by breaking its standard patterns of outreach and inclusion can gay rodeo reach its mission of "total nondiscrimination" and finally fulfill Phil Ragsdale's desire to create a rodeo "for ALL GAY PEOPLE."[120]

Conclusion

THE FUTURE OF GAY RODEO

"I really do not know where my life would be now if it were not for my rodeo family," said longtime IGRA member Bruce Roby.[1] Many participants express the same sentiment when they discuss the importance gay rodeo has played for them individually, the role it has held within the queer community, and the impact it has made on the mainstream rodeo world and broader American society. Gay rodeo has provided a familiar home for rural LGBTQ+ people and for queer cowfolx. It played a critical role in the fight against HIV/AIDS. Its fundraising efforts brought in hundreds of thousands of dollars to support research and to care for those diagnosed. It pushed back against popular conceptions of gayness in American society and made space for the queer cowboy and cowgirl as legitimate competitors in the rodeo arena. It achieved big-name sponsorships and received attention from professional rodeo organizations and straight competitors. It participated in the mainstreaming of the queer identity in the US while still celebrating alternative sexualities, gender identities, and sexual cultures. Gay rodeo was, without question, a success.

Even with these many accomplishments, it did not face an easy or clear path to acceptance. In the decades since Phil Ragsdale organized his first competition in 1970s Reno, gay rodeo as an institution faced opposition, hate, and threats of violence. Homophobic attacks based in "family values," morality, and religion attempted to stop the rodeos. AIDS-based fears provided further justification for these views, and as the epidemic expanded, so too did hostility against gay rodeo. It also endured internal strife in its developmental years. Some members only wanted it to offer a place for masculine competition modeled on mainstream rodeos. Others desired an inclusive environment that permitted anyone to participate, regardless of race, gender, sexuality, or rodeo experience. In these years, gay rodeo attempted to create a welcoming and inclusive arena, but the boundaries of that inclusion were also stretched and tested. Despite the ups and downs and the many obstacles that lay in its path in the 1970s, '80s, and '90s, it not only survived but expanded. The internal debates forced IGRA to look inward, to examine itself, and to survey members to identify what they needed the organization to be. The external attacks helped gay rodeo clarify its importance and its purpose. It met the opposition head on and usually came out stronger on the other side.

In terms of attendance, the circuit peaked in the 1990s and 2000s, when more than seventeen rodeos were offered annually between 1994 and 2008. But since that time, that number has dropped steadily, with an average of just eleven in the years prior to the COVID-19 pandemic. By 2013 there were more defunct IGRA associations than active ones.[2] The number of members also dropped precipitously. In 2018, IGRA estimated it had 1,250 members in nineteen local associations, and only sixteen remained active in 2021.[3] This has impacted IGRA's bottom line and its charitable mission. Corporate sponsors are less willing to take a risk on rodeos that attract fewer people each year. This has a damaging trickle-down effect, as the rodeos are more expensive to host without those sponsorship dollars. Increased costs cut into IGRA's ability to finish rodeos with a net profit that can be donated to community organizations. This puts more pressure on royalty to engage in almost constant fundraising and on members to donate more money and more time. But fewer members feel the same drive to give as they previously did, when donations funded HIV/AIDS organizations that were desperately needed in the darkest days of the epidemic. Gay rodeo in those days was a way for queer people to give back to their community and to support their own. As local associations increasingly donate to broader community organizations, including those without an LGBTQ+ focus, the need to participate and the desire to give back feels less urgent, so fewer people participate and even less money is raised. Similarly, as societal acceptance for LGBTQ+ people has increased, there is a more limited need for separate spaces. This means that fewer queer people are looking for a specifically "gay" rodeo. Caught in this vicious cycle, IGRA is scrambling to attract new members and questioning why it no longer holds the same relevancy for queer people.

In contrast, as gay rodeo began to retract in the late 1990s and early 2000s, other circuits continued to expand. College rodeo attracted a growing number of contestants, garnered new sponsorship deals, and professionalized. PRCA continues to award millions in prize money, with a record-setting payout at the 2022 National Finals Rodeo of more than $10.9 million, and the Professional Bull Riders tour has only grown since its formation in the early 1990s. By 2004, more than eight hundred cowboys competed for big prize money, including a $1 million bonus for whoever came out on top at the end of the season. As of 2022, forty-two PBR riders have earned more than $1 million over their careers, and five have earned more than $5 million.[4]

So, how did an organization that was so robust for decades see its fortunes reverse so quickly, and where does this leave IGRA today? As Bruce Roby notes, these are "the $25,000 questions!" and many in gay rodeo are searching for answers that will help IGRA regain the popularity and relevancy that it once held.

Even some of the most successful local associations have struggled in recent years. ARGRA, based in Canada, was established in 1991 and by 2007 had one of the largest memberships in IGRA, with more than three hundred active members.[5] Yet despite that success, ARGRA was anxious about its future, and its president, Heather Murray, noted in 2007, "Today we stand at a crossroads." A closer examination of its membership rolls reveals that the association was rightly concerned. While 136 new people joined ARGRA that year, the group had a retention problem, as only seven current members had been with it since its founding. Less than ten years later, it dissolved.[6] Other stalwart associations faced similar problems in that same decade. Diamond State confronted rumors that it was failing in 2007, and in 2008, the association had to move its popular Little Rock rodeo to every two years, specifically noting the recession of 2008 as the cause of its financial difficulties. The Heartland group in Nebraska canceled its rodeo the following year and similarly pointed to the poor economy, blaming it for a drop in sponsorships. In contrast, the Oklahoma association, one of the first five members of IGRA, blamed "apathy from the membership" for threatening its longtime rodeo. The group avoided the "tragic event" of canceling the rodeo that year but was forced to reorganize in 2016 in an attempt to expand membership. In 2017 the dreaded tragedy occurred: the rodeo was canceled for the first time since 1986.[7]

Though sometimes outside forces, like the recession of the 2000s, hurt the fortunes of gay rodeo, a more common problem was the one identified by OGRA. Like the Oklahoma group, many local associations had frequent problems drumming up enough support from within their ranks. Rodeos are substantial undertakings, and gay rodeo took its seriously. Without a paid, professional staff, this required significant volunteer support. Even in the golden age of gay rodeo in the 1990s, membership participation was often a challenge for local associations. Despite a membership of roughly a hundred people, SEGRA in Georgia went months without its meetings attracting the quorum of ten members. Associations' leadership regularly implored their groups to participate more. Atlantic States asked its members, "Are you doing your share to help ASGRA succeed or do you sit back and enjoy the fun times while others are making an investment of their time?" Following a rodeo with devastatingly low turnout, LGRA bemoaned, "The question we keep asking ourselves is where was the support from our community/membership." That support failed to appear, and the association folded the following year. The North Star association articulated this problem the most clearly when it said, "We all WANT a rodeo, but not enough people want to DO a rodeo."[8] People were excited to join so as to enjoy the rodeo, participate in the country-western scene, and meet like-minded LGBTQ+ people, but they rarely wanted to do the work to make an event happen.

Surveys of Arizona and Atlantic States association memberships are revealing in this respect. In the decade when gay rodeo grew rapidly, most members said they joined IGRA because of the social aspects, to meet people, and because of an interest in rodeo and the country-western scene. Separate LGBTQ+ spaces, such as gay bars and gay rodeo sites, historically functioned as communal social places and sites of interaction for queer people. However, as the acceptance of LGBTQ+ people increased in the twenty-first century, the US has moved into what some scholars have called a "postgay" era. As fewer queer people need to look for these separate spaces, places like gay bars have rebranded in order to survive. Some have done this by identifying themselves as a more inclusive space and by welcoming straight people, especially straight women, through their doors. Despite these efforts, 37 percent of gay bars in the US closed between 2007 and 2019, and COVID-19 caused another precipitous drop.[9] Gay rodeo functioned similarly to queer spaces like gay bars by offering LGBTQ+ people interested in country-western social activities a place to gather. It also followed a trajectory similar to the decline in gay bars. There was a 50 percent drop in the number of annual rodeos on the IGRA circuit and a 63 percent drop in membership between 2007 and 2019.[10]

The steeper decline in gay rodeo is for several reasons. First, it attracted a more limited and specific crowd than gay bars as a whole. Second, the interest in gay rodeo was tied to a wider interest in the country-western lifestyle that was popular, particularly in queer communities, in the 1970s, '80s, and '90s. As that enthusiasm waned, so too did that of the "wannabe cowboys," so only the people more devoted to the rodeo world remained involved. Third, and perhaps most importantly, gay rodeoers routinely identified the charitable mission of IGRA, especially its HIV/AIDS fundraising in the 1980s and '90s, as a significant motive for their participation.

Without that same urgent reason to participate, to volunteer, and to donate money, gay rodeo no longer holds the same central role as it did in the past. Carolyn Jones, a straight participant in IGRA, agrees. She said in 2015, "With AIDS becoming almost another chronic illness, the need for its charitable activities will fade. I believe that the upcoming generation will not need gay rodeo in many parts of America."[11] Kevin Hillman, who is HIV-positive, similarly identifies the passing of the critical years of the AIDS epidemic as leading to a decline in gay rodeo's popularity, but for another reason: "I'm looking at a generation of people who didn't have to do the fights like we did, didn't have to face the discrimination, so a lot of them don't understand the need or the reasoning behind gay organizations like gay rodeo, like the royal court, and those types of organizations, because their friends are so accepting of them and will party with them." He continued, "So it's going to be a difficult outreach to get these young people to understand the need for these organizations and the camaraderie and the family that they could be a part of, so we have a lot of work ahead of us as a gay rodeo . . . to bring those young people that word, that information, and try and get them involved, so that all these organizations can survive."[12] The generation gaps, both in how the cowboy is understood and the disease landscapes young queer people are experiencing, are creating new tensions for IGRA.

Forty years after the start of the AIDS epidemic, gay rodeo endured another disease crisis. The fight against AIDS unified the participants and fortified them against the onslaught of attacks they faced, but they could not react in the same way to COVID-19. With AIDS, the queer community was under attack—both devastated by the disease and confronted with homophobic vitriol, restrictive legislation, and threats to its very existence. Gay rodeo reacted by circling the wagons to protect the LGBTQ+ community and launching a counternarrative about it. AIDS gave gay rodeoers something to fight against and something to fight for: their lives and those of their friends, families, and lovers.

While AIDS brought more people to gay rodeo and gave it a greater purpose, COVID-19 did neither and effectively stopped it in its tracks. Like the rest of the world, gay rodeo shut its doors for more than a year. In 2021, IGRA slowly began to reopen, but recovery is far from assured. The Denver rodeo that year did see wall-to-wall attendees hungry for human interaction, and the packed arena and gay bars were reminiscent of the heady days of gay rodeo in the 1990s.[13] But despite this enthusiasm, member associations are struggling to host events. After two years with no finals rodeo and limited income, the IGRA board of directors debated the organization's ability to host an in-person annual convention in 2021.[14] While HIV/AIDS in many ways drove queer people together, COVID-19 physically restrained them from gathering. As people reevaluate the importance of such spaces, it remains to be seen if gay rodeo, or other queer spaces and events, can reignite already declining interest after such economic and physical devastation.

Gay rodeo's history illustrates how a group of people reviled by the political right and often viewed with suspicion on the political left painstakingly constructed an imperfect community dedicated to rural lifeways, country-western performance, and an idealized image of the cowboy. Created predominantly for white men, a new cowboy ideal emerged from this space—one who has sex with men and sometimes puts on a dress to complete. By troubling the predominant understanding of what it meant to be gay, a man, or western, gay rodeo presented a threat to a certain kind of American identity. Many people reacted with contempt, but gay rodeoers found their own path to walk, in the process enduring through epidemics, the end of the urban cowboy craze, and homophobic attacks. At the same time, in their pursuit of an "authentic," respectable rodeo, some opposed what they identified as threats to their claims to the cowboy identity—drag queens, camp events, female competitors, cowboy clones and wannabes, and other people who failed to fulfill societal expectations of hegemonic masculinity. At the same time that they were fighting for their own inclusion, gay rodeoers often redeployed aspects of the imagined West that prevented that of others. As a new generation inherits queer country-western culture, the tensions, debates, and experiences of their elders crafted a unique space that remains unsettled and unsettling to many.

GLOSSARY

There are many types of rodeos in the United States, and they can offer a myriad of different events. Listed in this glossary are those traditionally included at western rodeos and on the professional circuit. Many gay rodeo events are based on the western rodeo, but the circuit also includes some that appear outside the professional arena and others that are unique to it. Unlike the two categories of professional rodeo—roughstock events that are scored by a judge and do not require the use of a personal horse, and timed events that are scored based on speed alone—the gay circuit divides its competitions into four: roughstock, roping, speed, and camp events.

WESTERN RODEO EVENTS

ROUGHSTOCK EVENTS
(EVENTS SCORED BY A JUDGE AND NOT REQUIRING USE OF A PERSONAL HORSE)

bareback bronc riding—the rider must stay on the horse for eight seconds and remain in the proper riding position for the duration; judging is based on the performance of the rider and the horse

bull riding—the rider must stay on a bull for eight seconds and remain in the proper riding position for the duration; judging is based on the performance of the rider and the bull

saddle bronc riding—the rider must stay on a saddled and reined horse for eight seconds and remain in the proper riding position for the duration; judging is based on the performance of the rider and the horse

TIMED EVENTS
(EVENTS SCORED BASED ON TIMED SPEED)

barrel racing—the rider runs the horse around three barrels in a cloverleaf pattern (this is the only event for female competitors at PRCA rodeos and is sponsored by the Women's Professional Rodeo Association)

steer roping—the rider ropes a steer from horseback and, with the steer on the ground, ropes three legs together; steers are defined by the PRCA as 450–650 pounds

steer wrestling—the rider leaps from a racing horse onto the back of a running steer, grabs both of the steer's horns, jumps to the ground, and twists the steer's neck up to wrestle it to the ground; also called bulldogging

team roping—team event with a header and heeler on horseback; the header ropes a steer's horns, and the heeler ropes the steer's hind legs

tie-down roping—the rider ropes a calf from horseback and, with the calf on the ground, ropes three legs together; also called calf roping; calves are defined by the PRCA as 220–280 pounds

GAY RODEO EVENTS

CAMP EVENTS
(EVENTS OFTEN DESCRIBED AS MORE LIGHTHEARTED, COLORFUL, AND PLAYFUL)

goat decorating—a two-person event in which participants dress a goat in underwear; renamed goat dressing in 1989

steer decorating—a two-person team must rope a steer on foot and tie a ribbon to the steer's tail

wild cow milking—a three-person team—with one male, one female, and one "drag" (male or female rider in costume)—must rope a wild cow (defined as one that will not milk its young) and milk it; replaced by the wild drag race in 1986

wild drag race—a three-person team—with one male, one female, and one "drag" (male or female rider in costume)—must direct a steer on foot across a marked line, at which point the "drag" mounts the steer and must ride it back to the finish line

ROPING EVENTS
(EVENTS SCORED BASED ON TIMED SPEED)

calf roping on foot—like steer roping in in the western rodeo but done on foot rather than horseback

mounted breakaway roping—the rider ropes a calf's head on horseback; the rope breaks away from the saddle when the calf pulls it taut

ribbon roping—a two-person team ropes a calf and ties a ribbon to its tail; discontinued after 1985

team roping—same as team roping in the western rodeo

ROUGHSTOCK EVENTS
(EVENTS SCORED BY A JUDGE AND NOT REQUIRING USE OF A PERSONAL HORSE)

bareback bronc riding—like bareback bronc riding in the western rodeo; later replaced by saddle bronc riding

bull riding—same as bull riding in the western rodeo but with a six-second requirement

chute dogging—same as steer wrestling in the western rodeo but done on foot rather than horseback

steer riding—same as bull riding in the western rodeo but done on a smaller steer and with a six-second requirement

wild cow riding—same as bull riding in the western rodeo but using a wild cow and with a six-second requirement; replaced by steer riding in 1989

SPEED EVENTS
(EVENTS SCORED BASED ON TIMED SPEED)

barrel racing—same as barrel racing in the PRCA rodeos, but both men and women are permitted to participate

flag race—the rider follows pattern similar to the barrel race but picks up and plants flags in the process

pole bending—the rider must race a horse through linear pattern of six poles

speed barrels—the rider must race a horse through linear pattern of three barrels; discontinued after 1984

speed race—the rider must race a horse between two poles and round a barrel; discontinued after 1984

NOTES

ARCHIVES AND REPOSITORIES

ACC   IGRA Archives Collection Committee, Royalty Paperwork
Autry Archives   Autry Museum of the American West Archives, IGRA Collection
GRC   Gay Rodeo Collection, ONE Archives at the University of Southern California Libraries
GRH   Gay Rodeo History, http://gayrodeohistory.org, International Gay Rodeo Association
GSCC   Golden State Cowboys Collection, ONE Archives at the University of Southern California Libraries
RGRC   Reno Gay Rodeo Collection, Special Collections and Archives, University Libraries, University of Nevada at Las Vegas

ORAL HISTORY COLLECTIONS

This work draws extensively on the more than seventy oral history interviews collected by the two authors. We thank the many people who have spoken with us, both formally in interviews and informally on so many other occasions. Their trust in us and the access they provided to their stories and organizational archives made it possible to tell the story of queer cowfolx and gay rodeo. With that trust in mind, we approached this project as a form of community-engaged, collaborative practice. Our work is informed by scholars in the fields of oral history, Indigenous history, and public history. Michael Frisch in *A Shared Authority* (1990) was a leading voice for oral historians and public historians to work alongside oral history collaborators. Amy Lonetree explicitly located this conversation in public history spaces in *Decolonizing Museums: Representing Native America in National and Tribal Museums (2012)*. Benjamin J. Barnes and Stephen Warren in *Replanting Cultures: Community-Engaged Scholarship in Indian Country* (2022) more recently reminded scholars of the importance of working with communities, viewing them as participants and stakeholders in our work. We build on these practices and strive in this book to honor LGBTQ+ elders' experiences while also understanding how some practices of gay rodeo led to the problematic maintenance of a white, gender-normative West.

The interviews collected by Elyssa Ford were conducted in 2015 with six men and five women, including one trans man and one trans woman. The interviews collected by Rebecca Scofield and her team with the Gay Rodeo Oral History Project were conducted from 2016 to 2023. Of the sixty-five participants, forty-nine were men and fourteen were women. One narrator identified as a trans woman, and one as gender fluid. For both sets of interviews, narrators were overwhelmingly white; there was one Native competitor, one Hispanic competitor, and two of Asian descent. Two participants were white British immigrants. The lack of racial and ethnic diversity of narrators was reflective of the association itself at this time. However, these projects captured the voices of a broad range of experiences, from rookie riders to founders of the organization and from people reconnecting with rural lifeways to those seeking to live out cowboy dreams. Most were involved in national IGRA leadership or state executive committees, or were titleholders in royalty and rodeo events, and represented the full spectrum of IGRA associations, including some that no longer exist.

INTRODUCTION

1. IGRA Finals Rodeo Program, 1997, GRH, http://gayrodeohistory.org/index Programs.htm. For more on the queer community's use of the pink triangle as a statement of power, see Erik N. Jensen, "The Pink Triangle and Political Consciousness: Gays, Lesbians, and the Memory of Nazi Persecution," *Journal of the History of Sexuality* 11, no. 1/2 (January–April 2002): 319–49.
2. This man wrote to IGRA in 1994 asking for information on gay cowboys in the Michigan, Wisconsin, and Minnesota area. Letter from Pat Kaarite to IGRA, May 3, 1994, Autry Archives, Box 22.
3. Bobby Bridger, *Buffalo Bill and Sitting Bull: Inventing the Wild West* (Austin: University of Texas Press, 2002); Frederick Jackson Turner, "The Significance of the Frontier in American History," 1893, reprinted in *Does the Frontier Experience Make America Exceptional?*, edited by Richard Etulain (Boston: Bedford/St. Martin's, 1999); Richard White, "Frederick Jackson Turner and Buffalo Bill," in *The Frontier in American Culture*, edited by James Grossman (Berkeley: University of California Press, 1994); Richard W. Slatta, "Making and Unmaking Myths of the American Frontier," *European Journal of American Culture* 29, no. 2 (July 2010): 81–92; Richard Slotkin, *Regeneration through Violence: The Mythology of the American Frontier, 1600–1860* (Middletown, MA: Wesleyan University Press, 1973); Richard Slotkin, *The Fatal Environment: The Myth of the Frontier in the Age of Industrialization, 1800–1890* (New York: Atheneum, 1985); Richard Slotkin, *Gunfighter Nation: The Myth of the Frontier in Twentieth-Century America* (New York: Atheneum, 1992); Robert Athearn, *The Mythic West* (Lawrence: University Press of Kansas, 1986); Karen Jones and John Wills, *The American West: Competing Visions* (Edinburgh, UK: Edinburgh University Press, 2009).
4. For more on the racial diversity of the US West, ranching, and rodeo history, see the comparative work by Elyssa Ford, *Rodeo as Refuge, Rodeo as Rebellion: Gender, Race, and Identity in the American Rodeo* (Lawrence: University Press of Kansas, 2020).
5. There is a long history of American rodeo scholarship, including the

following: Wayne S. Wooden and Gavin Ehringer, *Rodeo in America: Wranglers, Roughstock & Paydirt* (Lawrence: University Press of Kansas, 1996); Melody Groves, *Ropes, Reins, and Rawhide: All About Rodeo* (Albuquerque: University of New Mexico Press, 2006); and Richard C. Rattenbury, *Arena Legacy: The Heritage of American Rodeo* (Norman: University of Oklahoma Press, 2010). For a more detailed discussion on the myth of the cowboy and the role it has played in American history and American identity, see William Savage Jr., *The Cowboy Hero: His Image in American History & Culture* (Norman: University of Oklahoma Press, 1979); Michael Allen, *Rodeo Cowboys in the North American Imagination* (Reno: University of Nevada Press, 1998); and Jeremy Agnew, *The Creation of the Cowboy Hero: Fiction, Film, and Fact* (Jefferson, NC: McFarland & Company, Inc., 2015).

6. Fred Schnell, *Rodeo! The Suicide Circuit* (New York: Rand McNally, 1971); Dirk Johnson, *Biting the Dust: The Wild Ride and Dark Romance of the Rodeo Cowboy and the American West* (Lincoln: University of Nebraska Press, 1994). For sports medicine studies on rodeo, see D. S. Ross, A. Ferguson, P. Bosha, and K. Cassas, "Factors that Prevent Roughstock Rodeo Athletes from Wearing Protective Equipment," *Current Sports Medicine Report* 9, no. 6 (November–December 2010): 342–46; Renée Crichlow, Steve Williamson, Mike Geurin, and Heather Heggem, "Self-Reported Injury Rate in Native American Professional Rodeo Competitors," *Clinical Journal of Sport Medicine* 16, no. 4 (July 2006): 352–54; D. J. Downey, "Rodeo Injuries and Prevention," *Current Sports Medicine Report* 6, no. 6 (October 2007): 328–32; M. C. Meyers and C. M. Laurent Jr., "The Rodeo Athlete: Sport Science: Part I," *Sports Medicine* 40, no. 1 (May 1, 2010); and M. C. Meyers and C. M. Laurent Jr., "The Rodeo Athlete: Injuries: Part II," *Sports Medicine* 40, no. 10 (October 1, 2010). Rodeoers themselves are also quick to acknowledge the danger inherent in their sport; see Foghorn Clancy, *My Fifty Years in Rodeo: Living with Cowboys, Horses, and Danger* (San Antonio: Naylor Co., 1952); and Susan Thurston, "Walk It Off, Partner: Injuries Are a Way of Life for Ryan 'Badcat' McConnel, One of Pro Rodeo's Toughest, and Most Popular, Bull Riders," *St. Petersburg Times*, January 29, 2010, 29. This understanding of the stoic strength of cowboys in the face of life-threatening danger has even extended to rodeo cultures globally; see Scott Feschuk, "Youngsters Steer Way to Their Rodeo Dreams IN THEIR BLOOD: There Is Real Risk of Injury but Participants Figure It Goes with the Territory," *Globe & Mail* (Toronto, Canada), November 12, 1993, D11; and Ashlea Pritchard, "East to West Coast Rodeo Injuries All Part of the 'Cowboy Code,'" *Central Western Daily* (Orange, Australia), October 18, 2015.

7. Susan Nance, *Rodeo: An Animal History* (Norman: University of Oklahoma Press, 2020).

8. See Peter Iverson, *When Indians Became Cowboys: Native Peoples and Cattle Ranching in the American West* (Norman: University of Oklahoma, 1997) and *Riders of the West: Portraits from Indian Rodeo* (Seattle: University of

Washington Press, 1999); Jan Penrose, "When All the Cowboys Are Indians: The Nature of Race in All-Indian Rodeo," *Annals of the Association of American Geographers* 93, no. 3 (September 2003): 687–705; Kathleen Sands, *Charrería Mexicana: An Equestrian Folk Tradition* (Tucson: University of Arizona Press, 1993); Laura Barraclough, *Charros: How Mexican Cowboys Are Remapping Race and American Identity* (Oakland: University of California Press, 2019); Joyce Gibson Roach, *The Cowgirls*, 2nd ed. (Denton: University of North Texas Press, 1990); Mary Lou LeCompte, *Cowgirls of the Rodeo: Pioneer Professional Athletes* (Urbana: University of Illinois Press, 1993); Rebecca Scofield, *Outriders: Rodeo at the Fringes of the American West* (Seattle: University of Washington Press, 2019); and Ford, *Rodeo as Refuge*.

9. For more on the masculine performance in gay rodeo, see Rebecca Scofield, "'Chaps and Scowls': Play, Violence, and the Post-1970s Urban Cowboy," *Journal of American Culture* 40, no. 4 (December 2017): 325–40; Elyssa Ford, "Becoming the West: Cowboys as Icons of Masculine Style for Gay Men," in "Fashion and Style Icons," special issue, *Critical Studies in Men's Fashion* 5, no. 1–2 (May 2018): 41–53; Scofield, *Outriders*; and Ford, *Rodeo as Refuge*. Also see other studies on gay rodeo, including Jonathan Hanvelt, "Cowboy Up: Gender and Sexuality in Calgary's 'Gay' and 'Straight' Rodeo" (MA thesis, University of British Columbia, 2004); Todd Heibel, "An Arena for Belonging? A Spatial Hingepoint Perspective on Citizenship at the Gay Rodeo" (PhD diss., Pennsylvania State University, 2005); Christopher Le Coney and Zoe Trodd, "Reagan's Rainbow Rodeos: Queer Challenges to the Cowboy Dreams of Eighties America," *Canadian Review of American Studies* 39, no. 2 (2009): 163–83; Katherine A. Kuvalanka, "From Ball Culture to the Gay Rodeo: Expanding Notions of Family," *Sex Roles* 67 (2012): 366–68; D'Lane Compton, "Queer Eye on the Gay Rodeo," in *Gender in the Twenty-First Century: The Stalled Revolution and the Road to Equality*, edited by Shannon Davis, Sarah Winslow, and David Maume (Oakland: University of California Press, 2017), 222–39; Moshoula Capous-Desyllas and Marina Johnson-Rhodes, "Collecting Visual Voices: Understanding Identity, Community, and the Meaning of Participation within Gay Rodeos," *Sexualities* 21, no. 3 (2018): 446–75; John Jeffery Auer IV, "Movement and Change: Perspectives on Urban Gay Tourism and Gay Community Building of the Past" (PhD diss., University of Nevada, Reno, 2019); and Nicholas Villanueva Jr., "A Rodeo to Call Their Own: LGBTQ Vaqueros and the Gay Rodeo of the American West," in *Decolonizing Latinx Masculinities*, edited by Arturo J. Aldama and Frederick Luis Aldama (Tucson: University of Arizona Press, 2020), 307–25.

10. Kathryn Alexander, "Politely Different: Queer Presence in Country Dancing and Music," *Yearbook for Traditional Music* 50, no. 1 (2018): 187–209.

11. See the glossary at the end of our work for definitions of standard and nonstandard rodeo events.

12. John D'Emilio, "Capitalism and Gay Identity," in *Queer Economics: A Reader*, edited by Joyce Jacobsen and Adam Zeller (London: Routledge, 2008), 181–94; Colin Johnson, *Just Queer Folks: Gender and Sexuality in Rural America* (Philadelphia: Temple University Press, 2013), 196; J. Halberstam, *In a Queer Time and Place: Transgender Bodies, Subcultural Lives* (New York: New York University Press, 2005), 36–38. For more on queer rurality, see Will Fellows, *Farms Boys: Lives of Gay Men from the Rural Midwest* (Madison: University of Wisconsin Press, 1996); Michael Riordon, *Out Our Way: Gay and Lesbian Life in the Country* (Toronto: Between the Lines, 1996); John Howard, *Men like That: A Southern Queer History* (Chicago: University of Chicago Press, 1999); Beth Bailey, *Sex in the Heartland* (Cambridge: Harvard University Press, 2002); Peter Boag, *Same-Sex Affairs: Constructing and Controlling Homosexuality in the Pacific Northwest* (Berkeley: University of California Press, 2003); Hugh Campbell, Michael Mayerfeld Bell, and Margaret Finney, eds., *Country Boys: Masculinity and Rural Life* (University Park: Pennsylvania State University Press, 2006); Brock Thompson, *The Un-Natural State: Arkansas and the Queer South* (Fayetteville: University of Arkansas Press, 2010); Scott Herring, *Another Country: Queer Anti-Urbanism* (New York: New York University Press, 2010); Andrew Gorman-Murray, Barbara Pini, and Lia Bryant, eds., *Sexuality, Rurality, and Geography* (Lanham, MD: Lexington Books, 2013); Mary L. Gray, Colin R. Johnson, and Brian J. Gilley, eds., *Queering the Countryside: New Frontiers in Rural Queer Studies* (New York: New York University Press, 2016); and Ryan Lee Cartwright, *Peculiar Places: A Queer Crip History of White Rural Nonconformity* (Chicago: University of Chicago Press, 2021).
13. For more on metronormativity and the queer suburban, see Katherine Browne, "Imagining Cities, Living the Other: Between the Gay Urban Idyll and Rural Lesbian Lives," *Open Geography Journal* 1, no. 1 (2008): 25–32; Karen Tongson, *Relocations: Queer Suburban Imaginaries* (New York: New York University Press, 2011); Alexis Annes and Meredith Redlin, "Coming Out and Coming Back: Rural Gay Migration and the City," *Journal of Rural Studies* 28, no. 1 (January 2012): 56–68.; Julie A. Podmore and Alison L. Bain, "'No queers out there'? Metronormativity and the Queer Suburban," *Geography Compass* (2020): 1–16; and Julie A. Podmore and Alison L. Bain, "Whither Queer Suburbanisms: Beyond Heterosuburbia and Queer Metronormativities," *Progress in Human Geographies* 45, no. 5 (2021): 1254–77.
14. Tales of the sanctuary of the urban idyll are countered with the anti-idyll of rural spaces, popularly perceived to be conservative and dangerous to queer people; see Kath Weston, "Get Thee to a Big City: Sexual Imagery and the Great Gay Migration," *Gay and Lesbian Quarterly* 2, no 3 (1995): 253–77; Chris Wienke, "Does Place of Residence Matter? Urban-Rural Differences and the Wellbeing of Gay Men and Lesbians," *Journal of Homosexuality* 60, no. 9 (2013): 1256–79; and Peter Boag, "Gay Male Rural-Urban Migrations in the American West," in *City Dreams, Country Schemes: Community and*

Identity in the American West, edited by Kathleen A. Brosnan and Amy L. Scott, Urban West Series (Reno: University of Nevada Press, 2011), 284–305.

15. Nadine Hubbs, *Rednecks, Queers, and Country Music* (Berkeley: University of California Press, 2014), 2. This is not to say there is no correlation between rural and urban geographies and political alignments. A rural-urban political fissure does exist in the United States, and this has grown since 2000; see James G. Gimpel, Nathan Lovin, Bryant Moy, and Andrew Reeves, "The Urban-Rural Gulf in American Political Behavior," *Political Behavior* 42, no. 4 (December 2020): 1343–68. We suggest that an examination of gay rodeo provides a more nuanced understanding of rural and urban political leanings and of how political identities do not always neatly align with sexual identities.

16. Letter from TGRA Member to IGRA, 1997, Autry Archives, Box 42.

I. ORIGINS

1. Patrick O'Driscoll, "10,000 Hoot, Holler at Gay Rodeo," *Nevada State Journal*, August 2, 1981, 1–4A, Autry Archives, Box 6.
2. Allen Kalchik, "IGRA Finals All Around Cowboy: Greg Olson," *Roundup* (Spring 1994): 17.
3. Todd Garrett expressed similar sentiments. He grew up on a ranch in Georgia and competed in various "straight" rodeo circuits. At his first gay rodeo, he encountered what he identified as "pretend cowboys" who did not know anything about the sport, and so he avoided gay rodeo for years. Eventually he returned to it and even founded the Florida Gay Rodeo Association. Todd Garrett, email interview with Elyssa Ford, July 28, 2015.
4. Roger Bergmann, interview with Rebecca Scofield, Gay Rodeo Oral History Project, November 19, 2016, Austin, TX.
5. Scott Samet, "Reno Rodeo Plays Host to the Seventh Annual National Gay Rodeo Show, and That's No Bull!" *Weekly News*, August 18, 1982, Autry Archives, Box 6.
6. Ford, *Rodeo as Refuge*.
7. Kurt Markus, "Western Standards," *Esquire* (September 1989): 180–99.
8. For more on cowboys and masculinity in the West, see Richard Slatta, *Cowboys of the Americas* (New Haven: Yale University Press, 1990); Paul Starr, *Let the Cowboy Ride: Cattle Ranching in the American West* (Baltimore: Johns Hopkins Press, 1998); Simon Evans, Sarah Carter, and Bill Yeo, *Cowboys, Ranchers, and the Cattle Business* (Calgary: University of Calgary Press, 2000); Matthew Basso, Laura McCall, and Dee Garceau, editors, *Across the Great Divide: Cultures of Manhood in the American West* (New York: Routledge, 2001); and Jacqueline Moore, *Cow Boys and Cattle Men: Class and Masculinities on the Texas Frontier, 1865–1900* (New York: New York University Press, 2010).
9. Allen, *Rodeo Cowboys*.

10. Steven E. Weil and G. Daniel DeWesse, *Western Shirts: A Classic American Fashion* (Salt Lake City: Gibbs Smith, 2004); Holly George-Warren and Michelle Freedman, *How the West Was Worn* (New York: Harry N. Abrams, 2001); Lynn Downey, "Blue Denim by the Bay: The Levi Strauss & Co. Archives," *Costume* 43 (2009): 150–65; Laurel Wilson, "American Cowboy Dress: Function to Fashion," *Dress: The Journal of the Costume Society of America* 28, no.1 (2001): 40–52.
11. Charles Gibson, "How Clothing Design and Cultural Industries Refashioned Frontier Masculinities: A Historical Geography of Western Wear," *Gender, Place & Culture* 23, no.5 (2016): 733–52; Jean E. Palmieri, "Hawkins Hankers to Get Western Retailer to Pull Together," *Daily News Record*, January 5, 1994, S22; Richard Corliss, "Season of the Nightsoaps," *TIME Magazine* (February 9, 1981): 74–75.
12. "Levi Strauss Profit Up 12% in Quarter," *New York Times*, September 16, 1980, D3; Ron Alexander, "New Boutiques Off and Running to Cater to the Needs of Sports-Minded Men," *New York Times*, July 12, 1980, 42.
13. Curtis W. Ellison, *Country Music Culture: From Hard Times to Heaven* (Jackson: University of Mississippi Press, 1995); Michael Bane, "The Outlaws: Revolution in Country Music" (1978), in Travis Stimeling, *The Country Music Reader* (New York: Oxford University Press, 2014), 208–22.
14. "Man of the Year," *TIME Magazine* (January 5, 1981), cover image. For more on the use of the frontier myth by American presidents, see David A. Smith, *Cowboy Presidents: The Frontier Myth and U.S. Politics since 1900* (Norman: University of Oklahoma Press, 2021).
15. George-Warren and Freedman, *How the West Was Worn*, 188; "Gap Stores Discusses Possible Sale of a Unit," *Wall Street Journal*, January 14, 1980, 27.
16. John-Manuel Andriote, *Hot Stuff: A Brief History of Disco* (New York: HarperCollins, 2001); Tim Lawrence, *Love Saves the Day: A History of American Dance Music Culture, 1970–1979* (Durham, NC: Duke University Press, 2003).
17. Peter Hennen, *Faeries, Bears, and Leathermen: Men in Community Queering the Masculine* (Chicago: University of Chicago, 2008), 9–13.
18. Interview on Gay Rodeo History, http://gayrodeohistory.org (hereafter GRH). In addition to the materials held by the Autry Archives, IGRA has meticulously gathered and shared publicly a significant amount of its institutional material on this website.
19. Golden State Cowboys Constitution and By-Laws, Golden State Cowboys Collection, 1969–76, C0112011.061, GSCC.
20. Golden State Cowboys Constitution and By-Laws, GSCC.
21. Brian Smith to Ernie Wilbanks, July 12, 1970, GSCC. For more on the gay motorcycle scene, see Hennen, *Faeries, Bears, and Leathermen*; Gayle Rubin, "Valley of the Kings," *Sentinel USA*, September 13, 1984, 10–11; and Scott Bloom, *Original Pride: The Satyrs Motorcycle Club* (San Francisco: Frameline, 2006).

22. Hennen, *Faeries, Bears, and Leathermen*, 135–36; Gayle S. Rubin, "Elegy for the Valley of Kings: AIDS and the Leather Community in San Francisco, 1981–1996," in *In Changing Times: Gay Men and Lesbians Encounter HIV/AIDS*, edited by Martin P. Levine, Peter M. Nardi, and John H. Gagnon (Chicago: University of Chicago, 1997), 101–43.
23. Marvin Taylor, "Looking for Mr. Benson: The Black Leather Motorcycle Jacket and Narratives of Masculinities," in *Fashion in Popular Culture*, edited by Vicki Karaminas, Toni Johnson-Woods, and Joseph Hancock (Bristol, UK: Intellect, 2013), 126.
24. The information presented here comes from the GSC constitution and by-laws, planning documents, letters from and to members, and event flyers (GSCC).
25. Brian Rogers, "It All Started with a Crazy Idea," GRH, http://gayrodeohistory.org/2012/PrideInTheSaddle/021.htm.
26. For more on the Imperial Court System, see Imperial Court System, https://internationalcourtsystem.org; H. M. Berberet, "In Service of Camp or the Campiness of Service: 'The Court' as Queer Civic and Fraternal Organization," *Journal of American Culture* 39, no. 1 (March 2016): 33–40; and Michael Gorman, *The Empress Is a Man: Stories from the Life of José Sarria* (New York: Haworth, 1998).
27. John Rice, "Reno Gay Rodeo Draws Big Crowd," *Nevada State Journal/Reno Evening Gazette*, August 5, 1979, GRH, http://gayrodeohistory.org/indexNewspapers.htm. This same article also appeared in the *Baltimore Sun*, *Mobile Register*, and *New Orleans Times-Picayune*. More details about the history and development of the Reno Rodeo are available in the National Reno Gay Rodeo Program, 1981, GRH, http://gayrodeohistory.org/indexPrograms.htm.
28. National Reno Gay Rodeo Program, 1981, GRH, http://gayrodeohistory.org/indexPrograms.htm.
29. Ivan Sharpe, "Reno's Eye-Opening Gay Rodeo," *San Francisco Examiner*, August 22, 1977, 9, GRC, Folder 6.
30. The history of gay rodeo and many archival materials are available at http://gayrodeohistory.org. Also see Bill Arsenaux, "Ride 'Em Cowboy: Reno's Gay Rodeo," *In Touch for Men* (November 1978): 74–77; John Calendo, "Gay Rodeo: Wild Time in Reno," *In Touch for Men* (January 1981): 34–35; "National Reno Gay Rodeo: An Editor's View," *Skin* 5, no. 1 (1983): 10–17; Charles Faber, "National Reno Gay Rodeo: And in the Saddle," *The Advocate* (September 16, 1982): 21; and Rice, "Reno Gay Rodeo Draws Big Crowd."
31. Pacific Coast Gay Rodeo Association materials, http://gayrodeohistory.org/Newsletters/pcgra/index.htm. This web page includes newsletters, letters, the agenda for a committee meeting, event flyers, and ephemera from PCGRA.
32. "Shortage of Money, Cancels Gay Rodeo," *San Francisco Chronicle*, July 28,

1981; Animal Rights Materials, 1981, GRC, Folder 5. See chapter 5 for an expanded discussion on gay rodeo and animal rights activists.
33. Unless otherwise noted, information about the founding and dissolution of the rodeo associations and the number of rodeos held annually is available at GRH.
34. Untitled newsletter document, circa 1981/1982, Autry Archives, Box 6; Comstock Gay Rodeo Association Newsletter, December 1980, GRC, Folder 5; National Reno Gay Rodeo Flyer, 1984, GRC, Folder 5.
35. Wayne Jakino to Mr. President, January 16, 1982, Autry Archives, Box 6.
36. Joseph Sedlack to Ron Jesser (CGRA), January 14, 1982, Autry Archives, Box 6; Joseph M. Sedlack to Wayne Jakino, February 10, 1982, Autry Archives, Box 6.
37. IGRA Timeline, GRH.
38. "Reno Gay Rodeo Canceled for 1985," *Reno Gazette*, August 1, 1985, 29; Laura Myers, "Gay Rodeo Will Return to Reno in October," *Reno Gazette*, June 7, 1988, RGRC, Folder 4; IGRA Annual Convention Program, 1992, GRH, http://gayrodeohistory.org/indexPrograms.htm.
39. IGRA Rodeo Rule Books, 1984, 1985, 1986, 2015, GRH, http://gayrodeohistory.org/indexRodeoRules.htm.
40. IGRA rule books are available at http://gayrodeohistory.org/indexRodeoRules.htm. The rule book continued to call it "goat decorating" in 1989 and 1990, but the finals rodeo programs switched to "goat dressing" in 1989. The rules stayed the same, so this was not a substantial change.
41. These instructions appeared in the very first rule book in 1984 and have remained the same in ensuing rule books. IGRA Rule Book, 1984, GRH, http://gayrodeohistory.org/indexPrograms.htm.
42. IGRA Newsletter, September 1987, Autry Archives, Box 2; GSGRA Newsletter, no month, 1985, Autry Archives, Box 2; GSGRA Newsletter, May 1994, GRH, http://gayrodeohistory.org/indexNewsletters.htm; IGRA Bylaws, Standing Rules and Rodeo Rules 1986–87, 7, Autry Archives, 94.79.41 MOAW; IGRA Finals Rodeo Brochure, 1987, Autry Archives, 94.79.48 MOAW.
43. IGRA Rodeo Programs, GRH, http://gayrodeohistory.org/index-programs-thumbs.htm.
44. Evelyn C. White, "5,000 See Dust Fly at Gay Rodeo," *San Francisco Chronicle*, September 21, 1987.
45. IGRA Newsletter, November 1987, Autry Archives, Box 2.
46. Rodney Foo, "Commissioner's Fight against Gay Rodeo 'Dead,'" *Nevada State Journal*, June 9, 1981, 1–12, Autry Archives, Box 6; "Gay Rodeo Opens Despite Opposition Due to AIDS Fear," *Los Angeles Times*, August 5, 1983, A2; "Coalition Using Health Threat," *USA Today*, July 28, 1983; "Unpaid Bill May End Gay Rodeo," *Las Vegas Review-Journal*, November 6, 1984; "The Future of This City's Famed Gay Rodeo," *The Advocate*, January 28, 1985; "Gay Rodeo Chairman Claims Plans Still Underway for 1986 Big Event," *Bohemian Bugle*, April 1986, GRC, Folder 6.

47. IGRA Bylaws 1986–87, 22–24. For the 1988 IGRA finals rodeo program, see GRH, http://gayrodeohistory.org/indexPrograms.htm.
48. UGRA Newsletter, April 1990, Autry Archives, Box 4.
49. The Arkansas group was founded in 1990 but did not join IGRA officially until 1991 at the national convention. This process was the same for all of the associations. They were founded and then would be officially seated at the next IGRA convention, which explains why sometimes there was a year's gap between a group's founding and its joining IGRA. Even though the Arkansas group did not officially join IGRA until the 1991 convention, it was active earlier. DSRA Newsletter, May 1990, Autry Archives, Box 4.
50. Letter from Reon Shelton to R. J. Newby, March 25, 1990, Autry Archives, Box 4. The Australian rodeo had a three-day program, with a tennis tournament, a bush dance (as opposed to the American barn dance), and a one-day rodeo. The organizer drew inspiration directly from IGRA and invited a representative to attend their version of the gay rodeo, although it is unclear if IGRA took up the offer.
51. IGRA Convention 1988–89 Newsletter, mailed 1990, Autry Archives, Box 4. Box 4 also contains IGRA meeting notes in which this newsletter was planned and concerns about participation and rodeo size were raised. On March 30, 1990, Roger Bergmann submitted his own list of suggestions to shorten the rodeos (also in Box 4). While the convention that year identified five hundred competitors, the organization commonly cited eight thousand members in internal correspondence to prospective sponsors; see, for instance, Letter to Miller Breweries from Wayne Jakino, Autry Archives, Box 15. Membership committee records, however, show the verified members in good standing to be 2,817 in 1993, 2,891 in 1995, and 2,641 in 1997; see IGRA Association and Division Membership Totals, Autry Archives, Box 47. Similar discrepancies appear in today's reporting of membership numbers. For instance, on February 12, 2015, *Echo Magazine* reported that IGRA had almost five thousand members. Official annual conference reports show a 2013 membership of 1,685, a significant dip in 2014 to 1,345, and a 2015 number of 1,600.
52. IGRA continued to grow in the early 1990s. In 1992 there was a new group, in Nevada; in 1993 three (Illinois, Alberta in Canada, and Heartland for Nebraska); and in 1994 one, in Michigan. IGRA Timeline, GRH.
53. Other examples include the Sooner State Rodeo Association, which split Oklahoma into two groups. It was founded in 2002 and folded in 2013. Those same years, the High Sierra Rodeo Association, made up of a single county in Nevada, also emerged and dissolved. The Liberty Gay Rodeo Association, located in Philadelphia, joined in 2006 and ended in 2011, following what its president called a "devastating" financial situation after a poorly attended 2009 association rodeo and a canceled 2010 rodeo; see LGRA Newsletter, March 2010, GRH, http://gayrodeohistory.org/indexNewsletters.htm.
54. Some of these rodeos were explicitly nontraditional. In 1990, an All People's

Rodeo held by the Tri-State Gay Rodeo Association included events not sanctioned by the IGRA rule book, like stud decorating, wild cowboy riding, and fastest "blow job." No subsequent rodeos were held by this association. TSGRA Program, 1990, GRH, http://gayrodeohistory.org/indexPrograms.htm.

55. Cedrick Heraux, "Homophobia in Sport: Who Can Play?" in *Playing on an Uneven Field: Essays on Exclusion and Inclusion in Sports*, edited by Yuya Kiuchi (Jefferson, NC: McFarland & Company, 2019). For a history of the Gay Games, see Caroline Symons, *The Gay Games: A History* (London: Routledge, 2010).

56. For a comparison of gay rodeo and the Gay Games, see Ford, "Becoming the West."

57. Quoted by contestant John King in White, "5,000 See Dust Fly." Despite King's quote, he was intimately involved in the bar scene, but one born out of the country-western enthusiasm of the late 1970s and early '80s. King owned Charlie's, a gay country bar in Denver, and it became a home to the nascent but rapidly growing Colorado Gay Rodeo Association, founded by his business partner Wayne Jakino. For more on Charlie's, see Chris Arneson, "Charlie's Looks Back on More than Three Decades of Business," *OutFront Magazine* (May 18, 2016), www.outfrontmagazine.com/charlies-looks-back-three-decades-business.

58. "Why a Gay Rodeo? Why Not!," *QC* (June–July 1995): 5–8, Autry Archives, Box 8; reprinted in *Roundup* (August 1995), Autry Archives, Box 25.

59. For examples of these rodeo schools, see these offerings from the Red River Rodeo Association, www.redriverrodeoassociation.com; and the Colorado Gay Rodeo Association, www.cgrarodeo.com/rodeo-school.

60. Quoted in John Marchese, "Bustin' Stereotypes," *New York Times*, September 26, 1993. For more information about privacy and anonymity in gay rodeo, see Rice, "Reno Gay Rodeo"; Comstock Gay Rodeo Association: Rules/Regulations for all Contestants/Events, 1983, GRC, Folder 5; PCGRA materials, GRH, http://gayrodeohistory.org/Newsletters/pcgra/index.htm; and IGRA Rule Book, 1984, GRH, http://gayrodeohistory.org/indexRodeoRules.htm.

61. Many IGRA members mention these concerns; see Bruce Roby, email interview with Elyssa Ford, July 30, 2015; Carolyn Jones, email interview with Elyssa Ford, July 27, 2015; Todd Garrett, email interview with Elyssa Ford, July 28, 2015; Amy Griffin, email interview with Elyssa Ford, July 27, 2015; and Laura Scott, email interview with Elyssa Ford, July 27, 2015.

2. "HOOKIN' UP" AT THE GAY RODEO

1. Susan Jeffords, *The Remasculinization of America: Gender and the Vietnam War* (Bloomington: Indiana University Press, 1989), 168. For more on discophobia and its roots in homophobia, see Gillian Frank, "Discophobia: Anti-Gay Prejudice and the 1979 Backlash against Disco," *Journal of the History of Sexuality* 16, no. 2 (May 2007): 276–306.

2. Chuck Browning, interview with Rebecca Scofield, Gay Rodeo Oral History Project, June 9, 2022, Denver, CO.
3. For more on buckle bunnies on the rodeo circuit, see DeAnn K. Gauthier and Craig J. Forsyth, "Buckle Bunnies: Groupies of the Rodeo Circuit," *Deviant Behavior* 21, no. 4 (July–August 2000): 349–65. For more on the sexualization of female rodeo participants, see Joan Burbick, *Rodeo Queens and the American Dream* (New York: PublicAffairs, 2002); and Renee Laegreid, *Riding Pretty: Rodeo Royalty in the American West* (Lincoln: University of Nebraska Press, 2006). Also see the 2013 A&E reality show *Rodeo Girls*, which featured barrel racers riding in bikinis on its promotional materials.
4. For more on the fitness and physique magazines, see Thomas Waugh, *Hard to Imagine: Gay Male Eroticism in Photography and Film from Their Beginnings to Stonewall* (New York: Columbia University Press, 1996); David Johnson, "Physique Pioneers: The Politics of 1960s Gay Consumer Culture," *Journal of Social History* (Summer 2010): 867–92; and Herbert Otto, "'The Pornographic Fringeland' on the American Newsstand," *Journal of Human Relations* 12 (1964): 375–90.
5. Tracy D. Morgan, "Pages of Whiteness: Race, Physique Magazines, and the Emergence of Public Gay Culture," in *Queer Studies: A Lesbian, Gay, Bisexual, and Transgender Anthology*, edited by Brett Beemyn and Mickey Eliason (New York: New York University Press, 1996), 289–91.
6. Jennifer Evans, "Queer Beauty: Image and Acceptance in the Expanded Public Sphere," in *Globalizing Beauty: Consumerism and Body Aesthetics in the Twentieth Century*, edited by Harmut Berghoff and Thomas Kuhne (New York: Palgrave Macmillan, 2013), 99; Morgan, "Pages of Whiteness," 287.
7. Micha Ramakers, *Dirty Pictures: Tom of Finland, Masculinity, and Homosexuality* (New York: St. Martin's Press, 2001), xi, 38–39.
8. Ramakers, *Dirty Pictures*, 64–65. This concept of gender presentation and the sexual role that men took equating to sexuality also is discussed in Craig Loftin, "Unacceptable Mannerisms: Gender Anxieties, Homosexual Activism, and Swish in the United States, 1945–1965," *Journal of Social History* 40 (2007): 577–96; and George Chauncey, *Gay New York: Gender, Urban Culture, and the Makings of the Gay Male World, 1890–1940* (New York: Basic Books, 1994).
9. Jeff Auer, "Cowboys on the Cover of a Magazine," *Gay & Lesbian Review Worldwide* 15, no. 6 (November 2008): 13–16; Waugh, *Hard to Imagine*, 150–51, 162–73, 265–66. Kris Studio released *The Hired Hand* in 1963, which featured a city slicker who was lured to a homestead by a tricky nude rancher; romantic and sexual love ensued. *The Fugitive*, also from Kris Studio in 1963, was hard-core porn about an outlaw on the run in the Wild West. For more on Chuck Renslow, see Tracy Baim and Owen Keehen, *Leatherman: The Legend of Chuck Renslow* (Chicago: Prairie Avenue Productions, 2001).
10. Chong-suk Han and Kyung-Hee Choi, "Very Few People Say 'No Whites':

Gay Men of Color and the Racial Politics of Desire," *Sociological Spectrum* 38, no. 3 (July 2018): 145–61.

11. Ramakers, *Dirty Pictures*, 106–7. Also see some of the work by Corey W. Johnson about country-western gay bars, including "'The First Step Is the Two-Step': Hegemonic Masculinity and Dancing in a Country-Western Gay Bar," *International Journal of Qualitative Studies in Education* 18, no. 4 (July–August 2005): 445–64; and "'Don't Call Him a Cowboy': Masculinity, Cowboy Drag, and a Costume Change," *Journal of Leisure Research* 40, no. 3 (2008): 385–403.

12. Loftin, "Unacceptable Mannerisms"; Derek Nystrom, *Hard Hats, Rednecks, and Macho Men: Class in 1970s American Cinema* (New York: Oxford University Press, 2009), 140.

13. Ramakers, *Dirty Pictures*, 65.

14. Les Wright, *The Bear Book: Readings in the History and Evolution of a Gay Male Subculture* (New York: Routledge, 1997), 24–29. Also see Iulian Suman, "Scruffy Masculinities: A Visual Analysis of Gay Bear Representations in Walter Van Beirendonck's Runways" (MA thesis, Stockholm University, 2021).

15. Randy Shulman, "This Cowboy's Life," *Metro Weekly*, October 1, 1998, 26–35, Autry Archives, Box 42.

16. Interview by Perry Brass, posted to *Gay Today*, January 1999, Autry Archives, Box 51.

17. For more on the way that masculine gay men threatened traditional understandings of homosexual inferiority and heterosexual superiority, see Theo Sonnekus, "Macho Men and the Queer Imaginary: A Critique of Selected Gay 'Colonial' Representations of Homomasculinity," *De Arte* 30 (2009): 37–53.

18. Mary McHale, letter to the editor, *Reno Gazette*, March 23, 1981, 4.

19. Email to IGRA Leadership, October 31, 1997, Autry Archives, Box 42. Other emails sent between 1997 and 2000 made similar claims, Autry Archives, Box 42.

20. Loftin, "Unacceptable Mannerisms," 578; Sonnekus, "Macho Men and the Queer Imaginary," 38.

21. Loftin, "Unacceptable Mannerisms," 582.

22. Reno Gay Rodeo Poster, 1979, accessed July 29, 2015, http://outhistory.org/exhibits/show/las-vegas/articles/rgr.

23. Ragsdale's quotes about the wild cow milking event come from "Wild Cow Milking Contest: 'Working Together,'" National Reno Gay Rodeo Program, 1981, GRH, http://gayrodeohistory.org/indexPrograms.htm. Ragsdale also made similar comments in a news article that same year in "Breaking Barriers, Building Bonds at Rodeo," *Go! Great Outdoors Magazine* (Fall 1981): 4–6, GRH, http://gayrodeohistory.org/indexNewspapers.htm. For information about the change from wild cow milking to wild drag race, see MGRA Newsletter, March 1987, Autry Archives, Box 2; and IGRA Rule Book, 1987, GRH, http://gayrodeohistory.org/indexRodeoRules.htm.

24. IGRA Finals Rodeo Audience Surveys, 1997, Autry Archives, Box 47. Of the twenty-eight total survey participants, three added comments specifically criticizing the involvement of drag queens and the royalty contest. No respondent wrote in support of this more feminine element, though 21 percent admitted they attended the rodeo primarily to see the royalty competition and entertainment.
25. Letter to GSGRA, San Francisco Chapter, October 15, 1997, Autry Archives, Box 38.
26. Letter to GSGRA, October 19, 1997, Autry Archives, Box 38.
27. Rice, "Reno Gay Rodeo Draws Big Crowd," GRH, http://gayrodeohistory.org/indexNewspapers.htm.
28. "'Not for Sissies' Gay Rodeo True to the West," *Denver Post*, July 12, 1999, B-01. Capous-Desyllas and Johnson-Rhodes, "Collecting Visual Voices" and Johnson, "'Don't Call Him a Cowboy" also discuss the presence of hegemonic masculinity in queer country-western spaces, including the gay rodeo and country-western gay bars.
29. Martin P. Levine, *Gay Macho: The Life and Death of the Homosexual Clone*, edited by Michael S. Kimmel (New York: New York University Press, 1998), 1–8.
30. John Calendo, "Interview with Dave Wilson," *In Touch for Men* (January 1981): 77, GRH, http://gayrodeohistory.org/indexMagazines.htm. Other examples of articles that promote an authentic western identity of gay rodeo contestants include Bob Morris, "Like a Rhinestone Cowboy," *Out Magazine* (April 1996), 120–23, 152, 154, 156, Autry Archives, Box 30; and "Contestant Profile: Tammy Crowder," *Roundup*, October 1996, 61, Autry Archives, Box 30.
31. Jan Klunder, "Homosexuals Stage State's 1st Gay Rodeo," *Los Angeles Times*, March 31, 1985, 3.
32. Quote in Celeste McGovern, "Homo on the Range: The Alberta Gay Rodeo Association Goes Public," *Alberta Report*, July 18, 1994, 29. In 2022 actor Sam Elliott similarly questioned the existence of gay cowboys, this time on the range, in comments he made about the gay Western *The Power of the Dog*, saying on a podcast that the film was a "piece of shit" for the "evisceration of the American West" with "all these allusions to homosexuality throughout the fucking movie"; see David Reddish, "Sam Elliott Goes on Epic Rant," *Queerty*, March 1, 2022, www.queerty.com/sam-elliott-goes-epic-rant-trashing-piece-sht-gay-movie-power-dog-20220301.
33. Letter from Wayne Jakino to Phil Ragsdale, January 15, 1982, Autry Archives, Box 6.
34. CGRA Newsletter, April 1984; CGRA Newsletter, August 1995, GRH, http://gayrodeohistory.org/Newsletters/cgra/index.htm; Allen Kalchik, "All Around Cowboy—Greg Olson," *Roundup* (Spring 1994): 16–17, Autry Archives, Box 17.
35. OGRA Newsletter, August 1995, GRH, http://gayrodeohistory.org/Newsletters/ogra/index.htm.

36. IGRA Board of Directors Meeting Minutes, January 12, 1996, Autry Archives, Box 32.
37. Letter from Panda Bear to IGRA, August 20, 1995, Autry Archives, Box 32.
38. ILGRA Newsletter, December 1996, Autry Archives, Box 38.
39. MIGRA Newsletter, January 2014, GRH, http://gayrodeohistory.org/Newsletters/migra/index.htm; PCGRA Newsletter, circa 1981, GRH, http://gayrodeohistory.org/Newsletters/pcgra/index.htm.
40. IGRA Board of Directors Meeting Minutes, Annual Convention, July 1998, Autry Archives, Box 43.
41. Dottie Indyke, "ABQ Welcomes Zia Rodeo," *Out Magazine* (August 2002): 14–15, Autry Archives, Box 72.
42. Emails to IGRA Leadership, October 14, 1997, and November 15, 1997, Autry Archives, Box 42.
43. Roundup Mail Bag, *Roundup* (October 1995): 4, Autry Archives, Box 25.
44. For examples of cowboy features in non-country-western gay erotica, see the "Bronc Busting" feature in *Numbers* (February 1983); "Cruising Cowboys," *Blueboy* 2, no. 1 (1981); and the "Bronc Bustin' Cowboy Issue," *Mandate* (July 1982).
45. Jay Clarkson, "'Everyday Joe' versus 'Pissy, Bitchy, Queens': Gay Masculinity on StraightActing.com," *Journal of Men's Studies* 14, no. 2 (Spring 2006): 203.
46. An audience survey at the 1997 IGRA finals rodeo showed that 74.1 percent of respondents identified as urban residents versus only 25.9 percent identifying as rural. IGRA Finals Rodeo Audience Surveys, 1997, Autry Archives, Box 47.
47. National Reno Gay Rodeo Program, 1979, GRH, http://gayrodeohistory.org/1979/ProgramReno.htm.
48. National Reno Gay Rodeo Program, 1980, GRH, http://gayrodeohistory.org/1980/ProgramReno.htm.
49. O'Driscoll, "10,000 Hoot," 1–4A, Autry Archives, Box 6.
50. Samet, "Reno Rodeo Plays Host," Autry Archives, Box 6.
51. Faber, "National Reno Gay Rodeo."
52. For more on the use of poppers by gay men, see John Lauritsen, "Political-Economic Construction of Gay Male Clone Identity," *Journal of Homosexuality* 24, no. 3–4 (1993): 227–28.
53. The mainstream LGBTQ+ publications referred to here include magazines such as *Genre, Instinct, Metro Weekly*, and *The Advocate*, rather than those intended as adult-oriented or erotica.
54. IGRA Board of Directors Meeting, Annual Convention, 1995, Autry Archives, Box 23; and 1998, Autry Archives, Box 59.
55. Letter from Wayne Jakino to IGRA and Responses from TGRA Members, 1997, Autry Archives, Box 42.
56. Patrick Moore, *Beyond Shame: Reclaiming the Abandoned History of Radical Gay Sexuality* (Boston: Beacon Press, 2004), 78–81; Deborah Gould, *Moving*

Politics: Emotion and ACT UP's Fight against AIDS (Chicago: University of Chicago Press, 2009), 311–13.

57. For instance, see Charles Yoo, "Gay Rodeo Rounds Up Charity Cash," *Atlanta Journal-Constitution*, July 26, 2004, B1.
58. Los Angeles Rodeo Programs, 1985, 1990, and 1991; and Denver Rodeo Program, 1990, GRH, http://gayrodeohistory.org/indexPrograms.htm.
59. Denver Rodeo Program, 1990, GRH, http://gayrodeohistory.org/index Programs.htm.
60. Benita Roth, *The Life and Death of ACT UP/LA* (New York: Cambridge University Press, 2017), 34–35. For more information about the condemnation of any gay male sex during the AIDS crisis, see Ephen Glenn Colter, Wayne Hoffman, Eva Pendleton, Alison Redick, and David Serlin, eds., *Policing Public Sex: Queer Politics and the Future of AIDS Activism* (Boston: South End Press, 1996). For more on gay bathhouses, see Allan Bérubé, "The History of Gay Bathhouses," also in *Policing Public Sex*, 187–220.
61. Douglas Crimp, "How to Have Promiscuity in an Epidemic," in *AIDS: Cultural Analysis, Cultural Activism*, edited by Douglas Crimp (Cambridge, MA: MIT Press, 1987), 270; José Esteban Muñoz, "Ghosts of Public Sex: Utopian Longings, Queer Memories," in Colter et al., *Policing Public Sex*, 357.
62. Thomas J. Linneman, "Risk and Masculinity in the Everyday Lives of Gay Men," in *Gay Masculinities*, edited by Peter Nardi (Thousand Oaks, CA: Sage Publications, 2000), 85. Also see Michael Shernoff, *Without Condoms: Unprotected Sex, Gay Men, and Barebacking* (New York: Routledge, 2006).
63. Richard Labonte, ed., *Country Boys: Wild Gay Erotica* (Jersey City, NJ: Cleis, 2007), 104.
64. Phil Julian, "A Bullrider's View in Less Than Six Seconds," *Frontiers* (May 23, 1996): 22.
65. Eric Rofes, *Dry Bones Breathe: Gay Men Creating Post-AIDS Identities and Cultures* (New York: Haworth Press, 1998), 3–4.
66. Quote in Rofes, *Dry Bones Breathe*, 132–33. Also see Eva Pendleton, "Domesticating Partnerships," in Colter et al., *Policing Public Sex*, 381–83; and Christopher Castiglia and Christopher Reed, *If Memory Serves: Gay Men, AIDS, and the Promise of the Queer Past* (Minneapolis: University of Minnesota Press, 2011), 45.
67. IGRA Rodeo Program Covers, 1990s–2000s, GRH, http://gayrodeohistory .org/indexPrograms.htm; IGRA Rodeo Brochures, 2000–2005, Autry Archives, Boxes 62 and 78.
68. Klunder, "Homosexuals Stage," 3.
69. Letter to IGRA, 1997, Autry Archives, Box 38.
70. UGRA Newsletter, April 1990, Autry Archives, Box 4. For other examples of gay rodeo participants who desired a "wholesome" social environment outside the gay bar scene and associations that presented their rodeos this way, see Sandy Hume, "Bum Steer," *American Spectator* 25, no. 12 (December 1992): 47; Indyke, "ABQ Welcomes Zia Rodeo"; Yoo, "Gay Rodeo Rounds

Up"; and NGRA Newsletter, October 2014, GRH, http://gayrodeohistory.org/Newsletters/ngra/index.htm.
71. National Reno Gay Rodeo Programs, 1979–84, GRH, http://gayrodeohistory.org/indexPrograms.htm.
72. IGRA Annual Convention, 1999, Autry Archives, Box 50; IGRA Annual Convention, 2000, Autry Archives, Box 59.
73. Los Angeles Rodeo Brochure, 2001, Autry Archives, Box 62.
74. Letter to GSGRA, San Francisco Chapter, October 15, 1997, Autry Archives, Box 38; Letter from Panda Bear to IGRA, August 20, 1995, Autry Archives, Box 32. These criticisms continued into the following decade. One anonymous survey following the 2002 San Diego rodeo said, "It is not about the rodeo. Cowboy circuit party." See 2002 Rodeo Surveys, Autry Archives, Box 72.

3. "A EUPHEMISM FOR AN ORGY"

1. "Culture of care" comes from the field of psychology. Don S. Browning described it in 1980 as developing concern and a system of care for oneself, one's community, and humanity more broadly. It calls for "an individual and collective sense of responsibility." Psychologists place the culture of care in opposition to the culture of control and the culture of joy. Don S. Browning, *William James and Some Contemporary Cultures of Psychology* (Lewisburg, PA: Bucknell University Press, 1980), 41–42.
2. Michael Bronski, *A Queer History of the United States* (Boston: Beacon Press, 2011), 218–19.
3. Bronski, *Queer History*, 219–20; Tina Fetner, *How the Religious Right Shaped Lesbian and Gay Activism* (Minneapolis: University of Minnesota Press, 2008).
4. Bronski, *Queer History of the United States*, 224; James Kinsella, *Covering the Plague: AIDS and the American Media* (New Brunswick, NJ: Rutgers University Press, 1989), 1–2, 8–9.
5. Most notably, the *New York Times* reported in early July on a rare cancer in forty-one gay men. Kinsella, *Covering the Plague*, 10–11; Bronski, *Queer History of the United States*, 224.
6. Kinsella, *Covering the Plague*, 90–91, 129–30.
7. Bronski, *Queer History of the United States*, 225.
8. Gould, *Moving Politics*, 50.
9. Jennifer Brier, *Infectious Ideas: U.S. Political Responses to the AIDS Crisis* (Chapel Hill: University of North Carolina Press, 2009), 78–79; Anthony Petro, *After the Wrath of God: AIDS, Sexuality, and American Religion* (New York: Oxford University Press, 2015), 55, 66–69.
10. Perry N. Halkitis, *The AIDS Generation: Stories of Survival and Resilience* (New York: Oxford University Press, 2014), 6, 56–57.
11. Bronski, *Queer History of the United States*, 225.

12. Simon Watney, *Policing Desire: Pornography, AIDS, and the Media*, 3rd ed. (London: Cassell, 1997, 1st ed., 1987), 18.
13. Colter et al., *Policing Public Sex*. For some of the debate within the LGBTQ+ community on sex, see Crimp, "How to Have Promiscuity" (1987) and Leo Bersani, "Is the Rectum a Grave?" (1987) as sex-positive advocates versus Randy Shilts's *And the Band Played On* (1987), Larry Kramer's *The Normal Heart* (1985), Michael Signorile, and Gabriel Rotello as gay neoconservatives who blamed AIDS on gay sexual culture and wanted to end public sex sites.
14. Susan Sontag, *Illness as Metaphor and AIDS and Its Metaphors* (New York: Anchor Books, 1990; constituent parts first published 1978 and 1989, respectively), 164.
15. Roth, *Life and Death* (New York: Cambridge University Press, 2017), 3.
16. Seth Dowland, "'Family Values' and the Formation of a Christian Right," *Church History* 78, no. 3 (September 2009): 606–31; J. Brooks Flippen, *Jimmy Carter, the Politics of Family, and the Rise of the Religious Right* (Athens: University of Georgia Press, 2011), 250–51.
17. By the early twenty-first century, the Independent American Party was Nevada's third-largest political party, with more than 14,000 registered voters, and it maintained its conservative values, including anti-LGBTQ+ beliefs. For more on the IAP, see Erin Neff, "Hansens Are Heart of the IAP," *Las Vegas Sun*, September 27, 2002; "About Us," American Independent Party, https://web.archive.org/web/20130321114535/http://www.iapn.org/newiap/2010aboutus.html.
18. National Reno Gay Rodeo Program, 1984, GRH, http://gayrodeohistory.org/indexPrograms.htm. By 1984 the fairgrounds were called the Nevada State Fairgrounds, but the location remained the same as it did under the earlier title, the Washoe County Fairgrounds.
19. National Reno Gay Rodeo Program, 1982, GRH, http://gayrodeohistory.org/indexPrograms.htm.
20. Sharpe, "Reno's Eye-Opening Gay Rodeo," 9, GRC, Folder 6; Gary Pederson, "Rodeo for Gays Fills Nevada Fair Ground," *Sacramento Bee*, August 21, 1977, GRC, Folder 6.
21. "Gays Hold a Rodeo to Counter Stereotype," *Boston Globe*, August 6, 1979, GRC, Folder 6. Ragsdale responded to these queer-led boycotts in the 1981 rodeo program, though it is unclear if these protests continued into 1981 or if Ragsdale just waited until that year's rodeo to make a statement. National Reno Gay Rodeo Program, 1981, GRH, http://gayrodeohistory.org/indexPrograms.htm.
22. Martin Griffith, "Leavitt Against Gay Rodeo," *Reno Gazette*, July 5, 1981, 1.
23. "Nevada's Governor Joins Rodeo Critics," no newspaper name, no date, GRC, Folder 6.
24. "Letters," *Reno Gazette*, March 23, 1981, 4.
25. Howard Smith and Lin Harris, "Western Gayla," *Village Voice*, June 16, 1981, GRC, Folder 6.

26. "Letters from Our Readers," *Reno Gazette*, July 5, 1981, GRC, Folder 6.
27. "Gay Rodeo," *The Advocate*, September 18, 1980, 18; "Gay Rodeo May Attract 20,000," *Reno Gazette*, July 29, 1981, GRC, Folder 6; O'Driscoll, "10,000 Hoot," 1–4A, Autry Archives, Box 6; Samet, "Reno Rodeo Plays Host," Autry Archives, Box 6.
28. "California AIDS Cases Double," *Reno Gazette*, June 23, 1983, 51.
29. While many newspapers refused to report on AIDS in its earliest years, the *Reno Gazette* discussed the disease soon after it first appeared in the *New York Times*, with one article in July 1981 and another in December 1981. At least five articles appeared in 1983, and the Washoe Medical Center offered a public program about AIDS that year, see "AIDS Program Planned," *Reno Gazette*, August 1, 1983, 31. Other AIDS-related articles appeared in the *Reno Gazette* in 1983 on June 23 (p. 51), July 20 (p. 4), and September 2 (p. 15).
30. Dennis McBride, *Out of the Neon Closet: Queer Community in the Sliver State* (North Charleston, SC: CreateSpace, 2016), 170; "AIDS Cases on the Rise in Washoe County," *Reno Gazette*, May 2, 1985, 1, 16.
31. Wayne Melton, "County Probably Can't Prohibit Reno Gay Rodeo," *Reno Gazette*, July 21, 1983; "Layoffs, Gay Rodeo-Ban," *Reno Gazette*, July 25, 1983; "Psychologist: Physicians Fear Reprisals from Gays," *Reno Gazette*, July 25, 1983; "Petition Opposes Gay Rodeo," *Las Vegas Sun*, July 26, 1983; "Gay Rodeo Debate," *Reno Gazette*, July 26, 1983; Helen Manning, "Gay Rodeo Foes Shot Down," *Reno Gazette*, July 27, 1983; Wayne Melton, "AIDS Focus of Arguments," *Reno Gazette*, July 28, 1983; "Gay Rodeo Won't Be Stopped," *Reno Gazette*, July 31, 1983; Tracey Wong, "Opposition Helping Gay Rodeo," *Nevada State Journal*, August 2, 1983 (all articles from GRC, Folder 6).
32. "Gay Rodeo Opens Despite Opposition," A2; "Coalition Using Health Threat," 7A, GRH, http://gayrodeohistory.org/indexNewspapers.htm; No title, *USA Today*, July 28, 1983; "Group Speaks Out Against Gay Rodeo," *Las Vegas Sun*, June 15, 1984, GRC, Folder 6.
33. Cory Farley, "Fear and Loathing in Reno: 'Patriots' Blither Anonymously," *Reno Gazette*, July 25, 1983, GRC, Folder 6.
34. Lee Adler, "Anti-Gay Activist Fails to See Governor," *Reno Gazette*, July 30, 1983; "Bryan Rejects Gay Proposal," *Las Vegas Sun*, August 10, 1983; "Rodeo Foes Undaunted," *Las Vegas Sun*, August 17, 1983; "No Trouble at Gay Rodeo," unnamed Reno paper, August 5, 1983; "Gay Rodeo Won't Be Stopped"; "Attendance Down at Gay Rodeo," *San Francisco Examiner*, July 24, 1984 (all from GRC, Folder 6).
35. "Group Speaks Out Against Gay Rodeo"; No title, *USA Today*, June 15, 1984. Arguments presenting gay men as child molesters have been used for decades. The cautionary film *Boys Beware* in 1961 and the Save Our Children campaign, with spokesperson Anita Bryant, in the late 1970s also made this same claim; see *Boys Beware*, directed by Sid Davis (Sidney Davis Productions, 1961) and Fetner, *How the Religious Right*, 25.
36. A small group of ten animal rights activists protested the 1984 Reno rodeo,

but no on-site opposition from the PFCC was noted in newspapers. "Attendance Down at Gay Rodeo"; "Unpaid Bill May End Gay Rodeo" (both from GRC, Folder 6). Scholars have discussed how protests by the Christian Right brought more press attention to LGBTQ+ rights and inadvertently helped to grow the gay rights movement. This aligns with the success of the Reno gay rodeo in 1981 and 1983, when increased opposition led to increased support and attendance, while the more limited 1984 protests led to little newspaper coverage and, accordingly, a drop in attendance. See Fetner, *How the Religious Right* and Chris Bull and John Gallagher, *Perfect Enemies: The Religious Right, the Gay Movement, and the Politics of the 1990s* (New York: Crown Publishing Group, 1996).

37. No title, *The Advocate*, January 22, 1985.
38. Lillian Faderman, *The Gay Revolution: The Story of the Struggle* (New York: Simon and Schuster, 2015), 416, 424. For more on the criminalization of HIV/AIDS, see Trevor Hoppe, *Punishing Disease: HIV and the Criminalization of Sickness* (Oakland: University of California Press, 2018).
39. Petro, *After the Wrath of God*, 187; Hoppe, *Punishing Disease*, 2.
40. IGRA Finals Rodeo Program, 1987, Autry Archives, Box 2.
41. Evelyn C. White," 5,000 See Dust Fly," GRH, http://gayrodeohistory.org/indexNewspapers.htm; Samet, "Reno Rodeo Plays Host," Autry Archives, Box 6.
42. Initial announcement: Myers, "Gay Rodeo Will Return," 17.
43. Mario Talkington, "Eagle Forum Organizers Against Gay Rodeo," *Reno Gazette*, July 6, 1988, 27.
44. Laura Myers, "Gay Rodeo Seeks Injunction Over Canceled Contract," *San Francisco Examiner*, September 19, 1988; "Gay Rodeo Hearing Set," *Reno Gazette*, September 7, 1988, 27; Michael Phillis, "Judge Opens Gay Rodeo Hearing," *Reno Gazette*, September 16, 1988, 32; Michael Phillis, "Judge to Rule on Gay Rodeo Contract," *Reno Gazette*, September 17, 1988, 18; "Judge Won't Force Gay Rodeo on Lawlor," *Reno Gazette*, September 20, 1988, 19; "Lawlor Again Rebuffs Gay Rodeo Organizers," *Reno Gazette*, September 21, 1988, 27; Lenita Powers, "ACLU: University Discriminated against Gay Rodeo," *Reno Gazette*, September 20, 1988, 1C–2C.
45. Jim Mitchell, "Organizers Say County Discriminated," *Reno Gazette*, October 7, 1988, 1C–2C.
46. Mike Henderson, "Event Set for This Weekend at Area Ranch," *Reno Gazette*, October 17, 1988, 1C–2C.
47. Doug McMillan, "Churchill County Officials Block Gay Rodeo," *Reno Gazette*, October 21, 1988, 1C.
48. Doug McMillan, "Churchill Officials Move to Block Gay Rodeo," *Reno Gazette*, October 20, 1988, 1C, GRH, http://gayrodeohistory.org/1988/1988-10-20-RenoGazetteJournal.htm.
49. In 1983 there was only one confirmed case at Washoe County hospitals. By 1985 there were six Washoe County cases confirmed locally, and most of

those patients died within the year. The health system said local numbers were even higher, as three to five people visited Reno hospitals monthly with symptoms but traveled to California cities for diagnosis and treatment. In August 1985 the Washoe County District Health Office set up an AIDS task force to better prepare health professionals and emergency personnel. By 1987 Washoe County had twelve reported cases and expected that to double in 1988, with seventeen new cases already reported by July of that year. "AIDS Cases on the Rise," 1, 16; "Washoe Task Force Sets Up AIDS Workshops," *Reno Gazette*, September 4, 1985, 49; Lila Fujimoto, "Area Hospitals Work on Dealing with AIDS," *Reno Gazette*, November 4, 1985, 1A, 6A; Jim Mitchell, "New AIDS Cases Predicted to Double," *Reno Gazette*, July 24, 1988, 1D, 4D.

50. "I Say There Will Be Confrontation: Interview with D. A. Kevin Pasquale of Churchill County, Nevada," *First Hand Events Magazine* 2 (1989): 67–68, GRH, http://gayrodeohistory.org/indexMagazines.htm.
51. "Tense Aftermath to Banned Gay Rodeo," *Reno Gazette*, October 23, 1988, 1C, GRH, http://gayrodeohistory.org/indexNewspapers.htm.
52. Reno Rodeo Program, 2004, GRH, http://gayrodeohistory.org/indexPrograms.htm. The rodeo program says, "Welcome back to the original home of gay rodeo" [. . .] "Phil . . . your dream has come home!"
53. Jennifer Comes, "Gay Rodeo to Make First Foray into Kansas," *Wichita Eagle*, July 19, 1991, 1D.
54. Lisa Agrimonti, "Gay Rodeo Group Turns to Wichita for Event Site," *Wichita Eagle*, August 17, 1991, 1D. Quotes are from Arizona Gay Rodeo Association Newsletter, September 1991, GRH, http://gayrodeohistory.org/Newsletters/agra/index.htm.
55. AGRA Newsletter, October 1991, GRH, http://gayrodeohistory.org/Newsletters/agra/index.htm; Jim Lynn, "Gay Rodeo to Use West Bank," *Wichita Eagle*, August 28, 1991, 2D; Arizona Gay Rodeo Association Newsletter, November 1991, Autry Archives, Box 1; "Gay Rodeo This Weekend," *Wichita Eagle*, October 20, 1991, 4B; "Officials Eject Reporter," *Wichita Eagle*, October 21, 1991, 3C. On the weekend of the rodeo, IGRA stood by its concerns as entry was denied to a television reporter, and a *Wichita Eagle* newspaper reporter was ejected.
56. CGRA Newsletter, November 1988, GRH, http://gayrodeohistory.org/Newsletters/cgra/index.htm.
57. GSGRA Newsletter, Greater LA Chapter, June 1994, GRC, Folder 6. Attached to the newsletter is a note from Stuart (no last name) to David (no last name) about the AIDS-focused opposition. Stuart asked that the note be retained for the group's historical records. None of the following Los Angeles newspapers reported on protests or opposition: *Times*, *Daily News*, *Evening Express*, *Herald*, and *Mirror News*.
58. OGRA Newsletter, February 1992, Autry Archives, Box 12.
59. BSGRA Newsletter, May 1991, Autry Archives, Box 6. The newsletter

included an article from the front page of the *Albuquerque Tribune*, April 29, 1991, which included the information about the NMGRA rodeo.
60. AGRA Newsletter, October 1991, GRH, http://gayrodeohistory.org/Newsletters/agra/index.htm.
61. AGRA Newsletter, November 1992, GRH, http://gayrodeohistory.org/Newsletters/agra/index.htm.
62. AGRA Newsletter, August 1992, GRH, http://gayrodeohistory.org/Newsletters/agra/index.htm. Other IGRA member associations adopted similar policies. For instance, the Tri-State Gay Rodeo Association of Indiana, Kentucky, and Ohio posted information that its 1990 rodeo would not allow any videos or cameras and that "'Straight Media' will not be allowed on premises"; see TSGRA Newsletter, February 1990, GRH, http://gayrodeohistory.org/Newsletters/tsgra/index.htm.
63. ASGRA Newsletter, July 1993, GRH, http://gayrodeohistory.org/Newsletters/asgra/index.htm; Letter from Roger Bergmann to IGRA Board, May 5, 1993, Autry Archives, Box 12; IGRA Board of Directors Minutes, May 28, 1993, Autry Archives, Box 12. IGRA leadership believed the Jerry Springer show would be an informational piece about gay rodeo that should show the rodeo and queer people in a positive light. Instead, the show changed the lineup at the last minute and used only three gay rodeo participants, alongside two PRCA cowboys who loudly stated that the IGRA rodeos should not be allowed to call themselves rodeos.
64. Cindy Patton, *Sex and Germs: The Politics of AIDS* (Boston: South End Press, 1985), 5.
65. Patton, *Sex and Germs*, 3.
66. Gould, *Moving Politics*, 122, 141.
67. Gould, *Moving Politics*, 114–15, 122.
68. Gould, *Moving Politics*, 140–41.
69. Rofes, *Dry Bones Breathe*, 97–104.
70. Avram Finkelstein, *After Silence: A History of AIDS through Its Images* (Oakland: University of California Press, 2018), 221.
71. National Reno Gay Rodeo Program, 1981, GRH, http://gayrodeohistory.org/indexPrograms.htm; National Reno Gay Rodeo Program, 1982, GRH, http://gayrodeohistory.org/indexPrograms.htm.
72. David Román, *Acts of Intervention: Performance, Gay Culture, and AIDS* (Bloomington: Indiana University Press, 1998), 14. The quote by Morris is from the *San Francisco Sentinel*, November 11, 1982, 4.
73. National Reno Gay Rodeo Program, 1983, GRH, http://gayrodeohistory.org/indexPrograms.htm. The rodeo program says only "the AIDS Foundation," which probably referred to the San Francisco AIDS Foundation.
74. National Reno Gay Rodeo Program, 1984, GRH, http://gayrodeohistory.org/indexPrograms.htm.
75. Roger Bergmann, interview with Rebecca Scofield, Gay Rodeo Oral History Project, November 19, 2016, Austin, TX.

76. Bruce Roby, interview with Rebecca Scofield, Gay Rodeo Oral History Project, September 11, 2016, Duncans Mills, CA.
77. David Renier, interview with Rebecca Scofield, Gay Rodeo Oral History Project, September 10, 2016, Duncans Mills, CA.
78. Laura, interview with Rebecca Scofield, Gay Rodeo Oral History Project, March 31, 2017, Denton, TX.
79. Frank Harrell, interview with Rebecca Scofield, Gay Rodeo Oral History Project, July 7, 2017, Denver, CO.
80. CGRA Newsletters, 1982–86, GRH, http://gayrodeohistory.org/Newsletters/cgra/index.htm.
81. ASGRA Newsletters, 1992–93, GRH, http://gayrodeohistory.org/Newsletters/asgra/index.htm; GSGRA Newsletters, 1995, GRH, http://gayrodeohistory.org/Newsletters/gsgra/index.htm. Rodeo programs often included a description of the riderless horse ceremony, which was held at most rodeos. It did not always include a reference to AIDS, but sometimes it did, such as in the IGRA Finals Rodeo Program, 2003, GRH, http://gayrodeohistory.org/indexPrograms.htm.
82. For more on the US government's limited response to AIDS, see Brier, *Infectious Ideas*; and Petro, *After the Wrath of God*.
83. David Renier, interview with Rebecca Scofield, Gay Rodeo Oral History Project, September 10, 2016, Duncans Mills, CA.
84. Laura, interview with Rebecca Scofield, Gay Rodeo Oral History Project, March 31, 2017, Denton, TX.
85. Miss Mae (Phil Fikel) Memorial, GRH, http://gayrodeohistory.org/2009/memorials/MissMae.htm.
86. For information about the royalty contests, see Desirey Benavides, email interview with Elyssa Ford, July 27, 2015; Candace Pratt, email interview with Elyssa Ford, July 28, 2015; "Breaking Barriers, Building Bonds," *Go! Great Outdoors Magazine* (Fall 1981); Ed Martinez, "First Texas Gay Rodeo Held at Simonton," *Texas Star* (Houston), November 9, 1984, front page, GRH, http://gayrodeohistory.org/indexNewspapers.htm; and TGRA Rodeo Programs, 1984 and 1985, GRH, http://gayrodeohistory.org/indexPrograms.htm.
87. AGRA Newsletter, July 1992, GRH, http://gayrodeohistory.org/Newsletters/agra/index.htm.
88. GSGRA Newsletter, August 1995, GRH, http://gayrodeohistory.org/Newsletters/gsgra/index.htm.
89. AGRA Newsletter, October 1991, GRH, http://gayrodeohistory.org/Newsletters/agra/index.htm.
90. IGRA Rule Book, 1986, GRH, http://gayrodeohistory.org/indexRodeoRules.htm.
91. CGRA Newsletter, August 1986, GRH, http://gayrodeohistory.org/Newsletters/cgra/index.htm.
92. Association Newsletters, GRH, http://gayrodeohistory.org/indexNewsletters.htm.

93. CGRA Newsletter, August 1995, GRH, http://gayrodeohistory.org /Newsletters/cgra/index.htm. Arizona was similarly criticized in 2001. A former AGRA board member said, "Awarding ourselves monies from our rodeo proceeds will look unprofessional, selfish, and be an embarrassment to AGRA" (AGRA Newsletter, August 2001, GRH, http://gayrodeohistory.org /Newsletters/agra/index.htm).
94. DSRA Newsletter, October 1990, GRH, http://gayrodeohistory.org /Newsletters/dsra/index.htm; AGRA Newsletter, October 1991, GRH, http:// gayrodeohistory.org/Newsletters/agra/index.htm.
95. GSGRA Newsletter, November 1995, GRH, http://gayrodeohistory.org /Newsletters/gsgra/index.htm.
96. ASGRA Newsletters, December 1995 and November 1997, GRH, http:// gayrodeohistory.org/Newsletters/asgra/index.htm.
97. ASGRA Newsletter, June 1998, GRH, http://gayrodeohistory.org/Newsletters /asgra/index.htm.
98. TGRA Rodeo Program, 1985, GRH, http://gayrodeohistory.org/index Programs.htm.
99. MGRA Newsletter, May 1991, Autry Archives, Box 1. Similarly, the HIV Wellness Center thanked the TGRA Austin chapter for a $10,000 donation, saying it was one of the largest donations they had received (TGRA Newsletter, May 1995, GRH, http://gayrodeohistory.org/Newsletters/tgra/index .htm. Many of the newsletters and rodeo programs available at the Autry Archives and GRH include similar acknowledgements of IGRA charitable donations.
100. TSGRA Newsletter, February 1992, Autry Archives, Box 12.
101. AGRA Newsletter, October 1991, GRH, http://gayrodeohistory.org /Newsletters/agra/index.htm.
102. CGRA Newsletter, December 1986, GRH, http://gayrodeohistory.org /Newsletters/cgra/index.htm.
103. AGRA Newsletter, October 1991, GRH, http://gayrodeohistory.org /Newsletters/agra/index.htm.
104. AGRA Newsletter, December 1991, GRH, http://gayrodeohistory.org /Newsletters/agra/index.htm.
105. MGRA Newsletter, March 1987, GRH, http://gayrodeohistory.org /Newsletters/mgra/index.htm; DSRA Newsletter, September 1990, GRH, http://gayrodeohistory.org/Newsletters/dsra/index.htm; BSGRA Newsletter, April 1991, Autry Archives, Box 1.
106. MGRA Newsletter, March 1987, GRH, http://gayrodeohistory.org /Newsletters/mgra/index.htm.
107. MGRA Newsletter, March 1987, Autry Archives, Box 2.
108. Denver Rodeo Program, 1983, GRH, http://gayrodeohistory.org/index Programs.htm.
109. Rofes, *Dry Bones Breathe*, 3–4, 69, 73–74. While AIDS may no longer feel as central to the LGBTQ+ community in the US, it remains a very real and

deadly disease. As of 2011, there were 1.1 million people living with HIV in the US, and 650,000 had died of AIDS. AIDS also has continued to be particular acute among gay men. Of the roughly two million people in the US with HIV/AIDS since it began to 2011, over 50% of those who have died are gay men, more than 50% of those today with HIV are gay men, and over 50% of new cases are gay men, mostly men of color, whereas gay men make up only 2–5 percent of the total US population; see Halkitis, *AIDS Generation*, 2–3.

110. AGRA Newsletters, 1990–2017, GRH, http://gayrodeohistory.org/Newsletters/agra/index.htm.
111. DSRA Newsletter, January 1998, GRH, http://gayrodeohistory.org/Newsletters/dsra/index.htm.
112. DSRA Newsletter, February 1998, GRH, http://gayrodeohistory.org/Newsletters/dsra/index.htm.
113. DSRA Newsletter, October 1998, GRH, http://gayrodeohistory.org/Newsletters/dsra/index.htm. Some of this lack of interest and corresponding chastisement appeared as early as 1997, when a DSRA fundraiser for the Ryan White Center raised just $35. The board asked in the newsletter, "Whatever the reason [for poor attendance] who is hurt? Ultimately the AIDS service organization. The DSRA clubhouse is not operated for profit. Every penny ultimately goes to the AIDS service organizations. All the DSRA keeps is for operating costs. You are hurting the people that need help the most. [. . .] Put your petty or profound problems behind you and help the DSRA help the AIDS service organizations by supporting the DSRA Clubhouse. Come on Folks, show us what you are made of." DSRA Newsletter, January 1997, GRH, http://gayrodeohistory.org/Newsletters/dsra/index.htm.
114. DSRA Newsletter, March 2000, GRH, http://gayrodeohistory.org/Newsletters/dsra/index.htm.
115. DSRA Newsletters, 2001–11, GRH, http://gayrodeohistory.org/Newsletters/dsra/index.htm.
116. For more on this generational gap in gay men after the AIDS epidemic, see Halkitis, *AIDS Generation*; Dion Kagan, *Positive Images: Gay Men & HIV/AIDS in the Culture of "Post-Crisis"* (London: I. B. Tauris, 2018); and Rofes, *Dry Bones Breathe*.
117. Brian Helander, interview with Rebecca Scofield, Gay Rodeo Oral History Project, October 21, 2017, Albuquerque, NM.

4. "DOLLARED TO DEATH"

1. Chili Pepper, interview with Revulai Detiv, Gay Rodeo Oral History Project, November 16, 2019, Denver, CO.
2. The authors would like to thank Saraya Flaig for her assistance in researching and thinking about the role of drag for this chapter.

3. Desirey Benavides, interview with Rebecca Scofield, Gay Rodeo Oral History Project, May 17, 2017, Palm Springs, CA.
4. See Fabio Cleto, ed., *Camp: Queer Aesthetics and the Performing Subject: A Reader* (Ann Arbor: University of Michigan Press, 1999).
5. Sara Warner, *Acts of Gaiety: LGBT Performance and the Politics of Pleasure* (Ann Arbor: University of Michigan Press, 2012); Susan Sontag, "Notes on 'Camp,'" quoted in Cleto, *Camp*, 53–65; J. Halberstam, *Female Masculinity* (Durham, NC: Duke University Press, 1998).
6. Marie Antoinette du Barry, interview with Rebecca Scofield, Gay Rodeo Oral History Project, April 1, 2017, Dallas, TX.
7. Scofield, "'Chaps and Scowls,'" 325–40.
8. Hennen, *Faeries, Bears, and Leathermen*. Also see Levine, *Gay Macho*; and Eric Anderson, *In the Game: Gay Athletes and the Cult of Masculinity* (Albany: State University of New York Press, 2005).
9. Patrick Terry, interview with Rebecca Scofield, Gay Rodeo Oral History Project, October 21, 2017, Santa Fe, NM.
10. IGRA Rodeo Rules, 2001, ii, IGRA Archives Committee Collection, Collection, ACC.
11. Heather Sykes, "Transsexual and Transgender Policies in Sport," *Women in Sport and Physical Activity Journal* 15, no. 1 (Spring 2006): 3–13; Eric Anderson and Ann Travers, eds., *Transgender Athletes in Competitive Sport* (New York: Routledge, 2017).
12. Arlie Russell Hochschild, *The Managed Heart: Commercialization of Human Feeling* (Berkeley: University of California Press, 1983), 23.
13. See Joan Acker, "Hierarchies, Jobs, Bodies: A Theory of Gendered Organizations," *Gender & Society* 4, no. 2 (1990): 139–58; and Christine L. Williams and Kirsten Dellinger, eds., *Gender and Sexuality in the Workplace* (Bingley, UK: Emerald, 2010). These dynamics have been particularly investigated in digital culture industries and academia; see Rosalind Gill, "Cool, Creative, Egalitarian? Exploring Gender in Project-Based New Media Work in Europe," *Information, Communication and Society* 5, no. 1 (2002): 70–89; Melissa Gregg, "The Normalisation of Flexible Female Labour in the Information Economy," *Feminist Media Studies* 8, no. 3 (2008): 285–99; Brooke Erin Duffy, "The Romance of Work: Gender and Aspirational Labour in the Digital Culture Industries," *International Journal of Cultural Studies* 19, no. 4 (July 2016): 1–17; Coleen Carrigan, Kate Quinn, and Eve A. Riskin, "The Gendered Division of Labor Among STEM Faculty and the Effects of Critical Mass," *Journal of Diversity in Higher Education* 4, no. 3 (September 2011): 131–46; J. Luke Wood, Adriel A. Hilton, and Carlos Nevarez, "Faculty of Color and White Faculty: An Analysis of Service in Colleges of Education in the Arizona Public University System," *Journal of the Professoriate* 8, no. 1 (2015): 85–109; Linda Babcock, Maria P. Recalde, Lise Vesterlund, and Laurie Weingart, "Gender Differences in Accepting and Receiving Requests for Tasks with Low Promotability," *American Economic Review*

107, no. 3 (March 2017): 714–47; Cassandra M. Guarino and Victor M. H. Borden, "Faculty Service Loads and Gender: Are Women Taking Care of the Academic Family?," *Research in Higher Education* 58, no. 6 (September 2017): 672–94; and Amani El-Alayli, Ashley A. Hansen-Brown, and Michelle Ceynar, "Dancing Backwards in High Heels: Female Professors Experience More Work Demands and Special Favor Requests, Particularly from Academically Entitled Students," *Sex Roles* 79, nos. 3–4 (August 2018): 136–50.

14. For a discussion on emerging gender identities and the power of naming, see Jack Halberstam, *Trans*: A Quick and Quirky Account of Gender Variability* (Oakland: University of California Press, 2018), 1–21.

15. Gorman, *Empress Is a Man*. For the role of medical philanthropy, also see Katie Batza, *Before AIDS: Gay Health Politics in the 1970s* (Philadelphia: University of Pennsylvania Press, 2018).

16. "Breaking Barriers, Building Bonds," *Go! Great Outdoors Magazine* (Fall 1981): 5.

17. Mipsy Mikels, interview with Saraya Flaig, Gay Rodeo Oral History Project, February 15, 2020, Phoenix, AZ.

18. Mipsy Mikels, interview.

19. Ron Neff, "He, She, & ?," *Roundup* (Spring 1993): 26; IGRA Handbook, 1986, Bylaws, Committees, 18, ACC; IGRA Handbook, 1989, Standing Rules, 31, ACC; IGRA Handbook, Bylaws, Committees, 1991, 19, ACC.

20. Tamara Marks, IGRA Royalty Etiquette Guide, Autry Archives, Box 81.

21. Personal correspondence, IGRA Archives Committee Chairman Roger Bergmann, 2020.

22. Bruce Roby, interview with Rebecca Scofield, Gay Rodeo Oral History Project, September 10, 2016, Duncans Mills, CA.

23. Roger Bergmann, interview with Rebecca Scofield, Gay Rodeo Oral History Project, November 19, 2016, Austin, TX.

24. T. X. Enoicaras, "Forget Vampires... Interview with a Cowboy," *Frontiers* (May 23, 1996): 25.

25. Desirey Benavides, interview with Rebecca Scofield, Gay Rodeo Oral History Project, May 17, 2017, Palm Springs, CA.

26. Colleen Ballerino Cohen, Richard Wilk, and Beverly Stoeltje, eds., *Beauty Queens on the Global Stage: Gender, Contests, and Power* (New York: Routledge, 1996), 2.

27. Bruce Roby, interview.

28. Bruce Gros, interview with Rebecca Scofield, Gay Rodeo Oral History Project, September 10, 2016, Duncans Mills, CA. Alex Hunt, scholar of the American West and ex–bull rider, asserts, when considering straight rodeo in the context of *Brokeback Mountain*, "In their exaggoration of masculinity beyond the bounds of the traditionally masculine, rodeo cowboys seem to be camp." In William R. Handley, ed., *The Brokeback Book: From Story to Cultural Phenomenon* (Lincoln: University of Nebraska Press, 2011), 141.

29. Judith Butler, "Performance Acts and Gender Constitution," *Theater Journal* 40, no. 4 (December 1988): 526.
30. IGRA Handbook, 1998, Standing Rules and Procedures, Exhibit D-2(a), ACC.
31. Sarah Tucker Jenkins, "Spicy. Exotic. Creature. Representations of Racial and Ethnic Minorities on *RuPaul's Drag Race*," in Niall Brennan and David Gudelunas, eds., *"RuPaul's Drag Race" and the Shifting Visibility of Drag Culture* (London: Palgrave Macmillan, 2017), 77–90.
32. Exhibit D-2(a), 1998. IGRA Handbook, 1998, Standing Rules and Procedures, Exhibit D-2(a), ACC.
33. Marks, IGRA Royalty Etiquette Guide, Autry Archives, Box 81.
34. Burbick, *Rodeo Queens*, 207. Also see Laegreid, *Riding Pretty*.
35. Bruce Roby, interview.
36. GSGRA Rodeo Program, 1989, Autry Archives, MOAW 94.79.46.
37. IGRA Handbook, 1986, Standing Rules and Procedures, 21, ACC.
38. Raeann Grow, interview with Rebecca Scofield, Gay Rodeo Oral History Project, July 8, 2017, Denver, CO.
39. Neff, "He, She, ?," 26.
40. Travis James, interview with Dusty Fleener, Gay Rodeo Oral History Project, November 22, 2019, Denver, CO.
41. Mipsy Mikels, interview.
42. Tony, virtual interview with Court Fund, Gay Rodeo Oral History Project, May 1, 2020.
43. IGRA Handbook, Standing Rules and Procedures, Attachment B: Rules Governing Selection of MR/MS/MISS IGRA, 1991, 41, (ACC).
44. Steven E. Weil and G. Daniel DeWesse, *Western Shirts: A Classic American Fashion* (Salt Lake City: Gibbs Smith 2004); Holly George-Warren and Michelle Freedman, *How the West Was Worn* (New York: Harry N. Abrams, 2001). For more on western dress see Scofield, "'Chaps and Scowls'"; Elyssa Ford, "Becoming the West."
45. Marie Antoinette Du Barry, interview with Rebecca Scofield, Gay Rodeo Oral History Project, 01 April 2017, Dallas, TX.
46. Marie Antoinette Du Barry, interview.
47. Chili Pepper, interview; Travis James, interview.
48. To some degree, this reflects a sustained critique about drag by women's liberationists. Robin Morgan stated in 1973, "We know what's at work when whites wear blackface; the same thing is at work when men wear drag." Quoted in Betty Luther Hillman, *Dressing for the Culture Wars: Style and the Politics of Self-Presentation in the 1960s and 1970s* (Lincoln: University of Nebraska, 2015).
49. Marie Antoinette Du Barry, interview.
50. IGRA Rodeo Rules, 1986; 1997; 2020, ACC.
51. One contestant mentioned that there is some level of choice as to whether

52. Chili Pepper, interview.
53. For instance, see Patrick "Cowboy Ram," interview with Dustin Fleener, Gay Rodeo Oral History Project, November 16, 2019, Denver, CO; and follow-up virtual interview by Saraya Flaig, June 24, 2020.
54. Mipsy Mikels, interview.
55. Baker A. Rogers, "Drag as a Resource: Trans* and Nonbinary Individuals in the Southeastern United States," *Gender and Society* 32, no. 6 (December 2018): 905.
56. Mipsy Mikels, interview.
57. Warner, *Acts of Gaiety*, 5, 11.
58. At the Texas State Prison Rodeo, for instance, incarcerated women were not allowed to participate at the rodeo at all until briefly in the 1970s, when they were allowed to ride donkeys and catch pigs. See Scofield, *Outriders*.
59. David Medzerian, "Goat Dressing," *Roundup* (July 1996): 39.
60. IGRA Bylaws, Standing Rules and Rodeo Rules, 1986–87, ACC.
61. Ford, "Becoming the West," 48–49.
62. Personal conversation, Santa Fe, NM, 2014.
63. This rule was included in rule books at least as far back as the mid-1990s.
64. D'Lane Compton reads current gay rodeo as a "spoof" of heteronormative rodeo, noting that the more invested the rodeo participants and workers are in a "serious" rodeo, the less invested the audience becomes. Few gay competitors would characterize their performances as a parody, but this interpretation captures gay rodeoers' dedication to play as potentially transgressive even as it often collapses into misogyny—as she notes, there is "a subtle line between spoofing masculinity and mirroring hypermasculinity." See Compton, "Queer Eye on the Gay Rodeo," 234.
65. "Send in the Clowns," *First Hand Events*, 1989 Gay Rodeo Souvenir Issue, 45.
66. Michael Szymanski, "Renaissance Cowboy," *Roundup* (August 1995): 26. "Nelly" was a slang term used to refer to an effeminate gay man.
67. NMGRA Newsletter, March 1991, Autry Archives, Box 4.
68. Health and Safety Committee Report, IGRA Annual Convention, 1995, Autry Archives, Box 35.
69. 2005 Southern Spurs Rodeo, video 2, Cowboy Frank Harrell.
70. The rules for this changed between the 1985 and 1986 rule books as camp events were formally created and codified. Previously, wild cow milking was included in the "roughstock" category. See IGRA Sanctioned Rodeo Rules, 1985, 4; and IGRA Bylaws, Standing Rules, and Rodeo Rules, 1986, 42, ACC.
71. Royalty Contestant Totals, IGRA Corporate Record Copy, 1989–2019, ACC.
72. Compton, "Queer Eye on the Gay Rodeo," 234–35.
73. Darrell Yates Rist, *Heartlands: A Gay Man's Odyssey across America* (New York: Dutton, 1992), 104.

74. Todd Heibel, "An Arena for Belonging? A Spatial Hingepoint Perspective on Citizenship at the Gay Rodeo" (PhD diss., Pennsylvania State University, 2005), 179–80.
75. Questionnaires, 1990, IGRA Annual Convention, 1995 Autry Archives, Box 4.
76. GSGRA Proposed Rule Book Changes, IGRA Convention, 1996, Autry Archives, Box 35.
77. Douglas Schrock and Michael Schwalbe, "Men, Masculinity, and Manhood Acts," *Annual Review of Sociology* 35 (2009): 277–95.
78. K. Bradford, "Grease Cowboy Fever: Or, the Making of Johnny T," *Journal of Homosexuality* 43, nos. 3–4 (2002): 25–30; Judith Halberstam, "Mackdaddy, Superfly, Rapper: Gender, Race, and Masculinity in the Drag King Scene," *Social Text,* no. 52–53 (Autumn/Winter 1997): 105–31; Thomas Piontek, "Kinging in the Heartland; Or, the Power of Marginality," *Journal of Homosexuality* 43, nos. 3–4 (2002): 125–43; Tristan Bridges, "A Very 'Gay' Straight? Hybrid Masculinities, Sexual Aesthetics, and the Changing Relationship between Masculinity and Homophobia," *Gender & Society* 28, no. 1 (2014): 58–82; Miriam J. Abelson, "'You Aren't from Around Here': Race, Masculinity, and Rural Transgender Men," *Gender, Place & Culture* 23, no. 11 (2016): 1535–46; Ashley A. Baker (aka Baker A. Rogers) and Kimberly Kelly, "Live like a King, Y'all: Gender Negotiation and the Performance of Masculinity among Southern Drag Kings," *Sexualities* 19, nos. 1–2 (2016): 46–63; Rogers Brubaker, *Trans: Gender and Race in an Age of Unsettled Identities* (Princeton, NJ: Princeton University Press, 2016); Rogers, "Drag as a Resource."
79. Halberstam, *Female Masculinity*, 1.
80. Patrick "Cowboy Ram," interview. For more on the history of drag kings, see Gilliam Rodger, *Just One of the Boys: Female-to-Male Cross-Dressing on the American Variety Stage* (Urbana: University of Illinois Press, 2018); Laura Cherrie Beaney, *Crossing the Catwalk: Transvestism in Contemporary Fashion and Culture* (London: Academica Press, 2019); Esther Newton, "Role Models," in *Camp: Queer Aesthetics and the Performing Subject: A Reader*, edited by Fabio Cleto (Ann Arbor: University of Michigan Press, 1972), 96–109.
81. Community Outreach and Fundraising Committee, IGRA Annual Convention, 2004, ACC.
82. Competitors are required to earn at least 75 percent of the total points to win a position on the royalty team. Even if there was only one competitor, they might not win, as was the case in the MsTer category for the first three years it was held. Travis James, interview; Royalty Contestant Totals, 1989–2019, ACC.
83. Community Outreach and Fundraising Committee, Proposal 1, Exhibit C1, Annual Convention, 2008, ACC.
84. Susan Sontag, "Notes on 'Camp,'" 53–65.
85. Bob Ames, "Rodeo Ramblin'," *Roundup* (Spring 1993): 14–16; Danny Lee,

interview with Rebecca Scofield, Gay Rodeo Oral History Project, May 12, 2017, Palm Springs, CA.

5. "IT'S MILLER TIME"

1. Kristine Fredriksson, *American Rodeo: From Buffalo Bill to Big Business* (College Station: Texas A&M University Press, 1985), 171–83.
2. Candy Pratt, interview with Rebecca Scofield, Gay Rodeo Oral History Project, September 10, 2016, Duncans Mills, CA.
3. Fredriksson, *American Rodeo*, 184–200.
4. While many scholars have shown the ways that progressive politics and a multiracial musical tradition helped create country music, scholars have demonstrated the appropriation of country music by right-wing politics in the 1970s and '80s; see Joshua Freeman, "Hardhats: Construction Workers, Manliness, and the 1970 Pro-War Demonstrations," *Journal of Social History* 26, no. 4 (Summer 1993): 725–44; Eileen Boris, "On Cowboys and Welfare Queens: Independence, Dependence, and Interdependence at Home and Abroad," *Journal of American Studies* 41, no. 3 (December 2007): 599–621; Daniel Geary, "'The Way I Would Feel about San Quentin': Johnny Cash & the Politics of Country Music," *Daedalus* 142, no. 4 (2013): 64–72; and Scofield, "'Chaps and Scowls,' 325–40. For a history of race and class in country music see Karl Hagstrom Miller, *Segregating Sound: Inventing Folk and Pop Music in the Age of Jim Crow* (Durham, NC: Duke University Press, 2010); and Aaron Fox, *Real Country: Music and Language in Working-Class Culture* (Durham, NC: Duke University Press, 2004).
5. Hubbs, *Rednecks*.
6. "Shooting from the Hip," *Los Angeles Times*, February 2, 1987, no page; Peter W. Kaplan, "The End of the Soft Line," *Esquire* (April 1980): 41–44.
7. Sarah Peterson, "Cowboy Fever Rises: and Merchants Cash In," *U.S. News and World Report* (February 16, 1981): 62.
8. Curt Westberg, virtual interview with Rebecca Scofield, Gay Rodeo Oral History Project, March 6, 2023.
9. For more on the development of consumer politics, see Liz Cohen, *A Consumers' Republic: The Politics of Mass Consumption in Postwar America* (New York: Knopf, 2003); and Robert E. Weems Jr., "African American Consumer Boycotts during the Civil Rights Era," *Western Journal of Black Studies* 19, no. 1 (1995): 72–79.
10. The Human Rights Campaign still produces an extensive list of companies deemed friendly to the LGBTQ+ community. Amy Corey, "Love Is Love Is Love Is Love: From Flaktivism to Consumer Activism in LGBTQ+ Communities," *Queer Studies in Media & Popular Culture* 4, no. 2 (2019): 122.
11. Milton Friedman and Rose Friedman, *Free to Choose: A Personal Statement* (London: Secker and Warburg, 1980), 222–23.
12. D'Emilio, "Capitalism and Gay Identity," 181–94.

13. Johnson, "Physique Pioneers," 867.
14. Alexandra Chasin, *Selling Out: The Gay and Lesbian Movement Goes to Market* (New York: St. Martin's Press, 2000), 23–24.
15. Grant Lukenbill, *Untold Millions: Secret Truths about Marketing to Gay and Lesbian Consumers* (New York: Harrington Park Press, 1999); Tracey Middleton, "A Queer Business: Brand Construction, Marketing Strategy and the Gay and Lesbian Consumer," *Journal of Brand Management* 4, no. 6 (1997): 390–400; Katherine Sender, *Business, Not Politics: The Making of the Gay Market* (New York: Columbia University Press, 2004); Whitney Ginder and Sang-Eun Byun, "Past, Present, and Future of Gay and Lesbian Consumer Research: Critical Review of the Quest for the Queer Dollar," *Psychology & Marketing* 32, no. 8 (2015): 821–41; Carlos A. Ball, *The Queering of Corporate America: How Big Business Went from LGBTQ Adversary to Ally* (Boston: Beacon, 2019).
16. Corey, "Love Is Love," 125.
17. Eric O. Clarke, *Virtuous Vice: Homoeroticism and the Public Sphere* (Durham, NC: Duke University Press, 2000), 61.
18. Tri-State Gay Rodeo Association, 1989, Gay Rodeo Collection, ONE Archives at the University of Southern California Libraries, GRC, Folder 1.
19. Denver Rodeo Program, 1985, Autry Archives, Box 1.
20. National Reno Gay Rodeo Program, 1981, GRH, http://gayrodeohistory.org/indexPrograms.htm.
21. Farber, "National Reno Gay Rodeo," 21.
22. Hume, "Bum Steer," 47.
23. Hennen, *Faeries, Bears, and Leathermen*.
24. Lisa Smith, interview with Rebecca Scofield, Gay Rodeo Oral History Project, November 20, 2016, Austin, TX.
25. Atlantic Stampede Program, 1993, GRH, http://gayrodeohistory.org/indexPrograms.htm.
26. AGRA Newsletter, July 2015, GRH, http://gayrodeohistory.org/Newsletters/agra/index.htm.
27. TGRA Rodeo Program, 1988, GRH, http://gayrodeohistory.org/indexPrograms.htm.
28. Letter from IGRA to Charlie Brydon, April 13, 1994, Autry Archives, Box 21.
29. For instance, see AGRA Newsletter, September 1991, GRH, http://gayrodeohistory.org/Newsletters/agra/index.htm.
30. AGRA Newsletter, July 1992, GRH, http://gayrodeohistory.org/Newsletters/agra/index.htm.
31. NGRA Newsletter, April/May 2001, GRH, http://gayrodeohistory.org/Newsletters/ngra/index.htm.
32. AGRA Newsletter, July 1992, GRH, http://gayrodeohistory.org/Newsletters/agra/index.htm.
33. Calendo, "Gay Rodeo," 91. These findings are supported by Craig McClain's

experiences doing ethnographic research in the early 2000s, see his "Gay Rodeo: Carnival, Gender, and Resistance" (MA thesis, University of New Mexico, 2005). Also see Rist, *Heartlands*, 110, about his uncomfortable experiences with the patriotism and religious aspects of the gay rodeo, even as he notes how dedicated gay rodeoers were to reclaiming a right to live different lives, in comparison to many gay people who abandoned their rural upbringings.

34. Greater Motown International Rodeo Program, 1995, GRH, http://gayrodeohistory.org/indexPrograms.htm.
35. For costuming, see, for instance, TGRA Newsletter, March 1992, Autry Archives, Box 11.
36. Jim Wilke, "My Lover Is a Cowboy," *Roundup* (May 1996): 6, Autry Archives, Box 30.
37. Canton Winer and Catherine Bolzendahl, "Conceptualizing Homonationalism: (Re-)Formulation, Application, and Debates of Expansion," *Sociology Compass* 15, no 5 (May 2021): 2. The term was first coined by Jasbir Puar in *Terrorist Assemblages: Homonationalism in Queer Times* (Durham, NC: Duke University Press, 2007). Also see Jasbir Puar, "Rethinking Homonationalism," *International Journal of Middle East Studies* 45, no. 2 (2013): 336–39.
38. Scholars such as Scott Lauria Morgensen have explained how this homonationalism of the early 2000s was deeply rooted in Euro-American settler-colonialism, through which queered bodies came into contact with other "queered populations in relation to which they also exert terrorizing control." See Scott Lauria Morgensen, "Settler Homonationalism," *GLQ* 16, nos. 1–2 (2010): 105; and Scott Lauria Morgensen, *Spaces Between Us: Queer Settler Colonialism and Indigenous Decolonization* (Minneapolis: University of Minnesota Press, 2011). For more on queer people's association with conservative issues, see Thatcher Phoenix Combes, "Queers with Guns? Against the LGBT Grain: Sociological Perspectives," *Sociological Perspectives* 65, no. 1 (2022): 58–76.
39. Alexander, "Politely Different," 187–209.
40. John Calendo, "Interview with Ron Brewer," *In Touch for Men* (January 1981): 77.
41. BSGRA Newsletter, April 1991, Autry Archives, Box 1.
42. Myra Ritter, "Tired of Gay Publicity," *Reno Gazette*, July 28, 1983, GRC, Folder 6.
43. Curtice Booth, "Nothing Pro Family about It," *Reno Gazette*, July 28, 1983, GRC, Folder 6.
44. "Gay Rodeo May Attract 20,000," *Reno Journal*, July 29, 1982, GRC, Folder 6.
45. O'Driscoll, "10,000 Hoot," 1, 4A, Autry Archives, Box 6.
46. Denver Rodeo Program, 1986, Autry Archives, Box 1.
47. Little Rock Bid for Annual Convention, 1993, Autry Archives, Box 14; Annual

Convention Packet from Denver, 1994, Autry Archives, Box 15; Town House Country Bar, Letter of Support for North Star Gay Rodeo Association's Bid for 1992 Annual Convention, July 1991, Autry Archives, Box 9.
48. Bylaw Change Proposals, 8th Annual Convention Welcome Packet, 1992, Autry Archives, Box 9.
49. Letter from Steve Higgins to IGRA, March 14, 1993, Autry Archives, Box 22.
50. Lukenbill, *Untold Millions*, 6.
51. For a review of the complexity and concerns about the potential of normativity within Pride and LGBTQ+ other events, see Clarke, *Virtuous Vice*, 21–29.
52. Letter from Roger Bergmann to IGRA Board of Directors, December 19, 1992, Autry Archives, Box 11.
53. IGRA Board of Directors Meeting Minutes, July 5, 1991, Autry Archives, Box 6.
54. IGRA Board of Directors Meeting Minutes, October 16 and 17, 1991, Autry Archives, Box 5; IGRA Board of Directors Meeting Minutes, Annual Convention, 1992, Autry Archives, Box 14.
55. Lawrence A. Wenner and Steven J. Jackson, *Sport, Beer, and Gender: Promotional Culture and Contemporary Social Life* (New York: Peter Lang, 2009). For the dynamics between beer and gay male identity in the media, see Steven M. Kates, "The Dynamics of Brand Legitimacy: An Interpretive Study in the Gay Men's Community," *Journal of Consumer Research* 31, no. 2 (September 2004): 455–64; Michael A. Messner and Jeffrey Montez de Oca, "The Male Consumer as Loser: Beer and Liquor Ads in Mega Sports Media Events," *Signs* 30, no. 3 (2005): 1879–1909; Blaine Branchik, "Queer Ads: Gay Male Imagery in American Advertising," *Consumption Markets, & Culture* 10, no. 2 (July 2007): 147–58; Wan-Hsiu Sunny Tsai, "How Minority Consumers Use Targeted Advertising as Pathways to Self-Empowerment: Gay Men's and Lesbians' Reading of Out-of-the-Closet Advertising," *Journal of Advertising* 40, no. 3 (2011): 85–97; and Carol Emslie, Jemma Lennox, and Lana Ireland, "The Role of Alcohol in Identity Construction among LGBT People: A Qualitative Study," *Sociology of Health & Illness* 39, no. 8 (2017): 1465–79.
56. National Reno Gay Rodeo Program, 1982, GRH, http://gayrodeohistory.org/indexPrograms.htm.
57. Jonathan Tasini, "The Beer and the Boycott," *New York Times*, January 31, 1988, 19. Also see Allyson Brantly, *Brewing a Boycott: How a Grassroots Coalition Fought Coors and Remade American Consumer Activism* (Chapel Hill: University of North Carolina, 2021).
58. CGRA Newsletter, April 1987, GRH, http://gayrodeohistory.org/Newsletters/cgra/index.htm.
59. IGRA/Miller Brewing Company Agreement, January 2, 1993, Autry Archives, Box 10.
60. Rodeo Director's Checklist, January 1, 1996, Autry Archives, Box 32.

61. Phoenix Rodeo Programs, 1992–98, GRH, http://gayrodeohistory.org/indexPrograms.htm. The "Hard Ride" ad appears in the 1993 program, and the 1997 program included another queer-coded ad, while most of the other programs that decade were more generically western focused.
62. "Put Your Money Where Your Mouth Is," *Gay Chicago Magazine*, December 31, 1992, Autry Archives, Box 11.
63. IGRA Sponsorship Committee Report, August 7, 1992, Autry Archives, Box 11.
64. Letter from Wayne Jakino to IGRA Board of Directors, May 25, 1993, Autry Archives, Box 12. Also see IGRA Board of Directors Meeting Minutes, May 22, 1992, Autry Archives, Box 10; IGRA Board of Directors Meeting Minutes, July 2, 1993, Autry Archives, Box 9; Letter from Greg Plowe to RJ Newby, April 21, 1993, Autry Archives, Box 12; and Letter from Miller Brewing to IGRA Board of Directors, June 9, 1993, Autry Archives, Box 13.
65. David, interview with Rebecca Scofield, Gay Rodeo Oral History Project, September 11, 2016, Duncans Mills, CA.
66. Fetner, *How the Religious Right*, 108.
67. Nance, *Rodeo*, 13–14.
68. "Women of Northside Assail Rodeo: Brand Sport Event Orgy of Brutality," *Northside Citizen*, July 10, 1925; "Against the Rodeo," *Chicago Tribune*, May 12, 1925; "The Rodeo in New York and London," *Chicago Tribune*, no date; "Humane Society Will Not Interfere with Roundup Program," *Chicago Illinois News*, May 13, 1925. All taken from Box 1, Chicago Scrapbook, Album #3, Tex Austin Collection, Museum of New Mexico, Fray Angelico Chavez History Library, Santa Fe, NM.
69. Raeann Grow, interview with Rebecca Scofield, Gay Rodeo Oral History Project, July 8, 2017, Denver, CO.
70. Shulman, "This Cowboy's Life," 29, Autry Archives, Box 42.
71. "Gay Rodeo?" Flyer, Gays and Friends for Animal Rights, GRC, Folder 3.
72. Hume, "Bum Steer."
73. Liz Galst, "Sacred Cows," *The Advocate*, July 27, 1993, 47–51.
74. Animal Rights Letters, 1994 (Autry Archives, Box 22.
75. Letter from Anna Moretto to IGRA, August 2, 1994, Autry Archives, Box 22.
76. IGRA President's Report, January 2001–April 2002, Autry Archives, Box 70.
77. PCGRA Newsletter, June 1981, GRH, http://gayrodeohistory.org/Newsletters/pcgra/index.htm.
78. IGRA Board of Directors Meeting Minutes, Annual Convention, 1994, Autry Archives, Box 19.
79. IGRA Board of Directors Meeting Minutes, July 25, 2002, Autry Archives, Box 70.
80. IGRA Public Relations Committee Report, October 20, 1995, Autry Archives, Box 23. In particular, they recommended that websites and programs exclude any photos of calf roping.
81. MIGRA Rodeo Program, 1998, Autry Archives, Box 43.

82. Sankar Sen, "Marketing and Minority Civil Rights: The Case of Amendment 2 and the Colorado Boycott," *Journal of Public Policy & Marketing* 15, no. 2 (Fall 1996): 311–18.
83. Sen, "Marking and Minority Civil Rights," 312.
84. "Colorado Boycott Picks Up Speed," *The Advocate*, January 12, 1993, 18–19; "Colorado Loss , Boycott Threats," *Windy City Times*, November 12, 1992, 1, 8, Autry Archives, Box 11.
85. Sen, "Marking and Minority Civil Rights," 311.
86. Letter from Robert Sweeney to IGRA, February 3, 1993, Autry Archives, Box 11.
87. Letter from Daniel Wood to IGRA, circa 1993–94, Autry Archives, Box 11.
88. "Colorado Loss Spurs Court Challenges."
89. Kelly Poorman, virtual interview with Rebecca Scofield, Gay Rodeo Oral History Project, June 5, 2021. For a fictionalized version of events at a Seattle rodeo, see Poorman's novel, *Roman and Jules* (San Jose, CA: Writers Club Press, 2000).
90. Gary L. Atkins, *Gay Seattle: Stories of Exile and Belonging* (Seattle: University of Washington Press, 2013); Marc L. Rubinstein, "Gay Rights and Religion: A Doctrinal Approach to the Argument That Anti-Gay-Rights Initiatives Violate the Establishment Clause," *Hastings Law Journal* 46, no. 5 (1995): 1585–1620.
91. IGRA Board of Directors Meeting Minutes, January 15–16, 1993, Autry Archives, Box 12.
92. IGRA Board of Directors Meeting Minutes, January 15–16, 1993, Autry Archives, Box 12.
93. Letter from Wayne Jakino to Texas Associations, circa 1993, Autry Archives, Box 15.
94. ASGRA, Newsletter, March 14, 1993, GRH, http://gayrodeohistory.org/Newsletters/ogra/index.htm.
95. *States News Service*, May 17, 1988.
96. N. Offen, E. A. Smith, and R. E. Malone, "From Adversary to Target Market: The ACT-UP Boycott of Philip Morris," *Tobacco Control* 12, no. 2 (June 2003): 203–7.
97. Offen, Smith, and Malone, "From Adversary to Target Market," 204.
98. Chasin, *Selling Out*, 174.
99. RJ Newby, Executive Office Duties, circa 1993, Autry Archives, Box 5.
100. IGRA Board of Directors Minutes, September 7, 1990, Autry Archives, Box 5.
101. IGRA Board of Directors Minutes, September 7, 1990, Autry Archives, Box 5.
102. RJ Newby, Executive Office Duties, circa 1993, Autry Archives, Box 5.
103. Lukenbill, *Untold Millions*, 3.
104. AGRA Newsletter, September 1991, GRH, http://gayrodeohistory.org/Newsletters/agra/index.htm.
105. AGRA Newsletter, October 1991, GRH, http://gayrodeohistory.org/Newsletters/agra/index.htm.

106. IGRA Sponsorship Committee Report and Letter from Jack Rooney to Wayne Jakino and Patrick Terry, July 22, 1998, Autry Archives, Box 43.
107. Email from D. Graff to IGRA, 1997, Autry Archives, Box 38.
108. IGRA Board of Directors Meeting Minutes, February 21, 1999, Autry Archives, Box 56; IGRA Rodeo Director's Information, 2000, Autry Archives, Box 60.
109. Laura, interview with Rebecca Scofield, Gay Rodeo Oral History Project, March 31, 2017, Denton, TX.
110. IGRA Board of Directors Meeting Minutes, Annual Convention, July 2003, Autry Archives, Box 81.

6. "FOR ALL GAY PEOPLE"

1. IGRA Website, www.igra.com.
2. National Reno Gay Rodeo Program, 1981, GRH, http://gayrodeohistory.org/indexPrograms.htm.
3. SEGRA Membership Brochure, 1991, Autry Archives, Box 1.
4. IGRA Website, www.igra.com.
5. CGRA Newsletter, November 2013, GRH, http://gayrodeohistory.org/Newsletters/cgra/index.htm.
6. HGRA Newsletter, June 2000, Autry Archives, Box 61.
7. IGRA Flyer, circa late 1990s, Autry Archives, Box 47.
8. CGRA Newsletter, November 2013, GRH, http://gayrodeohistory.org/Newsletters/cgra/index.htm.
9. HGRA Newsletter, July 2007, GRH, http://gayrodeohistory.org/Newsletters/hgra/index.htm.
10. Hennen, *Faeries, Bears, and Leathermen*, 96–97, 135. For more on the performative hypermasculinity of the gay leather community, see Andrew Childs, "Hyper or Hypo-Masculine? Re-Conceptualizing 'Hyper-Masculinity' through Seattle's Gay, Leather Community," *Gender, Place & Culture* 23, no. 9 (April 2016): 1315–28. For more on bear masculinity and the romanticized rural, see Wright, *Bear Book;* and Nick McGlynn, "Bears in Space: Geographies of a Global Community of Big and Hairy Gay/Bi/Queer Men," *Geography Compass* 15, no. 2 (2021): 1–13.
11. Sooner State, Atlantic States, Golden State, and Diamond State are examples of IGRA associations that worked closely with local bear groups. SSRA Flyer, no date, Autry Archives, Box 71; ASGRA Newsletters, 1993–97, GRH, http://gayrodeohistory.org/Newsletters/asgra/index.htm; GSGRA Newsletter, October 1996, GRH, http://gayrodeohistory.org/Newsletters/gsgra/index.htm; DSRA Newsletters, 1997–2003, GRH, http://gayrodeohistory.org/Newsletters/dsra/index.htm. In contrast, far fewer IGRA associations mentioned a connection with the Imperial Court System. CGRA in Colorado identified the close relationship to the ICS in its newsletters: an early

mention in 1982 regarding a contractual agreement for a joint event between CGRA and the Sovereign Court, and, in 2002, joint memberships offered by CGRA and the Court, along with the overlap between titleholders in both organizations; see Contractual Agreement, CGRA and Sovereign Court, January 29, 1982, Autry Archives, Box 6; CGRA Newsletter, March 2002, Autry Archives, Box 74; CGRA Newsletter, April 2002, Autry Archives, Box 71; and CGRA Newsletter, May 2002, Autry Archives, Box 71. The Nevada association also mentioned one joint fundraiser with the Imperial Court, which raised $4,000; see NGRA Newsletter, October 1999, Autry Archives, Box 61.

12. DSRA Newsletter, March 2002, GRH, http://gayrodeohistory.org/Newsletters/dsra/index.htm.
13. ASGRA Newsletter, September 1995, GRH, http://gayrodeohistory.org/Newsletters/asgra/index.htm.
14. ASGRA Newsletters, January and March 1992, July and August 1994, GRH, http://gayrodeohistory.org/Newsletters/asgra/index.htm.
15. Gary Schwartz, "The 1995 American Brotherhood Contest," *Roundup* (December 1995): 8–9, Autry Archives, Box 30; David Carlin, "The 1994 American Cowboy," *Roundup* (December 1995): 10–11, Autry Archives, Box 30.
16. IGRA Board of Directors Meeting, October 29, 1999, Autry Archives, Box 50; Leather Archives and Museum Newsletter, Winter 2000, Autry Archives, Box 61; IGRA Marketing and PR Committee Report, Annual Convention, 2000, Autry Archives, Box 63; IGRA Administrative Assistant Report, Annual Convention, 2002, Autry Archives, Box 69.
17. NWGRA Newsletter, June 1994, Autry Archives, Box 21.
18. O'Driscoll, "10,000 Hoot," 1–4A, Autry Archives, Box 6.
19. For references to straight contestants, see Perry Brass Interview with Thom Sloan, *Gay Today*, January 1999, Autry Archives, Box 51; ASGRA Newsletter, January–April 2001, GRH, http://gayrodeohistory.org/Newsletters/asgra/index.htm; Indyke, "ABQ Welcomes Zia Rodeo," 14–15; Blake Jackson, "Fear Keeps Many Winners Anonymous," *Oklahoman*, May 27, 2006; "Gay Rodeo Shows South Florida How West Was Fun," *South Florida Sun-Sentinel*, April 15, 2007; Krystina Martinez and Rick Holter, "Texas Gay Rodeo Event Features Cowboys, Cowgirls—and a Few Campy Twists," *KERA News*, May 1, 2015, http://keranews.org/post/texas-gay-rodeo-event-features-cowboys-cowgirls-and-few-campy-twists.
20. SSRA Flyer, circa 2002, Autry Archives, Box 71.
21. MIGRA Documents, 1998–99, Autry Archives, Box 43.
22. CGRA Newsletter, January 2014, GRH, http://gayrodeohistory.org/Newsletters/cgra/index.htm; Ryan Reed, email interview with Elyssa Ford, July 28, 2015.
23. GSGRA Newsletter, June 1995, GRH, http://gayrodeohistory.org/Newsletters/gsgra/index.htm.

24. Letter to IGRA, circa1996, Autry Archives, Box 33.
25. Candy Pratt, email interview with Elyssa Ford, July 28, 2015. IGRA member Laura Scott made a similar statement about the need to protect the queer community. She said, "We have several straight allies who compete who are very wonderful loving people. I am all for them being a part of this as long as they are kind and understanding. The moment they cross the line, they won't be made to feel welcome." Laura Scott, email interview with Elyssa Ford, July 27, 2015.
26. For examples of the inclusion of straight contestants, see the oral history interviews with Tennent Emmons, Roger Bergmann, David Hallwood, Lorry King, Jack Morgan, Bruce Roby, Joe Rodriguez, and Patrick Terry, Gay Rodeo Oral History Project interviews, 2016–17; and CGRA Newsletter, December 1983, GRH, http://gayrodeohistory.org/Newsletters/cgra/index.htm.
27. Todd Garrett, email interview with Elyssa Ford, July 28, 2015.
28. Bruce Roby, email interview with Elyssa Ford, July 30, 2015.
29. David Hallwood, Gay Rodeo Oral History Project, interview with Rebecca Scofield, November 19, 2016, Austin, TX.
30. Todd Garrett, interview.
31. Ryan Reed, interview.
32. Morris, "Like a Rhinestone Cowboy," 120–23, 152, 154, 156. IGRA member David Hallwood described a similar reaction by contractors and facilities they worked with; see David Hallwood, interview with Rebecca Scofield, November 19, 2016, Austin, TX.
33. ASGRA Newsletter, October 2002, GRH, http://gayrodeohistory.org/Newsletters/asgra/index.htm. IGRA also honored and remembered these rodeo workers, such as in 1999, when the TGRA newsletter included a memorial statement for a gay rodeo stock contractor who was robbed and killed (see TGRA Newsletter, Dallas Chapter, December 1999, Autry Archives, Box 61), and in 1996, when ASGRA recognized the sudden death of a "friend and supporter" who was its stock contractor and who taught at its roughstock schools (see ASGRA Newsletter, February 1996, GRH, http://gayrodeohistory.org/Newsletters/asgra/index.htm).
34. TGRA Newsletter, September/October 1984, GRH, http://gayrodeohistory.org/Newsletters/tgra/index.htm.
35. Contractor email to IGRA, September 1999, Autry Archives, Box 53.
36. Desirey Benavides, interview with Rebecca Scofield, Gay Rodeo Oral History Project, May 17, 2017, Palm Springs, CA.
37. David Hallwood, interview with Rebecca Scofield, Gay Rodeo Oral History Project, November 19, 2016, Austin, TX. For a perspective from a straight female contestant, see Lorry King, interview with Rebecca Scofield, Gay Rodeo Oral History Project, November 20, 2016, Denver, CO.
38. "Cowgirls Display Their Skill at State's First Gay Rodeo," *South Florida Sun-Sentinel* (Fort Lauderdale, FL), April 9, 2006.

39. Andrew Johnson, email interview with Elyssa Ford, July 28, 2015.
40. Bruce Roby, interview with Rebecca Scofield, Gay Rodeo Oral History Project, September 11, 2016, Duncans Mills, CA.
41. IGRA Bylaws, Standing Rules & Rodeo Rules, 1986–87, Autry Archives, MOAW 94.79.41.
42. IGRA Board of Directors Meeting Minutes, Annual Convention, 2000, Autry Archives, Box 63; IGRA Board of Directors Meeting Minutes, Annual Convention, 2001, Autry Archives, Box 71; ASGRA Newsletter, August 2001, GRH, http://gayrodeohistory.org/Newsletters/asgra/index.htm.
43. IGRA Gender and Sensitivity Committee Report, Annual Convention, 2002, Autry Archives, Box 71.
44. IGRA Gender and Sensitivity Committee Report, Annual Convention, 2002, Autry Archives, Box 71.
45. For more on the trans sport debates and the policing of gender, see, for example, Cheryl Cooky and Shari Dworkin, "Policing the Boundaries of Sex: A Critical Examination of Gender Verification and the Caster Semenya Controversy," *Journal of Sex Research* 50, no. 2 (2013): 103–11; Anderson and Travers, *Transgender Athletes*; and Joanne Harper, *Sporting Gender: The History, Science, and Stories of Transgender and Intersex Athletes* (Lanham, MD: Rowman & Littlefield, 2020).
46. IGRA Board of Directors Correspondence, 2002–2003, Autry Archives, Box 81.
47. IGRA Board of Directors Meeting Minutes, Annual Convention, 2001, Autry Archives, Box 71; IGRA Gender and Sensitivity Committee Report, Annual Convention, 2002, Autry Archives, Box 71; IGRA Board of Directors Meeting Minutes, Annual Convention, 2003, Autry Archives, Box 81; IGRA Finals Rodeo Program, 2003, GRH, http://gayrodeohistory.org/indexPrograms.htm.
48. Desirey Benavides, interview.
49. IGRA Newsletter, November 1987, Autry Archives, Box 2.
50. Allan Bérubé, *My Desire for History: Essays in Gay, Community, and Labor History* (Chapel Hill: University of North Carolina Press, 2011), 203. Bérubé's essay first appeared in Birgit Rasmussen, Eric Klineberg, Irene Nexica, and Matt Wrap, eds., *The Making and Unmaking of Whiteness* (Durham: Duke University Press, 2001), 235–65.
51. For more on the problems of exclusion and whiteness in the gay rights movement, see Roderick A. Ferguson, *One-Dimensional Queer* (Medford, MA: Polity Press, 2019); Kasie Hinkson, "The Colorblind Rainbow: Whiteness in the Gay Rights Movement," *Journal of Homosexuality* 68, no. 9 (2021): 1393–1416; and Darren Lenard Hutchinson, "Gay Rights for Gay Whites: Race, Sexual Identity, and Equal Protection Discourse," *Cornell Law Review* 85, no. 5 (July 2020): 1358–91.
52. Bérubé, *My Desire for History*, 204.
53. John King, interview with Rebecca Scofield, Gay Rodeo Oral History Project, July 8, 2017, Denver, CO; CGRA Programs, 1983–99, GRH, http://

gayrodeohistory.org/indexPrograms.htm; CGRA Newsletters, 1982–2014, GRH, http://gayrodeohistory.org/indexNewsletters.htm; TGRA Programs, 1984–2022, GRH, http://gayrodeohistory.org/indexPrograms.htm; TGRA Newsletters, Autry Archives; MIGRA Documents, 1998–99, Autry Archives, Box 43.

54. Joe Rodriguez, interview with Rebecca Scofield, Gay Rodeo Oral History Project, September 10, 2016, Duncans Mills, CA.
55. Bruce Gros, interview with Rebecca Scofield, Gay Rodeo Oral History Project, September 10, 2016, Duncans Mills, CA.
56. Scofield, *Outriders*; Ford, *Rodeo as Refuge*; Demetrius Pearson, *Black Rodeo in the Texas Gulf Coast Region: Charcoal in the Ashes* (Lanham, MD: Lexington Books, 2021).
57. GSGRA Los Angeles Rodeo Program, 1991, GRH, http://gayrodeohistory.org/indexPrograms.htm.
58. National Reno Gay Rodeo Programs, 1980 and 1984, GRH, http://gayrodeohistory.org/indexPrograms.htm. When Ragsdale refers to "the Gay Indians of America," he likely is referring the Gay American Indians (GAI), a gay rights organization formed in San Francisco in 1975. For more on the GAI, see Gregory Smithers, *Reclaiming Two-Spirits: Sexuality, Spiritual Renewal & Sovereignty in Native America* (Boston: Beacon Press, 2022).
59. IGRA Board of Directors Meeting Minutes, August 9, 2003, Autry Archives, Box 81.
60. AGRA Rodeo Programs, 1986–2009, GRH, http://gayrodeohistory.org/indexPrograms.htm.
61. Greg Begay, interview with Renae Campbell, Gay Rodeo Oral History Project, November 22, 2019, Denver, CO.
62. IGRA Flyer, circa late 1990s, Autry Archives, Box 47; CGRA Newsletter, October 1987, GRH, http://gayrodeohistory.org/indexNewsletters.htm; NSGRA Newsletter, November 1996, Autry Archives, Box 38; DSRA Newsletter, February 1997, GRH, http://gayrodeohistory.org/Newsletters/dsra/index.htm.
63. John King, interview.
64. AGRA Newsletter, November 1992, GRH, http://gayrodeohistory.org/Newsletters/agra/index.htm; Phoenix Rodeo Program, 1992, GRH, http://gayrodeohistory.org/indexPrograms.htm.
65. IGRA Sanctioned Rodeo Checklists, 1991, Autry Archives, Box 6; IGRA Rodeo Programs, GRH, http://gayrodeohistory.org/indexPrograms.htm; Bruce Roby, interview with Rebecca Scofield, Gay Rodeo Oral History Project, September 11, 2016, Duncans Mills, CA.
66. Alison Satake and William Love Correspondent, "A Pageant of Their Own: Gay Mexican Cowboy Contest Winner to Be Crowned Monday," *East Bay Times*, November 17, 2007, www.eastbaytimes.com/2007/11/17/a-pageant-of-their-own-gay-mexican-cowboy-contest-winner-to-be-crowned-monday; Miss Rosen, "A Night on the Town with LA's Queer Vaqueros: The

Cowboys of East Hollywood," *Huck*, November 1, 2017, www.huckmag.com/art-and-culture/photography-2/lgbt-latinx-cowboy.

67. Nadine Hubbs, "Vaquero World: Queer Mexicanidad, Trans Performance, and the Undoing of Nation," in *Decentering the Nation: Music, Mexicanidad, and Globalization*, edited by Jesus A. Ramos-Kittrell (Lanham, MD: Lexington Books, 2019), 75–96.
68. Hispanic people feel a similar tension between mainstream rodeo and the *charreada*, or Mexican rodeo, and many prefer the *charreada* because of the history, cultural pride, and community connections that it provides. See Ford, *Rodeo as Refuge*; and Barraclough, *Charros. Charreada* can be used to refer specifically to the rodeo itself, while the term *charrería*, which is also sometimes used, refers to the tradition as a whole.
69. Rick Phoummany, interview with Rebecca Scofield, Gay Rodeo Oral History Project, April 1, 2017, Dallas, TX.
70. Joe Rodriguez, interview.
71. Desirey Benavides, interview. For more on rodeo in Hawai'i, see Ford, *Rodeo as Refuge*.
72. Villanueva, "A Rodeo to Call Their Own," 307, 312.
73. IGRA leadership often framed their conversations of lesbian women around a gender framework, that is, the pursuit of men and women, versus a sexuality framework, that is, the pursuit of gays and lesbians. Despite the presence of straight women, lesbians have always formed the largest female population in gay rodeo and have been the subject of most IGRA conversations. Therefore, this section refers to women and lesbians interchangeably. The terms "women," "lesbians," and "female" are used inclusively in this section to mean anyone (cis or trans) who identifies under these categories.
74. Ann M. Ciasullo, "Making Her (In)Visible: Cultural Representations of Lesbianism and the Lesbian Body in the 1990s," *Feminist Studies* 27, no. 3 (August 2001): 577, 584–85.
75. Bill Carter, "ABC Is Canceling 'Ellen,'" *New York Times*, April 25, 1998, B16.
76. Kristin G. Esterberg, "From Accommodation to Liberation: A Social Movement Analysis of Lesbians in the Homophile Movement," *Gender and Society* 8, no. 3 (September 1994): 433.
77. Heather Murray, "Free for All Lesbians: Lesbian Cultural Production and Consumption in the United States during the 1970s," *Journal of the History of Sexuality* 16, no. 2 (May 2007): 251–53. For more on lesbian separatism, see Sarah Lucia Hoagland and Julie Penelope, *For Lesbians Only: A Separatist Anthology* (London: Onlywomen, 1988). *The Ladder* (1956–72) was the first national lesbian publication in the US, and by the 1970s, many other feminist-lesbian presses had been established. For more on lesbian publishing in the 1970s, see Kate Adams, "Built out of Books: Lesbian Energy and Feminist Ideology in Alternative Publishing," *Journal of Homosexuality* 34, no. 3–4 (1998): 113–41.
78. For more on rural lesbian separatist communities, see Catherine B. Kleiner,

"Doin' It for Themselves: Lesbian Land Communities in Southern Oregon, 1970–1995" (PhD diss., University of New Mexico, 2003); Heather Burmeister, "Women's Lands in Southern Oregon: Jean Mountaingrove and Bethroot Gwynn Tell Their Stories," *Oregon Historical Quarterly* 115, no. 1 (Spring 2014): 60–89; and Catriona Sandilands, "Lesbian Separatist Communities and the Experience of Nature: Toward a Queer Ecology," *Organization & Environment* 15, no. 2 (June 2002): 131–63.

79. See the discussion in chapter 1 on the Golden State Cowboys for more information about the group.
80. National Reno Gay Rodeo Program, 1981, GRH, http://gayrodeohistory.org/indexPrograms.htm. In the 1982 program, Ragsdale addressed his welcome to "Gay Men, Lesbian Women and Anyone," GRH, http://gayrodeohistory.org/indexPrograms.htm.
81. Wayne Jakino, "Rodeoing," *Roundup* (Spring 1994): 10, Autry Archives, Box 17. Not all Reno rodeo events were open to all participants. The events varied over the years, with greased pig catching in 1978, while 1984 included bull dogging for men and ribbon bull dogging for women; see National Reno Gay Rodeo Programs, 1979–84, GRH, http://gayrodeohistory.org/indexPrograms.htm.
82. National Reno Gay Rodeo Programs, 1979–84, GRH, http://gayrodeohistory.org/indexPrograms.htm.
83. An ad for Scissors appeared in the 1979 Reno program, while one for Scorpio's was included in the 1981 and 1982 programs, but only one year specifically identifies the bar as "the friendly! . . . women's bar"; see National Reno Gay Rodeo Programs, 1979–84, GRH, http://gayrodeohistory.org/indexPrograms.htm.
84. CGRA Newsletter, August 1982, GRH, http://gayrodeohistory.org/Newsletters/cgra/index.htm.
85. These programs are available at GRH, http://gayrodeohistory.org/indexPrograms.htm. Tracking women in leadership roles is difficult, but rough numbers can be estimated by using visual and naming cues of board members in programs and newsletters and by tracking those same names when gendered rodeo results are available. For instance, for its first seven years, from 1984 to 1991, AGRA listed between twelve and seventeen people in leadership positions annually, with just one to three women included each year. Most associations had similar gender ratios, often with only one or two women serving on boards and frequently none at all; see IGRA member association newsletters, GRH, http://gayrodeohistory.org/indexNewsletters.htm.
86. GSGRA Los Angeles Rodeo, 1986, GRH, http://gayrodeohistory.org/indexPrograms.htm. The California gay rodeo programs in the 1980s averaged one to three ads annually that targeted women.
87. Great Plains Rodeo, 1986–89, GRH, http://gayrodeohistory.org/indexPrograms.htm.

88. The poll received 108 responses, with 97 identified as men, 8 as women, and 3 unidentified. IGRA Newsletter, November 1987, Autry Archives, Box 2.
89. Only twenty-eight attendees completed the survey, and not all of them were IGRA members or rodeo contestants. Audience Survey Report, IGRA Finals Rodeo, 1997, Autry Archives, Box 47. Despite this limited survey, the IGRA media relations chair quoted a similar statistic in a media article, admitting that most of the contestants were men but claiming 30 percent were women; see Interview by Perry Brass, posted to *Gay Today*, January 1999, Autry Archives, Box 51.
90. CGRA Newsletter, January 2014, GRH, http://gayrodeohistory.org/Newsletters/cgra/index.htm.
91. The 1991 Albuquerque rodeo attracted 110 total contestants, of which 25 were women (23 percent female). IGRA rodeos at the end of that decade had similar ratios, such as one in 1999 with 135 contestants: 95 men and 40 women (29 percent female). *Albuquerque Tribune* article in BSGRA Newsletter, May 1991, Autry Archives, Box 6; IGRA contestant audit, 1999, Autry Archives, Box 54.
92. Personal experience at MGRA Kansas City Rodeo, 2014, attended by Elyssa Ford.
93. IGRA Contestant Audit, 1995, Autry Archives, Box 23; IGRA Contestant Audit, 1999, Autry Archives, Box 54; IGRA Contestant Audit, 2003, Autry Archives, Box 81.
94. IGRA Trustees Meeting Minutes, January 15, 1999, Autry Archives, Box 56. IGRA member Amy Griffin raised a related financial issue that may help to explain the smaller number of female participants. She pointed to income disparities between men and women, which are even greater between gay men and lesbians. See Amy Griffin, email interview with Elyssa Ford, July 25, 2015.
95. IGRA Board of Directors Meeting Minutes, October 11, 2002, Autry Archives, Box 70 and 74.
96. Letter to the Editor, *Roundup* (October 1995), Autry Archives, Box 25.
97. Email to IGRA, October 19, 1998, Autry Archives, Box 48.
98. NSGRA Newsletter, November 1996, Autry Archives, Box 38.
99. MGRA Newsletter, August–September 1991, Autry Archives, Box 1; DSRA Newsletter, March 1995, GRH, http://gayrodeohistory.org/Newsletters/dsra/index.htm.
100. GSGRA Newsletter, March 1993, GRH, http://gayrodeohistory.org/Newsletters/gsgra/index.htm.
101. DSRA Newsletter, August 1991, GRH, http://gayrodeohistory.org/Newsletters/dsra/index.htm.
102. ASGRA Newsletters, March 1992, September 1992, April 1994, November 1994, GRH, http://gayrodeohistory.org/Newsletters/asgra/index.htm.
103. IGRA Board of Directors Meeting Minutes, Annual Convention, November

14, 2009, www.igra.com/resources/Minutes_Board/2009/2009-11-14
_convention.pdf.
104. IGRA Women's Outreach Committee Meeting Minutes, Annual Convention, November 12, 2010, www.igra.com/resources/ConventionReports/2010/2010_WomensOutreach.pdf.
105. IGRA Women's Committee Meeting Minutes (ten representatives), Annual Convention, November 9, 2012, www.igra.com/resources/ConventionReports/2012/2012_WomensOutreach.pdf; IGRA Women's Committee Meeting Minutes (eight representatives), Annual Convention, November 15, 2013, www.igra.com/resources/Minutes_Board/2013/2013-11-16_convention.pdf.
106. DSRA Newsletters, August 1991, March 1995, December 1996, GRH, http://gayrodeohistory.org/Newsletters/dsra/index.htm.
107. DSRA Newsletter, February 1997, GRH, http://gayrodeohistory.org/Newsletters/dsra/index.htm.
108. IGRA Women's Outreach Committee Meeting Minutes, Annual Convention, November 12, 2010, www.igra.com/resources/ConventionReports/2010/2010_WomensOutreach.pdf. Fourteen representatives from twelve associations attended this first meeting.
109. "Dyke Dish: What Our Queer Sisters Really Think of Gay Boys," *Instinct* (April 2002): 36–41, Autry Archives, Box 72. For more on the exclusion and alienation that lesbians have experienced in gay bars, see Jaime Hartless, "'They're Gay Bars, But They're Men Bars': Gendering Questionably Queer Spaces in a Southeastern US University Town," *Gender, Place & Culture* 25, no. 12 (2018): 1781–1800.
110. Corey W. Johnson and D. M. Samdahl, "'The Night They Took Over': Misogyny in a Country-Western Gay Bar," *Leisure Sciences* 27 (July 2005): 331–48. The experience described by Johnson and Samdahl is dramatically different from the views that some other gay men had about the way women were treated in country-western bars. One gay rodeo member said he appreciated the queer country-western scene, because it did not have this same hostility as other gay bars. He explained that the country-western bars were "refreshingly different from a lot of other gay bars. There was more mixing of men and women, and that mixing felt easy and natural instead of enforced by political correctness. I noticed the lack of attitude." Steve Lenius, "Trail's End: Learning to Appreciate the West," *Roundup* (May 1996): 64, Autry Archives, Box 30.
111. Letter from CGRA to the ACLU, October 11, 1986, Autry Archives, Box 2.
112. IGRA Ethical Practices Review Board Meeting Minutes, October 22, 1995; December 5, 1995; January 12, 1996; January 22, 1996, Autry Archives, Box 32.
113. CGRA Newsletter, November 1988, GRH, http://gayrodeohistory.org/Newsletters/cgra/index.htm.

114. MGRA Newsletter, February 1987, GRH, http://gayrodeohistory.org/Newsletters/mgra/index.htm.
115. ILGRA Chicago Rodeo Brochure, 2001, Autry Archives, Box 62.
116. In 1993, Atlantic States divided equally the $10,000 of their rodeo proceeds to Brother Help Thyself, the Mautner Project for Lesbians and Cancer, Food and Friends, and the Northern Virginia Visiting Nurses Association; see ASGRA Newsletter, March 1993, GRH, http://gayrodeohistory.org/Newsletters/asgra/index.htm. Similarly, it gave $13,688 to six local charities in 1996: $2,797 each to Brother Help Thyself, Food and Friends, Pets DC, and the Mautner project, while the NAMES Project received $1,500 and the Sexual Minority Youth Assistance League $1,000. All but Mautner and SMYAL were AIDS-focused organizations; see ASGRA Newsletter, April 1996, GRH, http://gayrodeohistory.org/Newsletters/asgra/index.htm. In 1996, the New Mexico association noted that it had donated over $25,000 to New Mexico AIDS charities and the New Mexico Breast Cancer Coalition over the previous six years; see NMGRA Rodeo Program, 1996, GRH, http://gayrodeohistory.org/indexPrograms.htm.
117. Letter from Susan G. Komen Breast Cancer Foundation to IGRA, November 11, 1998, Autry Archives, Box 56. The Illinois, Arkansas, and Colorado associations all gave to breast cancer research in this period; see ILGRA Newsletters, January 1999, Autry Archives, Box 52; and February 1999, Autry Archives, Box 51; CGRA Newsletter, December 2000, Autry Archives, Box 65; and March 2000, GRH, http://gayrodeohistory.org/Newsletters/cgra/index.htm; and DSRA Newsletter, March 2000, GRH, http://gayrodeohistory.org/Newsletters/dsra/index.htm. The Arizona association considered the Susan G. Komen Breast Cancer Foundation for a donation in 2000; see AGRA Newsletters, August 2000 and October 2000, GRH, http://gayrodeohistory.org/Newsletters/agra/index.htm.
118. DSRA Newsletter, May 1990, Autry Archives, Box 4.
119. Dan Tracer, "All His Life People Said He 'Can't Do Things' but the Gay Rodeo Just Helped Him Prove Them All Wrong," *Queerty*, November 3, 2022, www.queerty.com/life-people-said-cant-things-gay-rodeo-just-helped-prove-wrong-20221103.
120. National Reno Gay Rodeo Program, 1981, GRH, http://gayrodeohistory.org/indexPrograms.htm; IGRA Website, www.igra.com.

CONCLUSION

1. Bruce Roby, email interview with Elyssa Ford, July 30, 2015.
2. In 2013, there were twenty-eight active associations versus thirty-one defunct groups. Eight more associations dissolved between 2014 and 2019. IGRA Timeline, GRH, http://gayrodeohistory.org/timeline.htm.
3. IGRA Press Release, IGRA Board of Directors Meeting Minutes, February

16, 2018, IGRA, http://igra.com/resources/Minutes_Board/2018; IGRA Board of Directors Meeting Minutes, February 14, 2021, IGRA, http://igra.com/resources/Minutes_Board/2021 (accessed Month day, year).

4. Sylvia Gann Mahoney, *College Rodeo: From Show to Sport* (College Station: Texas A&M University Press, 2004), 196–97; Rattenbury, *Arena Legacy*; "Wrangler National Finals Rodeo Payoff Climbs Again in 2002," ProRodeo, https://prorodeo.com/news/2022/2/22/general-wrangler-national-finals-rodeo-climbs-again-in-2022-now-at-a-record-14-1-million; Josh Peter, *Fried Twinkies, Buckle Bunnies, & Bull Riders: A Year Inside the Professional Bull Riders Tour* (Emmaus: PA: Rodale, 2005); "All Time Money Earners," PBR, https://pbr.com/athletes/riders/money.

5. Only GSGRA was larger, with just twenty-six more members; see ARGRA Newsletter, April 2007, GRH, http://gayrodeohistory.org/Newsletters/argra/index.htm.

6. ARGRA Newsletter, August 2007 and December 2007, GRH, http://gayrodeohistory.org/Newsletters/argra/index.htm; IGRA Timeline, GRH, http://gayrodeohistory.org/timeline.htm; IGRA Board of Directors Meeting Minutes, July 8, 2016, IGRA, http://igra.com/resources/Minutes_Board/2016/. ARGRA dissolved in 2016, but another Canadian association, CRGRA, joined IGRA two years later, in 2018.

7. DSRA Newsletters, November 2007 and December 2008, GRH, http://gayrodeohistory.org/Newsletters/dsra/index.htm; HGRA Newsletters, December 2007 and March 2009, GRH, http://gayrodeohistory.org/Newsletters/hgra/index.htm; OGRA Newsletter, August 2011, GRH, http://gayrodeohistory.org/Newsletters/ogra/index.htm; IGRA Timeline, GRH, http://gayrodeohistory.org/timeline.htm.

8. SEGRA Newsletter, July 1994, Autry Archives, Box 21; IGRA Board of Directors Meeting Minutes, Annual Convention, 1995, Autry Archives, Box 23. ASGRA had the same problem and had months without meetings its quorum for a business meeting in 1992, despite a membership of over 300 that year; see ASGRA Newsletters, 1992, GRH, http://gayrodeohistory.org/Newsletters/asgra/index.htm. For the other association references, see ASGRA Newsletter, May 1996, GRH, http://gayrodeohistory.org/Newsletters/asgra/index.htm; LGRA Newsletter, March 2010, GRH, http://gayrodeohistory.org/Newsletters/lgra/index.htm. LGRA dissolved in 2011; see IGRA Timeline, GRH, http://gayrodeohistory.org/timeline.htm; and NSGRA Newsletter, August 2014, GRH, http://gayrodeohistory.org/Newsletters/nsgra/index.htm.

9. Scott E. Branton and Cristin A. Compton, "There's No Such Thing as a Gay Bar: Co-Sexuality and the Neoliberal Branding of Queer Spaces," *Management Communication Quarterly* 35, no. 1 (2020): 69–95; Jaime Hartless, "Questionably Queer: Understanding Straight Presence in the Post-Gay Bar," *Journal of Homosexuality* 66, no. 8 (2019): 1035–57.

10. IGRA Timeline, GRH, http://gayrodeohistory.org/timeline.htm. The membership numbers are from 2007 to 2018, as numbers for 2019 are not available. See the table.
11. Carolyn Jones, email interview with Elyssa Ford, July 27, 2015.
12. Kevin Hillman, interview with Rebecca Scofield, Gay Rodeo Oral History Project, November 20, 2016, Austin, TX.
13. Rebecca Scofield, personal experience at CGRA Rodeo, 2021.
14. At a cost of $12,000, an in-person convention was deemed prohibitively expensive, and the IGRA board of directors investigated virtual meeting options instead. IGRA Board of Directors Meeting Minutes, June 24, 2021, and August 15, 2021, IGRA, http://igra.com/resources/Minutes_Board/2021.

INDEX

References to illustrations are italicized.

acceptance, 16, 40, 52, 72, 146, 169, 172, 177, 205, 207; finding, 54; goal of, 202; LGBTQ+ community, 35, 37, 171, 176, 180; societal, 6, 35, 180, 181, 206
ACLU, 77, 81, 198
activism, 144, 158; civil rights, 134; consumer, 8, 134, 135–36, 145, 146, 161–62; gay rodeo and, 102, 230n60; political, 9, 134; quiet, 144
ACT UP, 8, 73, 84, 159, 161; boycotts and, 134, 164; fundraising by, 162; silence equals death and, 160
advertisements, 39, 40, *49*, 57, 58, 60, *61*, *63*, 68, *98*, *141*, *142*, 148, 150, 152
Advocate, The, 57, 64, 150, 229n53
AGRA. *See* Arizona Gay Rodeo Association
AIDS, 8, 29, 30, 35, 59, 64, 65, 66–67, 69, 74–76, 94, 100, 145, 200, 204; concerns about, 77–83, 102; conference, 89, 96; deaths from, 91, 92, 96, 239n109; fear of, 85–87; fighting, 10, 92, 99, 209; fundraising for, 92, 93, 100, 102, 167, 208; impact of, 90–91, 101; infection with, 62, 70, 88, 239n109; medical advice for, 73, 91; medication for, 1, 74, 101; organizations, 93, 95, 96, 100, 101, 134, 235n49; protesting, 71, 72, 102; research, 90, 160, 162; spread of, 76, 77, 111; testing for, 73; transmission risk of, 62; treatment of, 70, 91; understanding, 73; warnings of, 60
AIDS crisis, 6, 8, 15, 35, 62, 64, 74, 83, 90, 92, 166; awareness of, 89;

Christian Right and, 30, 71; gay rodeo and, 30, 59, 67, 79, 85–87, 88, 91, 94, 99–102, 208, 209; growth of, 58, 160–61, 176, 200; impact of, 60; LGBTQ+ community and, 87, 88, 89, 94; pressure of, 9
AIDS Foundation, 89, 90
AIDS Project Los Angeles, 60, 73; advertisement from, *141*
AIDS Walk Arkansas, 100
Alexander, Kathryn, 5, 144
All People's Rodeo, 224–25n54
Amendment 2 (Colorado), 156
American Brotherhood contest, 175
American Psychiatric Association, homosexuality and, 72
Anaya, David, 86, 93
Anderson, Sue, 157
animal rights groups, 26, 100, 155–56; boycotts and, 136; IGRA and, 52; rodeos and, 154–55, 223n32, 233–34n36
Annie Oakley (television show), 17
antidiscrimination laws, 72, 140, 156, 161
antihomosexuality laws, 74, 75
Arizona Gay Rodeo Association (AGRA), 27, 29, 52, 93, 193, 206, 207, 298, 238n93, 257n85
ASGRA. *See* Atlantic States Gay Rodeo Association
Asian American community, gay rodeo participation and, 188
ASPCA (animal rights group), 100
assimilation, 4, 144
Atlantic Stampede, 138

263

Atlantic States Gay Rodeo Association (ASGRA), 31, 45, 94, 127, 139, 154, 155, 172, 174, 179, 181, 196, 207, 260n116
authenticity, 67, 172, 202; western, 113, 116, 122

"Ballet Mexicano" group, 186
bareback bronc riding, 28, 48, 211, 212
barebacking, 62, 64
barrel racing, 28, 115, 130, 167, 180, 189, 194, 211, 213, 226n3
bathhouses, 15, 39, 57, 60, 62, 65, 107
bears, 170–79, 180, 202
Bear State Cowboys, 19
Begay, Greg, 186
Benavides, Desirey, 112, 182, 188
Bergmann, Roger, 14, 90, 123–24, 148, 156, 158, 224n51
Bertram, Kat, 195
Bérubé, Allan, 183
Big Sky Gay Rodeo Association (BSGRA), 30, 144
bisexual people, 169
Black community, 4–5, 18, 41, 143, 144; participation in Black rodeo, 15, 130, 183, 184; participation in gay rodeo, 184
blackface, 123
BLK magazine, 185
Blueboy magazine, 55
bodybuilders, 41, 42, 43
Boston Lesbian and Gay Political Alliance, 88
Bowers vs. Hardwick (1986), 87, 88
bowling alleys, 39, 147
Boycott Colorado, 157, 159, 162, 164
boycotts, 134, 136, 137, 149; IGRA and, 153, 154, 161, 162, 164; impact of, 153–65; tourism and, 157
Boys Beware (film), 233n35
breakaway roping, 28, 167, 189, 212
Briggs, John, 72
Bronc magazine, 55

bronc riding, 109, 180
Brooks, Garth, 13
Browning, Chuck, 39, 54, *121*
Bryant, Anita, 72, 233n35
BSGRA (Big Sky Gay Rodeo Association), 30, 144
Bud Lite, 163
Budweiser, 148, 150
bullfighters, 123
bull riding, 14, 28, 48, 179–80, 191, 211, 212; mechanical, 107; women's, 195
Bullshot, 123
Bunkhouse magazine, 55
Burbick, Joan, 115
Butterfield, Craig, 51

calf roping, 14, 48, 249n80; on foot, 28, 212
Calvin Klein, 18
camp, 105, 109–12, 124–26
camp events, 6, 28, 29, 47, 55, 68, 106, 107, 108–9, 111, 112, 119, 126, 128, 181, 210; competing in, 122, 123
care, culture of, 87–96, 98, 231n1
Centers for Disease Control (CDC), 72, 73, 77
CGRA. *See* Colorado Gay Rodeo Association
charities, 3, 89, 91, 93, 101, 110; fundraising for, 20, 24; straight-identified, 71
Charlie's (gay country bar), 19, 34, 140, 186, 198–99, 225n57
charreadas, 15, 185, 187, 256n68
Chasin, Alexandra, 160
Christian Coalition, 157
Christian Right, 30, 71, 72, 76, 80, 87, 156; attacks from, 27, 234n36; family values and, 74; frustrations with, 158
Churchill County, Nevada, 81, 82
chute dogging, 28, 29, 31, 34, 213
Ciasullo, Anne M., 190
civil rights, 134, 139; gay rodeo and, 136; LGBTQ+, 9, 73, 143, 148

Clarke, Eric, 136
Clarkson, Jay, 55
Classic Rodeo Production, 179
Clinton, Bill, 139
clones, gay, 48, 50, 107, 210
clothing, 114, 133; black leather, 21, 171, 175, 222n23; cowboy/brown leather, 50; drag, 122; female, 118, 122; western, 17–19, 107
clowning, 122, 123, 125, 143
Cody, "Buffalo Bill," 4, 17
Colorado AIDS Project, 62
Colorado for Family Values (CFV), 156
Colorado Gay Rodeo Association (CGRA), 27, 28, 29, 33–34, 52, 84, 85, 93–94, 158, 169, 176–77, 186, 193, 198, 252n11; boycott and, 157; Coors and, 149; founding of, 26, 51
Colorado Tavern Guild, 161
competition, 35, 65, 107, 124, 189; drag, 116–17, 128, 194; fairness in, 183; professional, 53; western-wear, 116
Compton, D'Lane, 122–23, 125, 243n64
Comstock Empire Silver Dollar Court, 23
Comstock Gay Rodeo Association, 24, 26–27, 30, 185
condoms, 62, 98
conservatism, 7, 8, 15, 67, 71, 72
consumer citizenship, 134
Cook, Malcolm, 202
Coors, 150, 163; boycott of, 149; "Gay Day" at, 149
Copeland, Linn, 84
Corey, Amy, 135–36
COVID-19 pandemic, 35, 205, 209
cowboy ideal: gay masculinity and, 40–41, 44–48, 50–54; queering of, 112
cowboy mythology, 44, 123–24, 140, 217n5
Cowboy State Rodeo Association (CSRA), 30
Cowboys' Turtle Association, 5

cowboy up (term), 4
cowgirls, 28, 59, 65, 102, 115, 130, 154, 196, 204
Crimp, Douglas, 62
cruising, 44, 57
CSRA (Cowboy State Rodeo Association), 30
Cuff, The (gay leather bar), 175
culture of care, 87–96, 98, 231n1

Dallas (television show), 18
Dalton, Lisa LeAnn, 180
Danburg, Debra, 94–95
dancing, 5, 30, 31, 33, 44, 186, 198, 199; barn, 26, 224n50; clogging, 7, 29; country, 37; disco, 18–19, 39, 221n16, 225n1; line, 3, 19, 24, 146; square, 7, 21, 29, 196
Daughters of Bilitis, 190
Defense of Marriage Act, turnover of, 139
DeGeneres, Ellen, 190
D'Emilio, John, 7, 135
Democratic National Convention, 79
Denver rodeo, 27, 56, 60, 84, 176, 193, 209
Diamond State Rodeo Association (DSRA), 31, 53, 96, 100, 101, 172, 196, 198, 206–7; AIDS work and, 94; women's participation and, 197
Dick, Nancy, 146
Dickmann, Ken, 58, 191
discrimination, 35, 51, 175, 199; fighting, 159, 168
"Don't Ask, Don't Tell," 138–39
drag, 112, 117–18, 123, 168, 188, 191, 199, 242n48; cowboy, 128; eliminating, 47; female-style, 120
drag balls, 23
drag bars, 23
drag kings, 110, 118, 126, 127, 244n80
drag queens, 6, 9, 14, 16, 47–48, 52, 55, 68, 110, 114–16, 122, 210; banning, 125–26
DSRA. *See* Diamond State Rodeo Association

Du Barry, Marie Antoinette, 103, 117

Eagle Forum, 81, 157
Echo Magazine, 224n51
Eco Dykes, 155
economic issues, 34, 135, 146, 147, 153, 207; gay rodeo and, 10, 145
effeminacy, 9, 14, 19, 24, 50, 107, 124, 125, 138
Elliott, Sam, 228n32
Equality Colorado, 157
equal rights, 35, 159
Equal Rights Amendment (ERA), 75, 137, 138
erotica, 55, 62, 229n44, 229n53

Falwell, Jerry, 72
family values, 74, 158, 205
Feinstein, Dianne, 80
femininity, 48, 123, 128; definitions of, 112; exploring, 117; idealized, 115; lampooning, 126; masculinized, 127; performance of, 106, 108, 109, 114–15, 124, 125; white, 115
Fetner, Tina, 153
FGRA (Florida Gay Rodeo Association), 220n3
Finkelstein, Avram, 88
flag race, 195, 213
Florida Gay Rodeo Association (FGRA), 220n3
Focus on the Family, 157
Frediksson, Kristine, 133
Friedman, Milton and Rose, 134–35
Frontier magazine, 112
Fugitive, The (film), 226n9
fundraising, 10, 16, 20, 24, 48, 87, 88, 89, 90, 93–94, 109, 115, 140, 162, 167, 176, 209; gay community and, 94, 95; gay rodeo and, 9, 92, 94, 95, 99, 100, 111

Garrett, Todd, 178, 220n3
Gay American Indians (GAI), 255n58

Gay and Lesbian Animal Rights Caucus (PETA), 155
gay bars, 15, 20, 50, 66, 90, 107, 146, 153, 160, 195, 208, 209; advertisements for, 39, 49, 57, 60, 193; alienation at, 65, 198–99, 259n109; closing of, 208; country-western, 34, 60, 198, 259n110; mixing at, 259n110
Gay Chicago, 150
Gay Games, 33, 34, 225n56
gay liberation, 8, 64, 134, 190
Gay Men's Health Crisis, 73
Gay Oz Expo Rodeo, 31
Gay Pride events, 33, 64, 72, 77, 134, 146, 188; normativity with, 248n51; politics of, 138
gay rights movement, 72, 74, 93, 133, 134, 153, 165, 234n36; exclusion/whiteness in, 183, 254n51; IGRA and, 135, 203; urban cowboy boom and, 6–7
Gay Vaquero contest, 187
gender: ambiguity, 109, 118, 119, 123, 125; binary understanding of, 9, 107, 108, 109, 118, 119, 122, 125, 127, 128, 170, 181, 182, 188–89, 197, 198; complexity of, 6, 45, 107, 183; equality, 137, 194, 195, 203; fluidity, 109, 113, 119, 128; normative, 9, 181, 189; performance of, 60, 109, 110, 119, 122, 124, 128; play, 129, 181; policy, IGRA, 108, 119, 127, 128; presentation, 6, 39, 44, 46, 113, 117, 180, 226n8; sexuality and, 123
Genre magazine, 229n53
goat dressing, 13, 28, 29, 111, 120, 167, 212, 223n40
Golden Spike Gay Rodeo Association (GSGRA), 24, 30–31, 48
Golden State Cowboys (GSC), 16, 19, 20, 21, 23, 24, 191, 257n79
Golden State Gay Rodeo Association (GSGRA), 27, 47, 48, 90, 93, 94, 126, 163, 177

Gould, Deborah, 87
Great Plains rodeo, 193–94
Griffin, Amy, 258n94
Gros, Bruce, 184, 185, 187, 203
Grow, Raeann, 154
GSC. *See* Golden State Cowboys
GSGRA. *See* Golden Spike Gay Rodeo Association; Golden State Gay Rodeo Association
Gunsmoke (television show), 17, 113

Haggard, Merle, 133
Halberstam, J., 7, 127
Halkitis, Perry, 101
Hallwood, David, 178, 253n32
Hansen, Dan, 74, 75, 76, 77, 78, 81
Hansen, Janine, 81
Harrell, Frank, 90
Harvey Milk Gay Democratic Club, 137
Hays, Jason, 45
health and safety committee (IGRA), 124, 182
healthcare, 60, 69, 71, 92
Heartland Gay Rodeo Association (HGRA), 53, 169, 207
Helander, Brian, 101, 102, *121*
Helms, Jesse, 160, 161
heteronormativity, 40, 46, 54, 135
heterosexuality, 33, 39, 71, 227n17
HGRA (Heartland Gay Rodeo Association), 53, 169, 207
Hillman, Kevin, 208
Hispanic community, 4–5, 183, 256n68; participation in gay rodeo, 185–89. See also *charreadas*
HIV. *See* AIDS
Hochschild, Arlie Russell, 108
homonationalism, 144, 247n38
homophile organizations, 45, 46, 59, 190
homophobia, 6, 8, 44, 72, 75, 77, 79, 80, 82, 84, 87, 88, 99, 144, 154, 158, 163
Homosexual Bill of Rights, 46
Honcho magazine, 55
horse events, 28, 130, 176

horsemanship, 115, 116, 118, 119
Hubbs, Nadine, 8, 133, 187
humor, 9, 96, 105, 106–7, 109, 119, 120, 123, 128; camp events and, 125; gendered, 107, 125
Hunt, Alex, 241n28
Huttner, Elodie, 180
hyperfemininity, 39, 115, 119, 125
hypermasculinity, 15, 39, 63, 115, 116, 119, 137, 243n64; performative, 251n10; promotion of, 20
hypersexuality, 59, 63, 148

ICS. *See* Imperial Court System
IGRA. *See* International Gay Rodeo Association
Illinois Gay Rodeo Association (ILGRA), 53, 199
I Love Lucy (television show), 60
immigration, 40, 72
Imperial Court System (ICS), 23, 35, 110, 112, 116, 170, 171, 251–52n11
Independent American Party, 74, 232n17
Indigenous community, 4–5, 115, 143, 185–86; participation in gay rodeo, 185; participation in Native American and Indigenous rodeo, 15, 130, 185
Instinct magazine, 229n53
International Gay Bowling Organization, 33
International Gay Rodeo Association (IGRA), 8, 13, 16, 28, 29, 38, 45, 46, 50, 53–54, 59, 74, 80, 83, 84, 85–86, 88, 90, 96, 100, 106, 110, 113, 116, 117, 122, 123, 124, 130, 131, 132, 137, 143, 158, 159; growth for, 31–33, 107, 153; joining, 30, 48, 224n49; leadership of, 35, 134, 149, 163, 185; membership in, 31, 32 (table), 35, 64, 186, 201–2; mission of, 126, 149, 177, 180, 208; threats and, 84–85; women's outreach by, 196–98, 200–201

268 INDEX

International Gay Rodeo Association (IGRA) Board of Directors, 158, 262n14
International Gay Rodeo Association (IGRA) Finals Rodeo Program, 1, 152, 237n81
International Gay Rodeo Association (IGRA) Hall of Fame, 121
International Professional Rodeo Association (IPRA), 52
In Touch for Men magazine, 50, 144

Jakino, Wayne, 13, 26, 28, 15, 59, 148, 153, 158, 159, 225n57
Jeffords, Susan, 39
Jennings, Waylon, 18
Jerry's Kids (MDA), 89
Jerry Springer (television show), 86
Jim Beam, 150
Jim Crow, 17
Johnson, Colin, 7
Johnson, Corey W., 198, 259n110
Johnson, Magic, 96
Jones, Carolyn, 208
Joy of Gay Sex, The, 20

Kaepernick, Colin, 143
Kagan, Dion, 101
Kansas City rodeo, 178, 194
Kansas Gay Rodeo Association (KGRA), 29, 84, 193, 194
King, John, 34, 186, 189, 203, 225n57
Koop, C. Everett, 73
Kramer, Larry, 64
Kris Studio, 44, 226n9

Ladder, The, 190
Las Vegas, Nevada, 60; alternative lifestyles in, 66; Pride events in, 77
Laughery, Roger, 144
Lawlor Events Center (University of Nevada), 81
Leather Archives & Museum, 175
leather community, 10, 16, 20, 21, 24, 55, 170, 180, 197, 202, 251n10; bars and advertising, 63, 172, 175; gay rodeo and, 23, 171–79
Leatherman's Handbook, The, 20
Leavitt, Myron, 75, 76
Lee jeans, 50
Lesbian/Gay Rights Lobby of Texas, 139
lesbians, 6, 16, 70, 110, 122, 170, 180, 183, 189–91, 193–203; alienation of, 259n109; attracting, 181, 195; bars, 57, 95–96, 193; eliminating, 47; leadership roles for, 257n85
Levine, Martin, 48
Levi Strauss, 17, 18, 50, 107, 150, 172, 197
Levitt, Myron, 137
LGBTQ+ rights, 80, 88, 101, 139, 234n36
Liberty Gay Rodeo Association (LGRA), 207, 224n53
Linneman, Thomas, 62
List, Bob, 75
Little Rock rodeo, 172, 206–7
L. L. Bean, 18
Lonesome Cowboys (film), 44
Longacre, Justin, 63
Los Angeles, California, 13, 19, 36, 37, 72, 90, 187
Los Angeles Central chapter (GSGRA), 177
Los Angeles Gay and Lesbian Community Services Center, 88
Los Angeles rodeo, 27, 60, 66, 85, 88, 185
Lukenbill, Grant, 147

Macho Cowboys, 47, 52, 201
magazines: erotic, 55; fitness/physique, 41, 44, 45
Mandate magazine, 55
marginalization, 11, 18, 55, 107, 108, 160
Marks, Tamara, 169
Marlboro cigarettes, 133, 148, 150, 159, 160
Marlboro Wranglers, 19

marriage equality, legalization of, 139
masculinity, 1, 55, 66, 67, 68, 107, 116, 119, 143; acceptable, 48; authentic, 40, 41, 171; cowboy, 39, 40, 128, 143; female, 189; gay, 39, 40–41, 44–48, 50–54; gay rodeo and, 11, 29, 107, 108, 112–13, 218n9; gender presentation and, 46; hegemonic, 9, 59, 67, 171, 183, 194, 210; heteronormative, 14, 50, 54, 57; leather, 21, 45; muscular, 45, 189; normative, 11, 38, 39, 56; performance of, 11, 128; protecting, 109, 125–29; proving, 170; traditional, 5, 35, 39, 45, 46, 201; white, 107, 108, 143; working-class, 44, 46
Mattachine Society, 135, 190
McHale, Mary, 46, 51, 54
MDA (Muscular Dystrophy Association), 24, 89–90, 110
media, 34, 41, 57, 65, 74, 77, 81, 84, 85–87, 89, 111, 135, 158, 176
MGRA. *See* Missouri Gay Rodeo Association
Michigan International Gay Rodeo Association (MIGRA), 32, 53, 156, 169, 176, 177
Midnight Cowboy (film), 44
MIGRA. *See* Michigan International Gay Rodeo Association
Milk, Harvey, 137, 149
Miller Brewing, 17, 131, 132, 134, 149, 150–53, 156, 159; advertisements by, 150, *152*; boycott of, 134, 160, 161, 162–63
Mills, Amber Westin, 115
misogyny, 38, 243n64
Miss Mae, 92
Missouri Gay Rodeo Association (MGRA), 29, 92, 178, 193, 194, 199
morality, 77, 78, 79, 85, 113, 205
Moretto, Anna, 155
Morgan, Robin, 242n48
Morgan, Tracy D., 41, 44

Morrey, Joe, 148
Morrey Distributing Company, 148
Morris, Charles, 89
movie nights, women's, 195–96
Muñoz, José Esteban, 62
Murray, Heather, 206
muscular dystrophy, 71, 89, 91
Muscular Dystrophy Association (MDA), 24, 89–90, 110
music: country-western, 107, 245n4; mariachi, 188; politics and, 245n4

NAMES Project AIDS Memorial Quilt, 92, 94
Nance, Susan, 4, 154
National Gay and Lesbian Task Force, 134, 160
National Reno Gay Rodeo, 30, 34, 38, 47, 48, 50, 51, 57, *58*, 73, 80, 93, 144, 145, 148, 179, 186, 191, 201, 205; acceptance at, 176; AIDS and, 82, 90; attendance at, 76, 79; dominance of, 27; establishment of, 14, 24; fundraising at, 89, 90; growth of, 26; masculinity and, 138; opposition to, 76, 77, 79, 233–34n36; royalty competition at, 110; sexual celebration and, 56
Native Americans. *See* Indigenous community
Neff, Ron, 116
Nelson, Willie, 18
neoliberalism, 134–35, 162
neutrality, political, 133–34, 137
Nevada Families Eagle Forum, 81
Nevada Gay Rodeo Association (NGRA), 140
Nevada Indian Rodeo Association, 185
Nevada State Fair Board, 79
Nevada State Fairgrounds, 232n18
Nevada Supreme Court, 82
Newby, R. J., 161
New Mexico Gay Rodeo Association (NMGRA), 11, 29, 86, 236n59

Newsweek, 72, 190
New York Times, 231n5, 233n29
NGRA (Nevada Gay Rodeo Association), 140
NMGRA. *See* New Mexico Gay Rodeo Association
nondiscrimination, 169, 171, 186, 203
North Star Gay Rodeo Association (NSGRA), 31, 195, 207
Northwest Gay Rodeo Association (NWGRA), 31, 158, 175
NSGRA (North Star Gay Rodeo Association), 31, 195, 207
Numbers magazine, 55
NWGRA (Northwest Gay Rodeo Association), 31, 158, 175

obscenity laws, 41
OGRA (Oregon Gay Rodeo Association), 30, 207
Oklahoma Gay Rodeo Association, 29, 185, 193, 207
Olson, Greg, 14
Olympics, 33, 79
ONE, Inc., 46
Oregon Gay Rodeo Association (OGRA), 30, 207

Pacific Coast Gay Rodeo Association (PCGRA), 24, 27, 28, 29, 31, 53, 155, 193
Parents, Families, and Friends of Lesbians and Gays (PFLAG), 100
Parker's Western Wear, 145
Parton, Dolly, 115
Patrick "Cowboy Ram," 127
Patriots to Normalize Reno, 78
Patton, Cindy, 87
PCGRA. *See* Pacific Coast Gay Rodeo Association
Pendleton, Oregon, 115
Pennsylvania, Ohio, New York (PONY), 33, 53
People for the Ethical Treatment of Animals (PETA), 162; boycott by, 153, 154, 156, 164; IGRA and, 155, 156
Pepper, Chili, 106, 107, 111, 117
PFCC (Pro-Family Christian Coalition), 74, 77, 78, 79
Philip Morris, 148, 159, 160, 161
Phoenix City Council, 140
Phoenix General Hospital, 69
Phoenix rodeo, 27, 83–84, 193
Phoummany, Rick, 188
pink economy, 146
pink triangle, 216n1
pole bending, 28, 29, 167, 194–95, 213
police, 82, 140; brutality, 143
politics, 9, 56, 73–74, 134, 136–40, 142–45, 162; boycotts and, 154; consumer, 135, 148, 161, 245n9; corporate, 161; gay rodeo and, 102, 144; identity, 7; IGRA and, 136, 138, 139, 165; progressive, 245n4; socially conservative, 7, 8, 15, 56, 58, 60, 64, 65, 144, 169; urban/rural, 7, 15, 34, 56, 88, 154, 169, 220n15
PONY (Pennsylvania, Ohio, New York), 33, 53
pornography, 41, 55, 148
Power of the Dog, The (film), Sam Elliott on, 228n32
Pratt, Candy, 132, 134, 177
PRCA. *See* Professional Rodeo Cowboys Association
Pro-Family Christian Coalition (PFCC), 74, 77, 78, 79
Professional Bull Riders tour, 206
professionalism of gay rodeo, 5, 10, 28, 51, 58–59, 132, 146, 183
Professional Rodeo Cowboys Association (PRCA), 5, 10, 17, 59, 115, 236n63; IGRA and, 52; prize money and, 206
Puar, Jasbir, 247n37
public health, 73, 77–78, 81

queer suburbs, 7, 219n13

racial inequities, in rodeo, 183, 187
Ragsdale, Phil, 13, 24, 30, 33, 48, 51, 56, 65, 74–75, 76, 79, 81, 148, 168, 176, 179, 191, 193, 201, 203, 205; boycott and, 137; camp culture and, 110; as Emperor I, 23; fundraising and, 90; gender equality and, 195; homophobic attacks on, 80; media and, 85–86; political messaging/involvement and, 73–74; women's rights and, 138
Ralph Lauren, 18
Ramakers, Micha, 44
ranching, 4, 15, 50–51, 174, 184
Rawhide (gay bar), 60
Reagan, Ronald, 107; AIDS and, 73; cowboy persona of, 18, 133, 135
Rebel without a Cause (film), 41
Red River Rodeo Association, 225n59
Reinman, Tracy, 155
Remington, Frederick, 17
Renier, David, 90, 92
Renslow, Chuck, 44
respectability politics, 45, 51, 52, 53, 56, 58, 66, 67
ribbon bull dogging, 257n81
ribbon roping, 28, 29, 212
riderless horse ceremony, 92, 237n81
Rist, Darrel Yates, 126
Rivers, Joan, 24, 51, 76, 191
Roby, Bruce, 90, 113, 115, 178, 180, 204, 206
Rockmount, 17
rodeo circuits, 5, 41, 51, 52, 67, 184, 186, 187
rodeo clowns, 122, 123
rodeo queens, 107, 120, 124; Native American, 115; negative opinion about, 126
Rodriguez, Joe, 184, 188
Rofes, Eric, 88, 101
Roosevelt, Theodore, 17
Roper, 148
roping events, 28, 29, 34, 111, 212

Rotello, Gabriel, 232n13
roughstock events, 28, 29, 31, 111, 123, 179, 191, 211–12, 243n70; women's, 195
Roundup magazine, 55, 120, 148, 149, 195
royalty competition, 89, 94, 108, 120, 122, 125; decline of, 127; fluidity in, 112–19; IGRA, 110, 111; rules for, 127, 128; western identity and, 113
royalty pageants, 65, 228n24; drag-based, 16; western, 118–19
royalty titles: Miss titles, 86, 93, 106, 115, 116, 117, 118, 125; Mr. titles, 110, 115, 116, 118, 125, 138, 172–73, 188; Ms. titles, 92, 115, 116, 118, 125, 166, 167; MsTer titles, 110, 118, 125, 127, 244n82
Rubio, Paulina, 188

Sacramento, California, 75, 90, 184
saddle bronc riding, described, 211
sadomasochism (S/M), 20
safe sex, 60, 62, 64, 71, 98
Samdahl, D. M., 198, 259n110
San Francisco, California, 11, 13, 19, 23, 50, 72, 73, 75, 77, 80, 88–90, 184, 187
San Francisco AIDS Foundation, 73, 94
San Francisco rodeo, 56, 80, 94
Santa Fe Trail, 104
Save Our Children, 233n35
Schelkun, Sheryl, 85
Scissors (lesbian bar), advertisement for, *192*, 257n83
Scorpio's (bar), 257n83
Scott, Laura, 253n25
SEGRA. *See* Southeast Gay Rodeo Association
segregation, 5, 17, 160
Sen, Sankar, 156
sex clubs, 15, 62
sexual activity, 62, 67; at rodeos, 39, 54–57
sexual desire, 6, 7, 57, 64, 180; male gayness and, 41, 44

sexual freedom, 56, 60, 67
sexuality, 11, 34, 64, 68, 72, 140, 154, 186, 205; alternative, 204; female, 189; gay male, 62; gender and, 123; non-normative, 55
Sferrazza, Pete, 81
Shaffer, Robert, 76
Shanti Project, 88
Sheplers Western Wear, 148, 149, 150, 165
Shulman, Randy, 154
Signorile, Michael, 232n13
Silence=Death, 88; memorial, 97
Silver State Gay Rodeo Association (SSGRA), 81
slapping leather (term), 3
Sloan, Thom, 45
Smith, Brian, 20, 21
sodomy, 81, 87, 160; laws, 72, 78
Sontag, Susan, 73, 119
Sooner State Rodeo Association (SSRA), 176, 177, 224n53
Southeast Gay Rodeo Association (SEGRA), 31, 53, 168, 169, 207
speed barrels, 28, 29, 213
speed events, 28, 29, 111, 213
speed racing, 28, 29, 213
sponsorships, 15, 133, 134, 139, 145, 147–48, 149, 153, 156, 163, 164, 205
Springer, Jerry, 86, 236n63
SSGRA (Silver State Gay Rodeo Association), 81
SSRA. *See* Sooner State Rodeo Association
steampunk fashion, 104
steer decorating, 13, 28, 29, 120, 167, 212
steer riding, 29, 194, 213
steer roping, 211
steer wrestling, 211–12
Stockman-Farmer catalogue, 17
Stonewall riots, 72
straight rodeo, 16, 39, 40, 51, 52, 55, 57, 67, 105, 131, 163, 175, 179, 241n28

team roping, 28, 167, 212
Texas flag race, 28
Texas Gay Rodeo Association (TGRA), 27, 28, 29, 52, 59, 92, 94–95, 139, 163, 179, 193, 259, 238n99, 253n33
Thanksgiving Day Feed, 74
tie-down roping, 212
Time Magazine, Reagan and, 18
Tom of Finland, drawings by, 41
tourism, 146, 147, 157
Toys for Tots, 21
transgender people, 16, 112, 118, 128, 169, 170, 183, 194, 202; attracting, 181, 189; personal safety for, 181; rights for, 203
Tri-State Gay Rodeo Association (TSGRA), 31, 95, 225n54, 236n62
Turner, Frederick Jackson, 4
Twain, Shania, 115

UGRA (Utah Gay Rodeo Association), 30, 31, 65
United Airlines, 36, 163
urban cowboy, 3, 6–7, 107, 210
Urban Cowboy (film), 18
US Justice Department, 80
U.S. News and World Report, 133
US Supreme Court, 87, 139, 157
Utah Gay Rodeo Association (UGRA), 30, 31, 65

Vanity Fair, 190
vaqueros, gay, 187, 188, 202
Vietnam War, 12, 39
Village Voice, 76
Villanueva, Nicholas, 188
violence, 35, 108, 175, 205
virility, 38, 39, 40
visibility, 7, 77, 144, 145, 147, 158, 176; expansion of, 72, 76, 80, 101, 135, 143, 150, 163; queer, 138, 153
Vogue, 58

Waddell, Tom, 33

"wannabe" cowboys, 50, 54, 208, 220n3
Ward, Kathy, 169
Warhol, Andy, 44
Warner, Sara, 119
Washington Citizens for Fairness, 139
Washoe County, Nevada, 77, 78, 82; AIDS in, 80, 89, 234–35n49
Washoe County District Health Office, 235n49
Washoe County Fairgrounds, 74, 232n18
Washoe Medical Center, 233n29
Watney, Simon, 73
Wayne, John, 17
Westberg, Curt, 133
WGRA (Wyoming Gay Rodeo Association), 30
whiteness, 44, 183, 187, 188, 202
white supremacists, 143, 158
wild cow milking, 14, 28, 29, 47, 122, 212, 227n23, 243n70
wild cow riding, 28, 29, 213, 225n54
wild drag racing, 13, 29, 47, 106, 109, 120, *121*, 167, 181, 212, 214
Wild One, The (film), 41
Wild West shows, 4, 17
Williams, Belie, 75, 76, 78
Williams, Thelda, 140
Wilson, Pearl, 191
Wister, Owen, 17
women: participation in gay rodeo, 39, 40, 68, 191, 196–98, 199, 200–201
Wrangler jeans, 50, 148, 150, 165, 171, 174
Wyoming Gay Rodeo Association (WGRA), 30

www.ingramcontent.com/pod-product-compliance
Lightning Source LLC
Chambersburg PA
CBHW021341230426
43666CB00006B/362